More Luftwaffe
Fighter Aircraft
in Profile

Claes Sundin
& Christer Bergstrom

Schiffer Military History
Atglen, PA

Book design by Claes Sundin & Robert Biondi.

Copyright © 2002 by Claes Sundin and Christer Bergstrom.
Library of Congress Catalog Number: 2001096092.

Printed in China.
ISBN: 0-7643-1559-5

We are always looking for people to write books on new and related subjects. If you have an idea for a book, please contact us at the address below.

Published by Schiffer Publishing Ltd.
4880 Lower Valley Road
Atglen, PA 19310
Phone: (610) 593-1777
FAX: (610) 593-2002
E-mail: Schifferbk@aol.com.
Visit our web site at: www.schifferbooks.com
Please write for a free catalog.
This book may be purchased from the publisher.
Please include $3.95 postage.
Try your bookstore first.

In Europe, Schiffer books are distributed by:
Bushwood Books
6 Marksbury Ave.
Kew Gardens
Surrey TW9 4JF
England
Phone: 44 (0)208 392-8585
FAX: 44 (0)208 392-9876
E-mail: Bushwd@aol.com.
Free postage in the UK. Europe: air mail at cost.
Try your bookstore first.

Foreword by Claes Sundin

Since Christer Bergström's and my first profile book was published in 1997, I have had the opportunity to meet and correspond with fellow enthusiasts, pilots, artists, and researchers all over the world. Without their assistance, this work would never have matured into a book that I could be proud of. This higher standard is partly due to the fact that my own artistic learning curve has gone up, but also that new software has been introduced. By now I also have access to an abundance of spectacular profile subjects. The aircraft I've chosen to present in the form of 124 color profiles were all flown by Luftwaffe fighter aces, most of which are well known to the readers, while some still remain quite unknown despite their achievements in air combat. The reader will also notice that I tried to put more emphasis on the "successful years" of 1941-42, when the Luftwaffe fighter pilots dominated the skies wherever they appeared. To me as a profile artist, this definitely is the most interesting period. A period when new camouflage patters and colors was introduced and experimented with, but also an era when the ground crews and pilots painted their crates in a most individualistic and spectacular manner. Furthermore, it has also been my ambition to include each and every German single seated fighter model in service between September 1939 and May 1945. However, due to difficulties in finding photos of ace-piloted types such as the Fw 190 A-9 and Me 163, this has not been possible to fulfill.

Finally, I am quite aware that some of the profiles included in this book will be the subject of justified criticism, as I admit that there is an amount of uncertainty surrounding some profiles. This goes first and foremost with the profiles where the reference material is limited to photos only of parts of the airframe. This may also be said for the colors that I've chosen for the different profiles. As later chapter explains, the black-and-white photo nuances of the different camouflage colors are hard to separate from each other, why misinterpretations could have been made. But knowing that, together with my colleagues I have made the utmost in order to find out the actual appearance and coloring of the individual aircraft presented here. Furthermore I wish to state that these 124 color profiles are some of the best yet published and the absolute climax of what I could possibly accomplish. I conclude with the hope that the reader shall appreciate my color profiles together with Christer Bergström's fantastic pilot biographies. Enjoy the reading!

Claes Sundin
Förslöv, Sweden, June 3, 2001

Foreword by Christer Bergström

The purpose of this book is to display various painting schemes of the Luftwaffe's day fighters in World War II. The aircraft flown by some of the most successful German aces have been selected for this volume. Thus, the biographical text that accompany each pilot in this volume reflects above-average military achievements. It is not our aim to glorify the war or to promote any hero cult. The men whose war time careers are portrayed here, represent some of the most successful individuals among a German generation whose flight enthusiasm was exploited by a ruthless government to support the most tragic war mankind has ever witnessed. Today, the hostilities of those dark years are long since gone, and when pilot veterans from Germany, the USA, England, Russia, and other countries today meet, they feel united through their common passion for flying.

Christer Bergström
Eskilstuna, Sweden, June 3, 2001

The authors would appreciate any constructive criticism regarding this book. Furthermore, since the authors are continually working on many Luftwaffe related topics they would appreciate any suggestions together with new background materials (photos, documents etc.). Readers who like to contribute or comment please contact us trough some of the following addresses:

Claes Sundin
Torgvägen 26
S-260 91 Förslöv
Sweden

E-mail: sundin@swipnet.se
Website: http://hem2.passagen.se/galland/

Christer Bergström

christer.bm@telia.com
Website: http://www.blackcross-redstar.com

Acknowledgments

This book could not have been written without the help of Pilot veterans and a large number of historians, aviation history enthusiasts, and many others. The authors are deeply grateful for the interest, encouragement, and kindness of these people, who have shown that history and historical facts belong to all of us, and that it is in our common interest to cooperate in uncovering every part of Mankind's history. We wish to express our gratitude to:

Radek Adamec
Aleksey V. Andreev
Michael Balss
Kjell Bergström
Jan Bobek
Pawel Burchard
Don Caldwell
Michael Case
Paulo Dario
Drew Dorman
Nigel Eastaway
Carl-Fredrik Geust
Jürgen Grislawski
Tomislav Haramincic
Nick Hector
Ruy Horta
Ossi Juntunen
Stig Kernell
Christian Kirsch
Martti Kuvalainen
Håkan Linde
Per Martins
Andrey Mikhailov
Mike Mucha
Lennart Norman
Jim Perry
Martin Reid
Philippe Saintes
Yuri V. Shako
Hans Dieter Seidl
Peter Soltau
Harold E. Stockton
Tom Tullis
Peter Vollmer
Carl-Johan Westring
Jan Zdiarsky

Christian Allerman
Sergey V. Andreev
John Beaman
Lars-Eric Bergström
Andreas Brekken
Edgar Burford
Sven Carlsen
Yevgeniy Chizikov
Larry deZeng
Doug Drabik
Odd Eiterjord
Octavian Ghita
Pascal Guillerm
Thomas Hasselberg
Pär Henningsson
Ivanova Ivanovna
Vsevolod Kanaev
David Kohlen
Saso Knez
Yuriy Kvyatkovskiy
Kari Lumppio
George Mellinge
Kees Mol
Lennart Nilsson
Doug Norrie
Erik Pilawskii
Jean-Luis Roba
Pär Salomonson
Andreas Schmidt
Yuriy V. Shakhov
Paul Stipdonk
John Szirt
Dariusz Tyminski
Dave Wadman
Bo Widefeldt
Nicklas Östergren

Alfons Altmeier
Vlad Antipov
Holger Benecke
Dénes Bernád
David E. Brown
Otto Burkhard
Martina Caspers
Martin J. Cobb
Andrey Dikov (Korytov)
Chris Dunning
Santiago A. Flores
Robert Goebel
Håkan Gustavsson
Jim Haycraft
Carlos Herrera
Morten Jessen
Tor Karlsson
Siggi Kohlen
Petr Kubele
Knut Larsson
Raimo Malkamäki
Rolf Mewitz
Troy Molitor
Hans Nauta
Pye Palm
Dr. Jochen Prien
Günther Rosipal
Matti Salonen,
Anneluise Schreier
Mark Sheppard
Boris Sudny
Peter Taghon
Michael Ullman
Bob Wartburg
Björn Widmark
Manfred Wägenbaur

Ferdinando D'Amico
Vladislav Arkhipov
William Berge
Christian Berring
Eric Brown
Craig Busby
Brian Cauchi
John Crump
Tadeusz Dobrowecki
Olve Dybvig
Josef Fregosi
Franek Grabowski
Lutz Hannig
Joel Hayward
Michael Holm
James E. Johnson
Peter Kassak
Chuck King
Aleksandr Kudriavtsev
Sean Leeman
Alexey Matvienko
Yves Michelet
Eric Mombeek
David Nieto
Donald Pearson
Rune Rautio
Yuriy Rybin
Henk Sanders
Reinhard Schröder
Grzechu Slizewski
Hans E. Söder
Kevin Troha
Hannu Valtonen
Pierre Watteeuw
Bernd-Joachim Willmer

A special acknowledgment is owed to our friends and fellow researchers Mr. Günther Rosipal, Mr. Michael Ullman and Mr. Jim Perry, the authors are grateful for all their assistance.

World War II Luftwaffe airmen:

Leutnant Herbert Altner
Major Gerhard Barkhorn
Oberstleutnant Hansgeorg Bätcher
Hauptmann Hugo Dahmer
Generalleutnant Adolf Galland
Oberst Gordon M. Gollob
Leutnant Norbert Hannig
Hauptmann Wolfdieter Huy
Oberleutnant Otto Kath
Leutnant Walther Köhne
Major Heinz Lange
Leutnant Friedrich Lüdecke,
Oberst Eduard Neumann
Major Günther Rall
Oberfeldwebel Willi Reschke
Gefreiter Heinrich Scheibe
Hauptmann Hans Hermann Schmidt
Gerhard Schöpfel
Oberst Johannes Steinhoff
Oberleutnant Walter Wolfrum

Feldwebel Rudolf Artner
Unteroffizier Oscar Boesch
Major Hans-Ekkehard Bob
Feldwebel Franz Elles
Unteroffizier Arthur Gärtner
Major Alfred Grislawski
Oberst Hajo Herrmann
Oberfeldwebel Karl-Heinz Höfer
Leutnant Elias Kühlein
Felix Lademann
Oberleutnant Erwin Leykauf
Unteroffizier Friedrich Lühring
Leutnant Hermann Neuhoff
Feldwebel Heinz Radlauer
Major Erich Rudorffer
Leutnant Ernst Scheufele
Feldwebel Ernst Schröder
Oberleutnant Otto Stammberger
Oberst Hannes Trautloft
Oberfeldwebel Dieter Woratz

Oberst Gerhard Baeker
Oberfeldwebel Herman Buchner
Leutnant Hugo Broch
Leutnant Heinz Ewald
Oberleutnant Rudolf Gloeckner
Leutnant Gerhard Hanf
Leutnant Werner Hohenberg
Leutnant Udo Hünerfeld
Unteroffizier Gerhard Kroll
Major Friedrich Lang
Oberfeldwebel Walter Loos
Oberfeldwebel Heinz Marquardt
Feldwebel Horst Petzschler
Oberleutnant Ernst-Wilhelm Reinert
Oberleutnant Kurt Schade
Oberleutnant Willhelm Schilling
Leutnant Walther Schuck Major
Oberleutnant Ulrich Steinhilper
Unteroffizier Willy Unger

To any helpers whose names we may have missed, please accept our apologies and our implied gratitude.

Photo credits

Authors
Lorant
Saintes
Trautloft
Grislawski
Salomonsson
D'Amico

Bundesarchiv
Prien
Mol
Leykauf
Höfer
Brown
Neuhoff

Der Adler
Rodeike
Stipdonk
Bob
Rosipal
Crow

DAY FIGHTER CAMOUFLAGE

Edited by Michael Ullman

To fully appreciate and understand the various camouflages schemes and colors displayed by the aircraft profiles in this book; the reader should have a working understanding of the complex story of Luftwaffe camouflage schemes and colors. This brief summary covers the more important aspects of the subject but in no way should be considered comprehensive. Those wishing to learn more on the subject are advised to consult the various references quoted elsewhere in this book.

Introduction
On page 5 in both the 1938 and 1941 editions of the Luftwaffendienstvorschiften (L.Dv.) 521/1 document, the following description clearly and neatly summarizes the Reichluftfartministerium's (RLM) position on the reasons for painting aircraft:

> *Zweck der Lackierung* (Purpose of Painting)
> a) Surface-protection: Covering of aircraft construction materials against the influence of the weather, water and payload. Increases the service life of the aircraft.
> b) Making materials suitable for aeronautical use (e.g., fabric).
> c) Influences the visibility of an aircraft.

Pointedly, the RLM statements refer only to the surface protection aspects of painting, and not about the actual paints, their colors or their hues. To them, camouflage was the least important attribute of painting aircraft.

Of the almost 50 identified RLM paint colors and their variations, the RLM listed official color names for only 28, up to color 73 Grün. All numerically higher numbered colors did not have an official descriptive name. Only aircraft manufacturers such as Messerschmitt and Dornier used the names of well-known colors such as Grauviolett for their own internal purposes. For their identification purposes, the RLM used only the *Fliegwerkstoffnummer* (Aircraft Construction-Material Number), e.g., 7120.76 to describe a specific color.

The Pre-War Period 1935-1939
The first Luftwaffe aircraft were painted with a surface protection application in a hue referred to as *Hellgrau* (Light Gray) (This was, and continues to be, erroneously referred to in several publications as RLM 63 *Hellgrau* lacquer). *Hellgrau*, as initially used for civil aircraft, was acceptable within the then-current RLM-Specification requirements, but was never standardized as an official color within the RLM system. In late 1936, the RLM first issued regulation's defining how aircraft surfaces were to be protected with lacquers. This first universal finish was the now familiar overall 02 *Grau* scheme. *Hellgrau* and 01 *Silber*, used as an overall finish, were remnants of the painting system originally in force for civil aircraft, one that was subsequently superseded by overall 02. Overall, 63 was more unusual, this being the gray color used in the 61/62/63 camouflage scheme. The "real" RLM 63 had a hue very similar to 02, but just a bit lighter.

The Early War Period 1939-1940
From mid-1937, the Luftwaffe introduced a new camouflage consisting of two upper surface colors, 70 *Schwarzgün* (Black Green) and 71 *Dunkelgrün* (Dark Green), and an undersurface color 65 *Hellblau* (Light Blue). These paints were spray-applied to create a soft edge between the colors. When hostilities broke out in September 1939, German fighters were painted in this dark green defensive camouflage scheme (see profiles Nos. 1 and 2). Very soon however, the combination of these dark colors were found to be too conspicuous in air-to-air combat. Consequently, the RLM issued an order in the winter of 1939-40 instructing all single-engined fighter units to limit the dark upper surface camouflage on aircraft to the extreme plan-view as seen from above. The effect of this order was that units quite simply extended the *Hellblau* coloring up the fuselage sides. At the same time new uppersurface camouflage patterns with contrasting colors emerged. The pattern consisted of a combination of Color 71 and colors 02 RLM *Grau* or 70/02 (see profiles Nos. 3, 4 and 5). With these changes, the German fighter pilots at last had a better and more appropriate offensive camouflage that made their aircraft harder to detect in the air.

The Battle of Britain 1940
During the Battle of Britain, new Gray colors emerged. Most, if not all, were mixed at the unit level from German paints, but it is possible that in some cases they were created from captured stocks of French paint. A significant change in the fighter camouflage occurred in August 1940. Due to the long flight over the English Channel and combat over water, the light-colored *Hellblau* fuselage sides were found to be too conspicuous. The remedy was to mottle the fuselage sides in a wide variety of greens and Gray colors. These were often sprayed on resulting in a soft mottled finish, however in some cases the colors were applied with brushes, rags or sponges (see profiles Nos. 9, 10 and 11).

The Mid-War Period 1941-1944
During this period the Luftwaffe was operational over a vast portion of the globe, from the Arctic conditions of the North Cape to the deserts of North Africa, over both land and sea. In response to these tremendously varied climatic conditions and changing operational challenges on men, aircraft and units, the RLM was forced to provide colors and paints that would meet these demands. Once the German forces were forced on the defensive on all fronts and eventually lost command of the skies, concealment on the ground became paramount to the Luftwaffe's survival. Further, the Allied bombing offensive was beginning to cripple German industries which was manifested in severe shortages of raw materials, interrupted transportation networks, declining fuel stocks, loss of technical personnel and the like. Germany responded to this crisis by ruthlessly streamlining and decentralizing weapons production, and reduction, simplification and substitution of manufactured components and raw materials. Thus, because of these events and responses to them, this period experienced the greatest changes and variability in the manufacturing and painting of Luftwaffe aircraft.

On June 24, 1941, two days after the beginning of the Russian campaign, the RLM issued an order that ratified the new color scheme for fighter aircraft, consisting of an all Gray "offensive" scheme. The uppersurfaces were painted in two Gray shades, colors 74 and 75. The paint was sprayed on, creating a soft edge appearance between the colors. All undersurfaces were painted in Color 76, a light blue-Gray, which extended up the fuselage sides to a point slightly below the fuselage spine. On the fuselage sides, including the vertical tailplane, a variety of different colors were applied. These colors varied during the course of the war, but an early and common mix was RLM 02 *Grau*, 70 *Schwarzgrün*, and Color 74. These three colors were sprayed as a spotted soft mottle pattern in roughly equal proportions (see Profiles No. 14, 27 and 72).

The Mediterranean and North African Theatres
At the beginning and throughout the African campaign, many aircraft operating over the Mediterranean and North Africa regions retained their standard European Gray scheme used (see profiles

Nos. 36, 61 and 62). This camouflage was, of course, quite unsuitable over desert and semi-arid terrain. Until such time as their own desert paints became available, the Luftwaffe was forced to use stocks of older Italian camouflage colors for the uppersurface of its aircraft, though undersurfaces were left in their original light blue 65 or 76 colors (see Profile No. 25).

During the autumn of 1941, the RLM introduced a tropical scheme that consisted of a bright blue undersurface in Color 78, and uppersurfaces in the colors 79 and 80, a medium brown and dark green respectively. These latter two colors were similar to the Italian colors, with the greens being almost indistinguishable used (see profiles Nos. 59 and 64). Color 79 could be applied in two ways, either over the entire fuselage side surfaces, or, down to roughly the horizontal middle line of the fuselage used (see Profiles No. 26 and 44). Color 80 was to be applied as a mottle over 79 although in actual practice this color was seldom. Both colors were on occasion applied in a meandering or spotted scheme over older pre-existing gray or green European schemes.

In mid-1943 when the German forces where were forced back to the Italian mainland, the European became more and more common and gradually reintroduced as the it matched well with the local coloration. Furthermore, since the fighter replacements wore the standard Gray-toned upper camouflage there was no need to re-paint the aircraft

The Russian Campaign
Aircraft operating on the Russian front initially retained the European scheme of uppersurface Grays. However, due to the fronts ever changing climate conditions, rapid movement of units between different climate zones, and the fact that most of the missions where flown at lower altitudes, new demands were put on the German fighter camouflage. In response, different units started to experiment in the field with new patterns and blends of colors used (see profiles Nos. 20, 21 and 22), and during the course of the war eventually new camouflage schemes and colors were officially introduced. In addition, different styles of winter camouflage were created, but mainly a wide variation of green colors emerged, colors, which later in the war were developed into new defensive camouflage colors (see profiles Nos. 32, 57 and 100).

The Late War Period 1944-1945
On July 1, 1944 the RLM introduced two new uppersurface colors, 81 and 82. This did not have an immediate effect on the colors already in use, but an order shortly thereafter on August 15 would. That order demanded the withdrawal of colors 65, 70, 71 and 74 and mentioned for the first time new uppersurface paint, Color 83.

Some written descriptions of these three new colors were made during the war but none by the RLM. In November 1944, the Dornier firm described both the colors 81 and 82 with the single name of *Dunkelgrün* (Dark Green). In September 1944 Blohm & Voss described color 81 as *Olivbraun* and Color 82 as *Hellgrün*. Later, in February 1945 Messerschmitt described color 81 as *Braunviolett* (Brown-Violet) and color 82 as Hellgrün (Light Green). Unfortunately, there are no contemporary written color descriptions that include color 83. However, the results of the latest research investigations reveal that color 81 was dark brown, color 82 a light green and 83 a dark green color (see profiles Nos. 109, 112 and 120).

To overcome possible shortages of the new colors during the period of their introduction, the RLM approved the use of older discontinued standard colors with the newer ones. Authorized color combinations of 70 + 82 and 71 + 81 were ordered. In this context it should be mentioned that color combination of 83 and 75 could be regarded as the standard upper camouflage scheme for the Fw 190 D and most late production Bf 109 G/Ks and Fw 190 As (see Profile No. 124). By combining these colors the German fighters also received a most effective semi-defensive camouflage pattern, but these changes make it very difficult for today's researcher to determine in which colors a particular aircraft was painted.

Variations in RLM Colors
The most significant problem in the appearance of RLM colors in existing black and white and color photographs is that they reveal a wide range of different hues for the supposed same color, most particularly the late-war colors 81/82/83. Surprisingly, research has revealed that the "older" colors like 70 or 74 also have a wide range of possible hues, and that the RLM several times changed the specifications for the hue of various colors. Clearly revealed in the 1938 and 1941 editions of the L.Dv.521/1 color charts are the changes for colors RLM 27 yellow, 65 light blue and 66 Gray-black. Indeed, spectrographic analysis of nearly a dozen different samples of mainstream colors like 70 or 74 has revealed that no two samples are identical! Sometimes the difference in appearance is clearly visible; other times the samples look almost identical but differs in their analysis profiles.

The consequence of this is obvious: It is impossible to recreate an exact, scientifically verifiable copy of the RLM color paint. It is only possible to recreate an example of the RLM-color that closely approximates the original hue. This begs the question: What was the cause of these observed color variations of the same RLM color? The answer is a simple one. The variations were due to the production process of the lacquers. The different production processes of each manufacturer and the raw materials available to them caused the different appearances of the same RLM color.

Finally, the observed late-war underside green-Gray and blue-Gray camouflage colors, collectively misidentified as "RLM 84", represent the best attempts of different lacquer manufacturers to produce a paint matching the appearance of RLM color 76 and thus are not new colors (see profiles Nos. 111, 118 and 121). It is important to note that no late-war documents, including the likely last one published for the He 162, dated 28 February 1945, indicate the use of an undersurface color other than the standard 76. Also, there is no evidence to support the hypothesis that these new hues were trial paints of future RLM colors introduced during the last months of the war. Therefore, the RLM undoubtedly did not issue any new colors because by of the end of the war conditions were such that the German industry was simply incapable of producing them.

Profile colors

The following are the colors used on all of the profiles – please note that all colors have been significantly lightened in order to give the aircraft profiles an accurate scale effect camouflage.

In black and white, the same colors appear as follows:

02	04	21	23	24	25
26	27	Hellgrau 65/1938	65/1941	70	
71	74	75	75/Variation	76/1941	76/1944
76/Variation	76/Variation	78	79	80	81
81/Variation	81/Variation	82	82/Variation	83	83/Variation

02	04	21	23	24	25
26	27	Hellgrau 65/1938	65/1941	70	
71	74	75	75/Variation	76/1941	76/1944
76/Variation	76/Variation	78	79	80	81
81/Variation	81/Variation	82	82/Variation	83	83/Variation

MARKINGS

National markings

When the war broke out in September 1939, the national markings of the German fighter aircraft were made up of *Balkenkreuz* (Girder Cross) and *Hakenkreuz* (Swastika). The first mentioned had a thin white outline of the cross with an additional black outline and was painted on both sides of the fuselage and on the upper and lower wing surfaces. The last mentioned was positioned on the center of the upper vertical fin area and painted in black and white, with a thin black outline. During late 1939 and early 1940, a modification of the national insignia was introduced by widening the thin white outline of all *Balkenkreuze* except those positioned on the upper wing surfaces. At the same time, the Nazi symbol *Hakenkreuz* was repositioned to the forward part of the fin.

In 1942, simplified versions of both the *Balkenkreuz* and the *Hakenkreuz* were introduced, whereby the outer thin black border line was dropped altogether. But the earlier used crosses and swastikas were common as late as 1944, though exclusively on Fw 190 A aircraft! During 1942, another simplified cross was introduced. This time, the black cross disappeared completely, leaving only the white contours of the cross, painted on a contrasting camouflage color. These re-paintings were made after a larger overhaul or respray at depots or on unit level.

In order to save further time and toil, this type of cross and a simplified *Hakenkreuz* without its white outline were introduced on plant level during 1943. The simplified crosses were first and foremost applied to the fuselage sides and the upper surface of the wings, but not uncommonly even on the under surface of the wings. They were made in either black or white, depending on the surrounding camouflage color. However, in some cases the older type of black cross was kept on the under surface of the wings, still without the white outline.

Towards the end of the war, the sizes of the crosses and swastikas were reduced in order to attract less attention.

Recognitions and Theatrical markings

Due to the continued war on new theaters of operations, the Luftwaffe had to introduce new theatrical markings on its aircraft from 1941 on.

Certain parts of the aircraft were painted in a specific theatre-color as a recognition signal both from the ground and in the air. The parts chosen for these recognition paintings were mainly spinners, (a belt around) the stern part of the fuselage, rudders and wing tips. During the campaigns in North Africa and the Mediterranean, including Italy, white color was used, whereas it was yellow on the Eastern Front. Certain differences existed between the different operational areas, e.g. a white belt around the cowling just behind the spinner was used in North Africa, while the yellow belt usually was wrapped around the fuselage (partly hidden under the cross) on the Eastern Front. Apart from these differences, practice varied, often depending on which unit the aircraft belonged to, which is also clearly shown on the profiles in this book.

During the fall of 1943, the units belonging to the *Reichsverteidigung* (Home Defense) applied white on rudders or even on the whole vertical tail surfaces in order to identify the aircraft of a unit leader. However, this practice was soon abandoned and replaced by new additional recognition markings. These markings, a series of one-color fuselage bands painted on the rear fuselages, were introduced to the Home defense units late 1943: e.g. red for JG 1, white for JG 3, yellow for JG 11 and green for JG 27. During 1944 and 1945, each *Jagdgeschwader* in the Luftwaffe was allotted an individual single or two to three rows of colors for their fuselage bands: e.g. yellow-white-yellow for JG 2, black-and-white for JG 26 and all-black for JG 53. But in reality this was never fully applied, especially by units fighting on the eastern front.

The yellow underside engine cowling

The ever increasing and furious aerial combats over the British Isles in the summer of 1940 called for instant recognition in the air. During this period, the German fighters started to assume large areas of yellow distemper. The application could be found on wingtips, tailplane-tips and spinners, but the most common practice was to paint the engine cowling and rudders in yellow.

This practice of painting recognition markings, covering the whole of the engine cowling as well as the rudder, continued until new regulations appeared in the summer of 1941. It was soon realized that an all-yellow engine cowling was too conspicuous and a revision was called upon, which led to only the underside of the engine cowling and the rudder being painted yellow.

The painting of the underside of the engine cowling was made at depot and unit level, but there are evidence on hand that it was in fact also undertaken at the different aircraft plants. It should be noted that this regulation was followed with German perseverance; the yellow underside of the engine cowling characterized the appearance of German single-engined day-fighter aircraft on all fronts until the beginning of 1945.

Following the disastrous German fighter attack on the air bases on the Western Front on New Year's Eve 1945, the yellow color of the underside gradually disappeared. There is some evidence (e.g. recent findings of shot down aircraft from this period) that some units painted over the yellow underside cowling with color 76 *Weissblau*. The picture is further complicated by the fact that the yellow underside of the engine cowling in some cases was replaced with a yellow band around the cowling just behind the spinner. This practice could be verified by several well known photos taken of Bf 109s from II./JG 52 and J.Gr. 101 at the Neubiberg air base after the war.

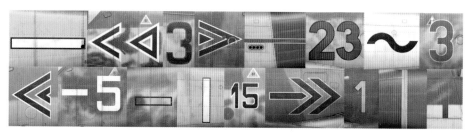

Individual numerals and unit markings

Each German day-fighter aircraft was to be identified by a colored numeral or staff symbol in front of the cross on the fuselage side. This identification code together with a roundlet, a wavy line or a bar indicated to which *Gruppe* the individual aircraft belonged. This practice was exclusively used among the day-fighter units.

Early in the war, the absence of any marking behind the cross on the fuselage side indicated *Gruppe* No. I, a horizontal bar indicated *Gruppe* No. II, and a wavy line or a vertical bar, *Gruppe* No. III. Later in the war, as several *Jagdgeschwader* were expanded by a fourth *Gruppe*, only the vertical bar came to indicate *Gruppe* No. III, while the roundlet or the wavy line became the symbol for *Gruppe* No. IV.

The color of the individual markings of the aircraft displayed the *Staffel* to which the aircraft belonged. There was no total standard for this practice. Still, even if some variations existed between different units, the most common color system was the following:

- White (normally black trim) for the first *Staffel* within a *Gruppe*.*
- Red or black (red normally black trim and black normally white trim) for the second *Staffel*.
- Yellow or brown (black or white trim) for the third *Staffel*.

Where there was a fourth *Staffel* in each *Gruppe*, this was given the call-code color blue. Finally, the green color was normally reserved for the *Stabsstaffel* of the *Gruppe* and the *Geschwader*.

Staffelkapitäne quite commonly flew the No. 1 aircraft, although this practice was more or less abandoned during the course of war.

The Staff Flight aircraft usually did not carry a number, but a symbol. The staff symbols mentioned above also differed from *Geschwader* to *Geschwader*. They consisted of different combinations of bars, chevrons and roundlets, normally black with a thin white outline. One common practice was to indicate the aircraft flown by a *Gruppenkommandeur* with a double chevron (*Doppelwinkel*), whereas a single chevron indicated the aircraft flown by the *Gruppenadjutant* (aide-de camp). In the *Geschwaderstab*, a single chevron followed by a vertical bar often indicated *Geschwaderadjutant*, but could also indicate the *Geschwaderkommodore's* aircraft.

* Since the normal outfit was three *Staffeln* in each *Gruppe*, and a *Geschwader* consisted of three *Gruppen* with a total of nine *Staffeln* (numbered 1-9), the "first *Staffel* within a *Gruppe*" consequently implies the *Staffeln* Nos. 1, 4 and 7 in a certain *Geschwader*.

Unit insignias

At the beginning of the war, most German fighter aircraft carried certain unit insignias, either the insignia of the *Geschwader*, the *Gruppe* or the *Staffel*, or a combination of two or even all three. These unit crests would be painted mainly on the engine cowlings or under the cockpit, but early in the war they even appeared on the rear fuselage. As early as 1940, these badges started to be removed. The reason for this, and the official banning in 1945 of painting unit insignias on combat aircraft, mainly was intelligence reasons, but the simple fact that time on the combat units became more and more expensive also played a rule.

Another way of identifying the aircraft of the same unit was to paint the noses of the aircraft in the same way. One interesting example is I./JG 1 of the Home Defense, whose Fw 190s originally carried white/black, yellow/black or red/black combination of checker-board cowlings. However, when the Thunderbolts of U.S. 78th Fighter Group, carrying the same checker-board painting on their cowlings, started to appear over the Low Countries and north-western Germany (the operational area of I./JG 1) during spring and summer in 1943, the German pilots had to have their

checker-board markings over-painted – as the German AA crews very quickly learned to identify "the checker-board noses" as enemies to be shot at!

Individual markings

Normally (especially during the early years of the war), the fighter pilots enjoyed the luxury of disposing over individual aircraft. Through this, the pilots and his ground crew had an inclination for decorating their aircraft with their personal "crate", which often resembles to modern "tags" in graffiti. These personal marks, common in most air forces with the practice of aircraft marked for individual pilots, could be anything, such as a name "tag", cartoon figures, etc. This practise also faded away towards the end of the war, partly due to the same reason as mentioned above (the ban against unit insignias), but also because it became less and less common with a personal aircraft reserved for each pilot.

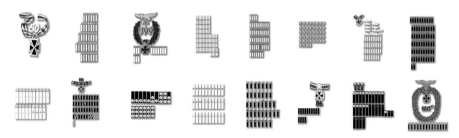

Kill markings

The well-known German "kill bars" (*Abschussbalken*) painted on the fighter aircraft started to emerge early during the Polish campaign in 1939. These bars were painted on the tailplane. In the beginning, it was only a question of simple bars, without any given specification such as national insignia or date. But already in 1940, the *Abschussbalken* started to be supplemented with small national insignias and dates. At the same time, the kill markings were repositioned to the rudder area; a practice that would remain unchanged for the rest of the war. As the number of victories achieved by some individuals grew higher, certain aces "started all over again" with the victory bars, having received a certain decoration for a certain number of victories: e.g. having been decorated with the Swords to the Knight's Cross with Oak Leaves after achieving his 69th victory in June, 1941, Adolf Galland had the number "69" and a laurel wreath painted on top of the rudder of his Bf 109F. His 70th victory was then indicated by a first kill bar, etc.

Both superiors and the Nazi propaganda machine encouraged the practice of painting kill bars on the rudders. Pictures of this after all rather cynical way of bookkeeping kills, were frequently published in German papers and youth magazines during the war. (The use of kill markings in one way or another was, nevertheless, common practice in most air forces. The most conspicuous form was used by the U.S. fighter pilots.)

As the fate of war eventually turned against Germany, the use of *Abschussbalken* became less and less frequent. The Allied counterparts were well aware of the meaning of *Abschussbalken*, and once the Mustangs, the Thunderbolts and the Spitfires had gained air superiority in the skies over Germany, the Allies fighter pilots started hunting the German *Experten* with great eager, identifying them by the rows of *Abschussbalken*. The removal of these bars soon became nothing less than a matter of self-preservation.

The making of a Profile

The aim of this work has been to create color profiles supplemented with facts as accurate as possible. Of course, this has been a laborious work. I shall only mention some difficulties and sources of mistakes, which encounters anyone who starts such a project.

One of the main problems is finding a complete photo documentation, displaying a whole aircraft or as large part of an aircraft as possible. Quite commonly, you find yourself restricted to parts of a fuselage; when that's all documentation at your disposal, you may commit lots of errors trying to make a complete color profile.

Once you have found an interesting aircraft, you face next problem: To identify the exact aircraft as an aircraft flown by an ace, when and where the photo where taken and so forth. Of course, an ocean of literature on this subject exists, but at large extent this literature has proven to be rather deficient.

To choose colors

The first task in the making of a profile is to settle the different black-and-white nuances in the original photo prints, in order to apply the correct colors of the camouflage and markings.

When it comes to this, one has to considerate purely photo-technical matters, such as how the exposure was executed when the picture was shot. The photos may be right exposed, over-exposed or under-exposed, which may be quite decisive for the judgment of the true original colors, later used in the making of the color profile. Furthermore, the profile-maker must take into consideration the light when the picture was shot – the sharp difference between an object in sunlight and a shadowed object is obvious.

Another source of trouble for the profile-maker is the melancholic fact that the most commonly used type of photographic film during World War II, is the Orthochromatic film, where the nuances of the pictures continuously change. Light nuances such as yellow are today, after 60 years, apprehended as dark gray or even black on the copies. This kind of problem also is applicable on the relatively few color prints which exist from this period, since color films of different manufacturers have different durability, and the colors of these films simply blur with the years. But naturally, color prints are of far greater use, although rather rare. A further important factor is that the original camouflage of the aircraft naturally grew paler with time.

Artwork

First of all it should be mentioned that all color profiles in this book are made in the scale 1:42, a size decided by the final size of the book and the demand of space put up by the aircraft with the longest fuselage, the Ta 152.

In order to make an aircraft profile of high quality, it is essential to have full line drawings of profiles available. Many profiles produced earlier are simply not quite proportional. Once this demand is fulfilled, the coloring starts.

Regarding artwork, the author started by making all the different colors used by the German Fighter Air Arm during World War II. Since all 124 profiles are made in a digital environment with the help of a Macintosh computer with Adobe Photoshop software, all this time-consuming adjustment-work is made on screen until a satisfactory result is achieved.

When it comes to the making of the profile, these colors have to be lightened by several degrees, taking the scale-effect into consideration.

The exact way of making these profiles will remain the illustrator's little secret, furthermore, it is too complicated to be described here and now. What can be said, is that the process used resembles to the older airbrush technique using masks, masking the color surfaces about to be colored.

As the illustrator I would like to point out that I have chosen to present all profiles exactly in the same condition as the original aircraft where in when the picture the profile is based on was taken.

Common questions

Since my first profile book was published in 1997, I've been contacted by and have corresponded with thousands of fellow enthusiasts around the world. And since they have asked me a number of questions during those years I though it could be interesting for the reader to know what I've had replied to some of their most common questions, which are as follows:

- Why I don't display my profiles from all sides: upper, lower, left and right hand side.
- Why I don't add landing gear or props to my profiles.
- Why I have a pilot figure in the cockpit.

My answer to all those enthusiasts is that if we as profile artists would like to keep the speculations down to a minimum, any display of upper, lower, left and right hand sides is impossible to make. That's because there are no (or very few indeed) Luftwaffe aircraft photographed and documented from all those directions. Furthermore, my personal "artistic" belief is that an aircraft should be portrayed flying and that landing gears and props simply spoil the sleek lines of a fighter. In addition to this, when meeting with Luftwaffe fighter pilots veterans, their most frequent comment is that a flying fighter without its pilot figure in the cockpit looks ridiculous, something I myself of course am inclined to agree upon. I would like to mention that not two of the pilot figures displayed are identical, and that they all help to illustrate the development of the Luftwaffe's pilot equipment. However, since I try to accommodate all enthusiasts out there, I'll choose to portray some of my profiles with propeller blades and landing gears.

The Profiles

1. Bf 109 E-1

Flown by *Oberleutnant* Eduard Neumann, 8./JG 26, Werl/Germany, September 1939.

"Edu" Neumann drew his first blood as a fighter pilot during the Spanish Civil War, where he shot down an I-153 on September 4, 1937 and an I-16 on June 11, 1938. On September 23, 1939, he was assigned *Staffelkapitän* of 8./JG 26 on the Western Front. After serving as *Geschwaderadjutant* in JG 27 for four months – whereby he achieved his first three victories in World War II – *Hauptmann* Neumann assumed command of I./JG 27 in July 1940. His first victory with I./JG 27 was achieved over the English Channel on July 20, 1940 against an RAF Blenheim I (L 1300) of 236 Squadron, with the crew Sergeants E.E. Lockton and H. Corcoran. By the end of the Battle of Britain, Neumann had achieved a total of nine confirmed victories. In April 1941, I./JG 27 arrived to Libya as the first Luftwaffe fighter unit in North Africa. It was under Neumann's command that the ace Hans-Joachim Marseille rose to fame. On June 8, 1942, Neumann became the *Geschwaderkommodore* of JG 27, which by that time had all three Gruppen based in North Africa. He commanded JG 27 until April 1943, and then served in various senior command positions, including Jafü Romania in early 1944. Eduard Neumann's final score was thirteen confirmed victories.

2. Bf 109 E-3

Flown by *Unteroffizier* Heinz Bär, 1./JG 51, Speyer/Germany, September 25, 1939.

On September 25, 1939, six 1./JG 51 pilots were involved in their first air combat, with six French Curtiss Hawk 75 fighters The first airkill of JG 51 was scored by *Hauptmann* Douglas Pitcairn, the *Staffelkapitän* of 1./JG 51, at 1230 hours. A few minutes later, *Unteroffizier* Heinz Bär brought down a second French plane. Four days later, the two successful German pilots were awarded with the Iron Crosses of the Second class. After the Battle of Britain, the seventeen victories on Bär's killboard rendered him the place as the second most successful pilot in I./JG 51. The colorful Heinz Bär was a most gifted but also rather non-militaric fighter pilot. He earned his nickname "Pritzl" due to his fondness of Pritzl candy bars. Bär started his fighter pilot career as an *Unteroffizier* in 1939, and ended the war as an *Oberstleutnant* with Adolf Galland's jet fighter unit JV 44. Significant to Bär's character is a meeting that he had with the commander in chief of the Luftwaffe, *Reichsmarschall* Hermann Göring, in late 1940. Göring was informed that Bär recently had survived being shot down in the English Channel. As Göring asked if it had been a tough experience, Bär replied: "No, sir, I kept reminding myself that *Herr Reichsmarschall* had said that the English Channel no longer is a channel!"

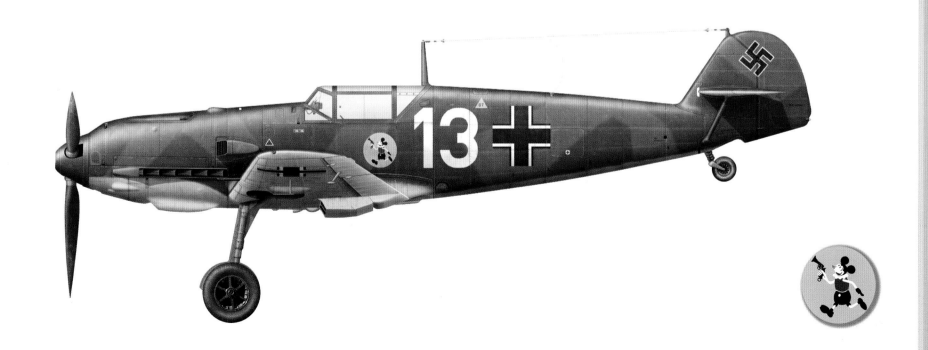

3. Bf 109 D-1

Flown by *Oberleutnant* Johannes Steinhoff, 10./(NJ)JG 26, Bonn-Hangelar/Germany, December 1939.

Johannes "Mäcki" Steinhoff started his military career in the German Navy in the mid-1930s. Between 1936 and 1938, he served as a fighter pilot with I./136, thereafter in the position as *Staffelkapitän* of the experimental night fighter *Staffel* 1.(N)/LG 1 prior to the war. Later, this *Staffel* – equipped with obsolescent Bf 109 D and Arado Ar 68 fighters – was redesignated into 10.(N)/JG 26. The task assigned to Steinhoff and his pilots was to operate in areas illuminated by searchlights in support of the AAA. But due to a lack of radar guidance and even without any ground control support, this unit was unable to achieve any success against the irregular nocturnal intrusions by French and British bombers over western Germany. Steinhoff's two first victories were achieved against RAF Wellingtons during the British air raid against Helgoland on December 18, 1939. In late December 1939, 10.(N)/JG 26 was incorporated into the new IV.(N)/JG 2. On February 1, 1940, Steinhoff was posted to JG 52, where he assumed command of the 4. *Staffel*. He was credited with eight kills during the Battle of Britain, and during the invasion of the Soviet Union in 1941, Steinhoff developed into the most successful pilot of II./JG 52. On August 25-29, 1941 he brought home seven victories, reaching a total of thirty-five – for which he was awarded with the Knight's Cross. In February 1942, when the *Gruppenkommandeur Hauptmann* Erich Woitke was relieved from his command, Steinhoff took charge of II./JG 52. From then on, he would achieve an impressive victory string over the southern combat zone of the Eastern Front.

4. Bf 109 E-3

Flown by *Unteroffizier* Hugo Dahmer, 4./JG 26, Dortmund/Germany, February 1940.

Hugo Dahmer belonged to the most successful NCOs of the German fighter air arm during the early stage of the war, and this resulted in repeated friction with his superiors. He scored his first victory as an *Unteroffizier* with 6./JG 26 on May 16, 1940, and on June 6, 1940 he reached a total of five kills by bagging two RAF 43 Squadron Hurricanes over Dieppe/France. Shortly afterward, the Luftwaffe's C-in-C arrived to inspect the *Staffel*, and Göring was amused to find that an Unteroffizier was more successful in terms of victories than several of the officers – including the *Staffelkapitän*, *Oberleutnant* Walter Schneider, who could only file two victories. On February 1, 1941, when Dahmer had amassed a total of 12 victories (still more than his *Staffelkapitän*), the *Geschwaderkommodore* of JG 26, *Oberstleutnant* Adolf Galland, had him transferred to 1./JG 77 in Norway. When the war against the Soviet Union opened in June 1941, Dahmer flew against the Soviets in the Murmansk area, in the Far North, with considerable success. He developed the so-called *Sauhaufen* ("higgledy-piggledy") tactic against Soviet bombers – German fighters attacking Soviet bomber formations from all directions, at irregular intervals, thus creating confusion and chaos among the bomber crews. In this way he brought down 25 Soviet aircraft in s short space of time. On August 1, 1941, he became the first pilot in the Far North to be awarded with the Knight's Cross. In early 1942 he returned to the English Channel, first with JG 26, later with III./JG 2, where he developed to *Staffelkapitän*. Dahmer carried out his last combat sortie on October 10, 1943, when he was shot down by Spitfires in the Rouen area and was severely injured. (Quite extraordinary, there are no RAF or USAAF claims in that area on that date.) Hugo Dahmer carried out a total of 307 combat sorties and was credited with 57 victories. Dahmer is still alive.

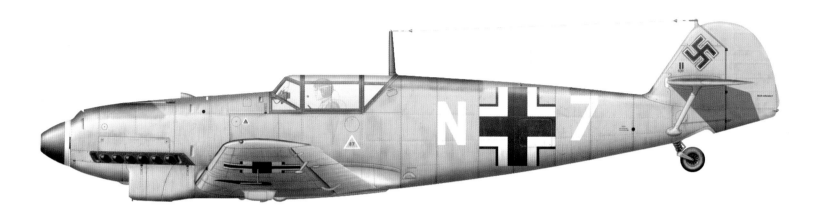

5. Bf 109 E-1

Flown by *Oberfeldwebel* Kurt Ubben, 6. (J)/JG 186, Wangerooge/Germany, late March 1940.

In late 1937, an aircraft carrier aviation *Gruppe*, *Trägergruppe* 184, was formed within the framework of the German program for the carrier *Graf Zeppelin*. In late 1938, the *Trägerjagdstaffel* 4./136 was renumbered into 6.(J)/186. Among the first pilots in the new 6./186 was *Feldwebel* Kurt Ubben. Early on September 1, 1939, 6./186 carried out its first wartime mission, to cover the cruiser *Schleswig Holstein* that fired some of the first shells against Westerplatte in the war against Poland. During the winter of 1939/1940, the *Staffel* was tasked to provide the German Bight with air cover against RAF bombing intrusions. In May 1940, it participated in the invasion of the Netherlands, and *Oberfeldwebel* Kurt Ubben scored his first victory – against a Fokker D-XXI – on May 10. In July 1940, when Hitler had disbanded the carrier programme, 6.(J)/186 was renumbered 9./JG 77. "Kuddel" Ubben took part in the Battle of Britain as *Staffelkapitän* 8./JG 77. Carrying out fighter-bomber missions against British shipping in the Aegean Sea in the spring of 1941, he scored a hit on the battleship *Warspite* on May 22. During the invasion of the Soviet Union, 8./JG 77 was assigned to the southern sector, and Ubben was assigned to command III./JG 77 from September 1941, although he only held the rank of an *Oberleutnant* by that time. On October 2, 1941, he scored his fortieth victory against a MiG-3.

6. Bf 109 E-4

Flown by *Oberleutnant* Josef Priller, 6./JG 51, Dinant/France, May 28, 1940.

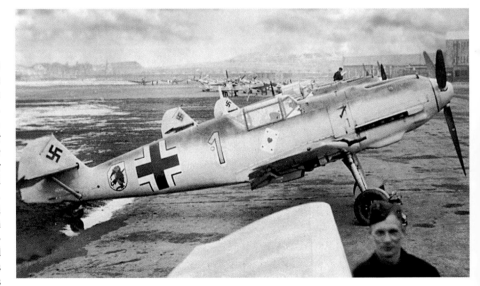

Josef Priller was both a deadly skillful fighter pilot, and a gifted accordion player who amused his comrades with music between the combat missions. From October 1939 he was assigned as *Staffelkapitän* of the new 6./JG 51 on the Western Front. During the air fighting over Dunkirk on May 28, 1940, Priller scored his two first victories against a Spitfire and a Hurricane over Dunkirk. During the Battle of Britain, he soon emerged into one of the most successful fighter pilots of JG 51. Following his twentieth victory Priller became the fourth member of the *Geschwader*, on October 19, 1940, to be awarded with the Knight's Cross. On November 20, 1940, the *Geschwaderkommodore* of JG 26 *Schlageter*, *Oberstleutnant* Adolf Galland, used his influence in the RLM to have Priller posted to JG 26 to assume command of the 1. *Staffel*. Priller's first victory with JG 26 was attained on June 16, 1941, when he led his *Staffel* in an attack against six RAF Coastal Command Blenheims. Two of the bombers were shot down – one by Priller – and a third was badly damaged. From then on, Priller achieved an amazing victory row against the RAF intrusions over northern France. On July 7, 1941, he defeated the famous RAF ace Group Commander Harry Broadhurst (fifteen victories) in a dogfight near Dunkirk. Broadhurst nevertheless was able to return his badly crippled Spitfire to England. One week later, Priller pounced on a formation of RAF 72 Squadron Spitfires from above and rapidly shot down one – his fortieth victory. The British pilot bailed out and was captured. He later told the Germans that he had not even seen his attacker. On July 20, 1941, Priller was awarded with the Oak Leaves.

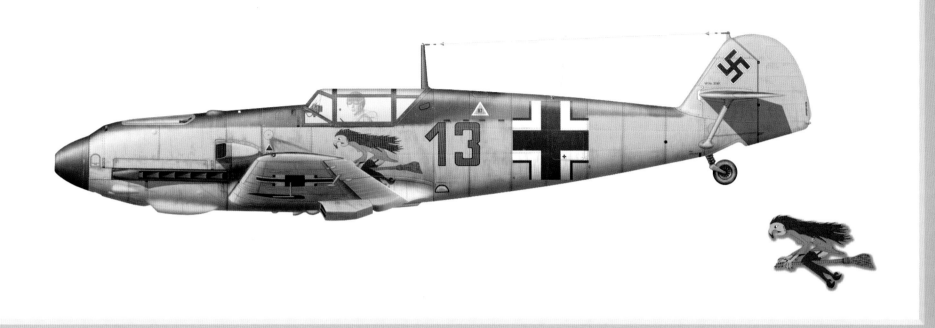

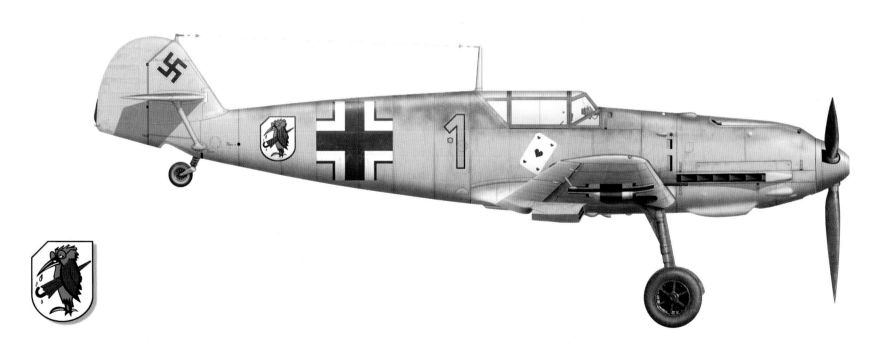

7. Bf 109 E-4
Flown by *Hauptmann* Günther Lützow, *Stab* I./JG 3, Berneuil/France, June 6, 1940.

"Franzl" Lützow was the son of a famous military family and became known as one of the leading personalities of the Jagdwaffe. Like his friend Werner Mölders, Lützow always took great care in the men under his command, and although he advanced to high command positions, he remained firm against Göring's accusations against the fighter pilots. Just as in the case with Mölders, Lützow grew increasingly concerned over the policy of the Third Reich. In the summer of 1942, he publicly humiliated two SD servicemen who had asked him to assign men from his JG 3 to executions of Jews. Before that, Lützow also was one of the most famous Luftwaffe fighter pilots, and on October 24, 1941, he was the second fighter pilot to surpass the 100-victory-mark. But he also grew concerned over the irrational "pure victory-hunting mentality" of the *Jagdwaffe*, and he urged his pilots to stop "flying for fun and seeing who can shoot down the most enemy aircraft." Lützow told them: "The position of Germany is more than critical in every respect and the position of the air force is catastrophic. Every machine, every drop of gas, every hour's flying is irreplaceable. The easy ground life we are leading is irresponsible; in the air even more so. Every shot must go to assist the infantry, if there is no target for it in the air. Every available bomber must be usefully employed at all times." Having led I./JG 3 with success, he was appointed *Geschwaderkommodore* JG 3 in August 1940. Two years later, he left JG 3 to serve in various staff positions. At the end of the war, he served with Galland's Me 262-equipped JV 44, and on April 24, 1945, he failed to return from a combat sortie. Günther Lützow was credited with a total of 103 victories in World War II, plus five in the Spanish Civil War.

8. Bf 109 E-4
Flown by *Major* Adolf Galland, *Stab* III./JG 26, Audembert/France, August 1940.

The colorful Adolf Galland probably is the best known pilot of the Luftwaffe. Born on March 19, 1912 in Westfalia, Galland struggled with both his unwilling father and the Luftwaffe bureaucracy to become a fighter pilot. When he received his "wings" he was, to his disappointment, posted to a ground-attack aviation unit. Galland took part in the Spanish Civil War, where he carried out 300 daring low-level attacks, and flew an Hs 123 biplane against ground targets during the war with Poland. In 1940 he finally made it to a fighter unit, and there he soon proved to have a great talent in fighter combats. His name will forever be associated with the Battle of Britain, where he led JG 26 "Schlageter." During the Battle of Britain, Galland gave proof of both immense flying skills and high ambitions for achieving personal victories. He described himself as "World War II's von Richthofen," and not without reason. In August 1940, ten RAF fighters fell before his guns, followed by another fifteen during the following month. He was awarded with the Knight's Cross on August 1, 1940, and the Oak Leaves less than two months later. On June 21, 1941, Galland became the first man to be awarded with Hitler's new highest military award, the Swords to the Knight's Cross with Oak Leaves. By that time he had achieved 69 victories. During the following five months, Galland carried out about ninety sorties over the English Channel, adding another twenty-seven victories to his killboard. On November 18, 1941, he achieved his ninety-fourth and last victory with JG 26 – a claim that nevertheless can not be substantiated through RAF records. Shortly afterwards Galland was appointed successor of the late Werner Mölders as Inspector of the Fighter Air Arm. At the end of the war, he led the Me 262-equipped JV 44. His total victory score reached 104. Adolf Galland passed away on February 9, 1996.

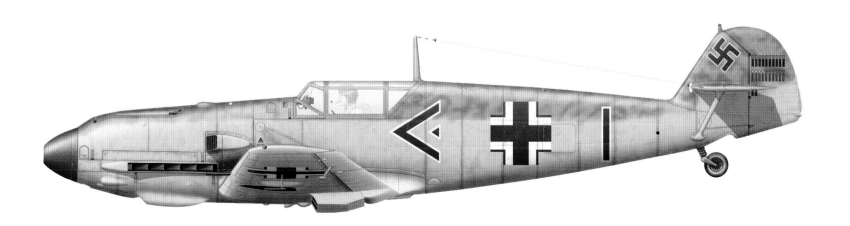

9. Bf 109 E-4

Flown by *Oberleutnant* Werner Machold, 9./JG 2, France, September 1940.

The outbreak of World War II saw Werner Machold as an NCO pilot with I./JG 2 *Richthofen*. Born on July 29, 1911, Werner Machold was among the oldest of the first fighter aces of the Luftwaffe. However, his *Gruppenkommandeur*, *Hauptmann* Erich Mix, was a veteran pilot from World War I who in 1940 was in his forties. But the 13 victories achieved by Mix in a two-month period is a clear evidence that he was still going strong. Mix soon noticed the talent of *Oberfeldwebel* Machold and placed him in the position of a section leader. On May 14, 1940, when JG 2 achieved twenty victories, *Oberfeldwebel* Werner Machold achieved his first two kills against French M.S. 406 fighters. Five days later, he shot down an RAF Hurricane, and brought home two victories each on May 20 and May 21, 1940. His eighth victory was scored against a Spitfire over Calais on May 26, 1940. His ninth and tenth were achieved against a Morane and a Bloch 150 on June 3, 1940. During the subsequent Battle of Britain, Machold rose to become one of the most notable German aces. He knocked down three Hurricanes in a row on August 30, 1940. Three days later he repeated the same feat, only this time against three Spitfires. Having achieved 20 victories, all but six against RAF Spitfires and Hurricanes, Machold was awarded with the Knight's Cross on September 5, 1940. Later, Machold was promoted to *Oberleutnant* and put in charge of 7./JG 2. Machold's last two victories were attained against RAF Spitfires over the English Channel on May 19, 1941. During a low-level attack against a British convoy in the English Channel on June 6, 1941, Machold's Bf 109 received a hit in the radiator, and the pilot had no other option but to belly-land on the British southern coast. The victor in 32 aerial combats would spend the remainder of the war in a POW camp.

---

10. Bf 109 E-4

Flown by *Hauptmann* Wilhelm Balthasar, *Stab* III./JG 3, Desvres/France, September 27, 1940.

Wilhelm Balthasar drew his first blood with J.88 in the Spanish Civil War, where he was credited with seven kills. At the outbreak of World War II he served as *Staffelkapitän* of 1./JG 1 (later 7./JG 27) and would soon prove to be one of the most talented fighter pilots of the Luftwaffe, placing himself in second place after Werner Mölders. During the Battle of France in May-June 1940, Balthasar took a heavy toll of the Armée de l-Air. On May 11, he claimed four victories in two separate combats: First three Gladiators of Belgian Military Aviation's 1st Escadrille, I Group/2d Regiment (1/I/2) at Maastricht at around 1700 hours; then a French M.S. 406, possibly piloted by Adjutant Leclercq of GC II/6, west of Maastricht at 1951 hours. Another five victories followed on June 5, and the next day Balthasar contributed with four to the day's total of twenty-seven victories by JG 27. In total, Balthasar scored twenty-three kills during the Battle of France. He almost shot down twenty-four – but narrowly escaped shooting down Adolf Galland by mistake only through Galland's excited radio call. On September 1, 1940, he was appointed *Gruppenkommandeur* of III./JG 3. Four days later he claimed a Spitfire of 222 Squadron but was himself hit and injured by another aircraft from the same squadron. Five months later, Balthasar returned to operational duty as *Geschwaderkommodore* of JG 2 *Richthofen*. During a series of intense air fighting over northern France on June 22, 1941 through June 27, 1941, he shot down nine RAF aircraft. Balthasar was killed during an aerial combat with Spitfires of RAF Northolt Wing near Aire on July 3, 1941. Two pilots of RAF Northolt Wing each claimed a Bf 109 during that engagement – Wing Commander Johnny Kent and Polish Pilot Officer Boleslav Drobinski of 303 Squadron. Wilhelm Balthasar achieved a total of 47 victories (seven in Spain) and was awarded with the Knight Cross with Oak Leaves.

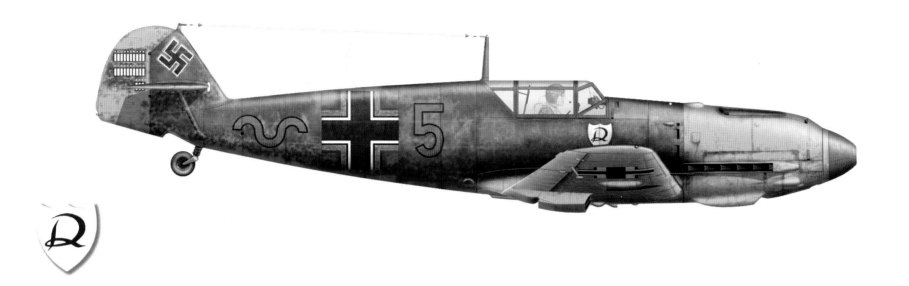

11. Bf 109 E-4/B

Flown by *Oberleutnant* Hans-Ekkehard Bob, 7./JG 54, Guines/France, September 30, 1940.

One of the main disadvantages to the Luftwaffe during the Battle of Britain was the limited operational range of the Bf 109. The single-engine Messerschmitt fighter was originally designed as a local interceptor (*Objektschutzjäger*). Normally, the Bf 109 could not carry out combat missions further than the British capital. This is one of the main reasons to the German failure in the air offensive against the British Isles. Increasing losses among the bombers flying against London compelled the commanders of the fighter units to carry out hazardous long escort missions. Frequently, the Bf 109s returned to France with the last drops of fuel. The return flight to France, with the red warning lamp glowing, put a heavy pressure on the German fighter pilots. On one occasion, the entire III./JG 54 became disorientated during a return flight. Pilot after pilot reported: "My red lamp is glowing!" And still no land in sight. The contours of the French coast appeared in the haze. *Oberleutnant* Hans-Ekkehard Bob couldn't resist switching on the transmission button and to joyfully exclaim: "Cape Horn ahead!" The *Geschwaderkommodore* threatened the "joker" with heavy punishment for disobeying radio discipline. Only after the war did Bob dare to confess the identity of the joker to Trautloft. Shortly afterward, one-third of all Bf 109s in the *Jagdgeschwader* on the English Channel were assigned to carry out fighter-bomber missions against the British Isles. There were no bombsights available, nor did there exist any methods for dropping bombs from Bf 109s. Everything had to be improvised. *Oberleutnant* Bob set out to test bomb dropping against a small, almost deserted coastal strip at Dungeness. There, Bob and his pilots carried out one test bombing after another, learning in which angle and at what speed the bombs had to be dropped in order to achieve greatest precision. Many years after the war, when Bob was invited to participate in RAF,s fiftieth anniversary in England, a former pilot from Fighter Command approached him and said: "What I can't understand is why you Germans dropped so many bombs at Dungeness. There was absolutely nothing there!"

12. Bf 109 E-4

Flown by *Oberleutnant* Friedrich-Karl Müller, *Stab* III./JG 53, Etaples/France, October 1940.

October 1940 was an inglorious month to the Luftwaffe. It was obvious that the momentum of the air offensive against the United Kingdom had been lost. JG 53 recorded a total of twenty-five victories against sixteen combat losses during the month. By that time, Friedrich-Karl Müller served as a relatively anonymous *Oberleutnant* with III./JG 53. He managed to achieve a total of eleven victories between May 1940 and May 1941. Not even the air fighting against obsolete Soviet aircraft in the summer of 1941 brought Müller any remarkable success. Until May 1942, he had carried out more than 300 combat sorties and was credited with 25 victories. It was not until the Battle of Stalingrad in late summer and fall of 1942 that Müller, now serving as *Staffelkapitän* 1./JG 53, broke the spell. By that time, the Soviet Air Force had replaced its old I-16s, I-153s, and SBs for more modern aircraft, but the shortened pilot training – an imperative measure to keep in pace with the immense losses in 1941 – rendered most Soviet airmen helpless against the experienced Luftwaffe veterans. Müller scored 25 victories through August 1942. But his most successful month was September 1942, when 35 Soviet aircraft fell before his guns. I./JG 53 was credited with no less than 918 victories during the summer and early fall of 1942. Thus, against Müller's record claim of six Il-2s shot down on September 9, 1942, Soviet statistics only confirm the loss of three. Approximately five hundred aircraft actually shot down by a single *Jagdgruppe* in only four months may still be regarded as a splendid performance – although it also lost twenty-six pilots in the course. In April 1944, Müller was appointed *Geschwaderkommodore* of JG 3 in the Home Defense, but was killed on May 29, 1944, in a landing accident at Salzwedel. Friedrich-Karl Müller's final score was 140 victories.

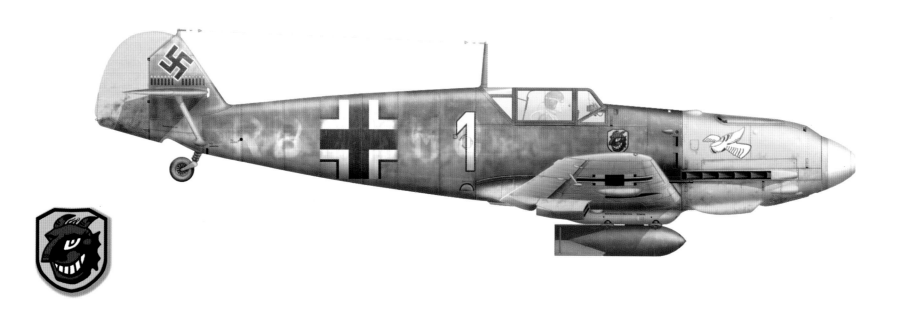

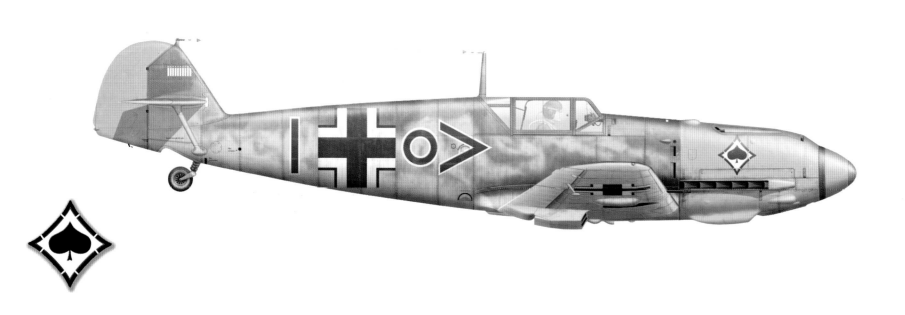

13. Bf 109 E-4
Flown by *Oberleutnant* Egon Troha, 9./JG 3, Desvres/France, October 29, 1940.

Egon Troha was born in Croatia, by then a part of Austria, on March 1, 1916, as the second eldest child of an Officer of the Kaiser's Army. He started his pilot training in Austria, and was included into the Luftwaffe after the Anschluss of Austria to Germany in 1938. On the very same day as the war broke out, Troha was posted to 1./JG 26 with the rank of a *Leutnant*. Two weeks later he was shifted to the new 7./JG 26. On February 25, 1940, he was again posted to a new unit, this time to III./JG 3, where he was assigned as *Gruppenadjutant*. Troha achieved his first victory on May 10, 1940, when he bounced a formation of seven Dutch Fokker G-1s and shot down the aircraft piloted by Lieutenant J. Van der Jagt. His second victory, an RAF Blenheim, fell before his guns on June 8, 1940. From July 1940, he flew over the English Channel, shooting down a Spitfire each on August 26, 1940 (possibly of 610 RAF Squadron) and August 30, 1940. His fifth and last victory was achieved on October 26, 1940, when he destroyed a Hurricane – probably piloted by 229 Squadron's Pilot Officer G.M. Simpson, who was attacking a He 59 air-sea-rescue aircraft. Simpson was killed. At 1715 hours on October 29, 1940, Troha was shot down by Pilot Officer George Marland, flying an RAF 222 Squadron Spitfire. Troha belly-landed at the West Court farm close to Boothen cross road near Shepherdswell and was immediately captured by angry British farm workers armed with flails and scythes. Troha was transported to a POW camp in Canada, and during a riot in the camp, he was severely wounded and lost one eye. This allowed Troha to benefit from a prison exchange, and on September 13, 1944, he boarded the Swedish luxury liner *Gripsholm* in New York, which arrived ten days later at Gothenburg/Sweden. He returned to Germany and ended the war as a fighter pilot trainer for former bomber pilots in JG 108.

14. Bf 109 E-4
Flown by *Oberleutnant* Joachim Müncheberg, 7./JG 26, Chaffiers/France, November 14, 1940.

"Jochen" Müncheberg was described as "one of the great figures of the Luftwaffe" by JG 27's "Edu" Neumann. Born on December 31, 1918, he was posted to III./JG 132 Schlageter (later III./JG 26) as an *Oberfähnrich* in 1938. On November 7, 1939, he attained the *Geschwader*'s second victory by knocking down an RAF 57 Squadron Blenheim over the Rhine River. On May 14, 1940, Müncheberg took part in the wiping out of an entire Hurricane section from RAF 504 Squadron. During the subsequent Battle of Britain in the summer and fall of 1940, he proved to be one of the *Geschwader*'s most gifted fighter pilots. On November 14, 1940, Müncheberg – now *Staffelkapitän* 7./JG 26 – brought down a Spitfire as JG 26 and JG 51 escorted III./St.G. 1 during the last Stuka sortie over the English Channel. When *Oberstleutnant* Galland early in 1941 was instructed to shift one of his *Staffeln* against Malta, he picked Müncheberg. Although the British had reinforced their Malta fighter force considerably, the RAF fighter pilots stood no chance against Müncheberg's men. When 7./JG 26 returned to France in September 1941, it had amassed a total of fifty-two victories – without losing a single pilot – in the Mediterranean theater. Nearly half the victories, twenty-five, were scored by Müncheberg. Counted among Müncheberg's victims over Malta were two of the best RAF fighter aces in that area, 261 Squadron's Flying Officers James Archibald Findlay MacLachlan (sixteen kills) and Eric Taylor (seven kills). Shortly afterward, 261 Squadron was withdrawn from Malta for "fatigue," and returned to England to rest. During his stay in the Mediterranean area, Müncheberg was awarded both with the Oak Leaves to his Knight's Cross, and (on April 15, 1941) Italy's highest military award, the Medaglia d'Oro.

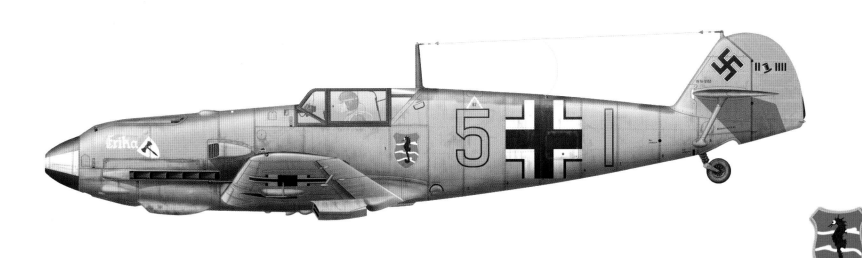

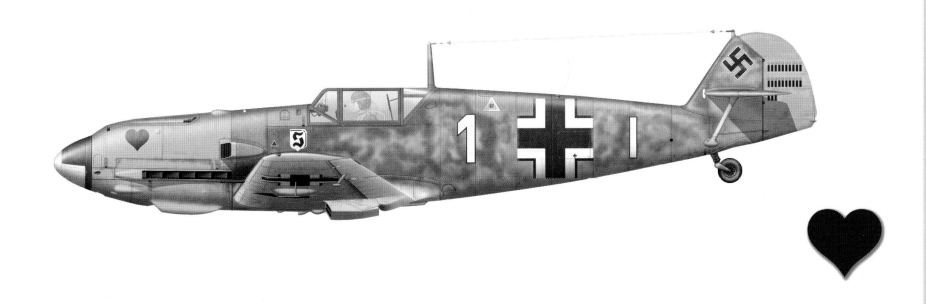

15. Bf 109 E-4

Flown by *Hauptmann* Rolf Pingel, *Stab* I./JG 26, St. Omer-Clairmairais/France, December 1940.

Rolf Peter Pingel participated as a fighter pilot with J. 88 in the Spanish Civil War, where he shot down four Republican aircraft. At the beginning of World War II, he served as *Staffelkapitän* 2./JG 53 on the Western Front, and became one of the most successful fighter pilots during the "Phony War" in 1939. His first victory in this conflict was attained on September 10, 1939, when he hit a French Mureaux reconnaissance aircraft of Groupe I/520. The Mureaux crashed near Saarbrücken, killing the crew. On September 26, 1939, he led his *Staffel* to wipe out an entire formation of five RAF 150 Squadron Battle bombers. The fateful August 15, 1940, when the Luftwaffe lost 71 aircraft in a fruitless attempt to knock out RAF Fighter Command on the ground, *Hauptmann* Pingel participated in escorting one hundred Ju 87s and Ju 88s against Portland. In the ensuing dogfight, I./JG 53 claimed to have shot down five Hurricanes while six bombers went lost. RAF 87, 234, and 601 squadrons filed eight losses. Pingel returned to base with two victories – his eighth and ninth. One week later, Pingel was shifted to JG 26 to take command of its I. Gruppe. On September 14, 1940, *Stab* and I./JG 26 clashed with the Hurricanes of 253 Squadron south of the Thames Estuary. The Germans claimed four Hurricanes shot down – including Pingel's fifteenth and *Major* Adolf Galland's thirty-second victories. Actual 253 Squadron losses were confined to one aircraft that was shot down and another that collided with a Bf 109. That evening, Hauptmann Pingel was awarded with the Knight's Cross. On July 10, 1941, Pingel came across an RAF four-engine Stirling bomber and followed it across the English Channel, where he was shot down by the Stirling's upper gunner. Rolf Pingel, credited with 26 victories, would spend the remainder of the war in British captivity.

16. Bf 109 E-4

Flown by *Major* Hannes Trautloft, *Stab*/JG 54, Le Mans/France, March 1941.

In March 1941, JG 54 was stationed in Le Mans on a well-deserved rest and recuperation after the hard times during the Battle of Britain. The *Geschwaderkommodore Major* Hannes Trautloft and the other officers of JG 54 spent most of the time at Le Mans with pheasant hunting trips or walks in the old town of Le Mans. According to Hannes Trautloft, his main preoccupation at this time was a series of visits to the dentist – fearful for Trautloft, who had greater fear for the dentist than for any Spitfire. The only hostile activity that met the men of JG 54 at Le Mans were French chocolate bars that were found to be stuffed with small, sharp metallic pieces. Trautloft celebrated his 29th birthday in Le Mans on March 3. The only noteworthy flight incident during this stay in Le Mans occurred when *Major* Trautloft was forced to punish *Oberleutnant* Hans-Ekkehard Bob for failing to report that he had crashed a Bücker training plane in the harbor of Cherbourg.

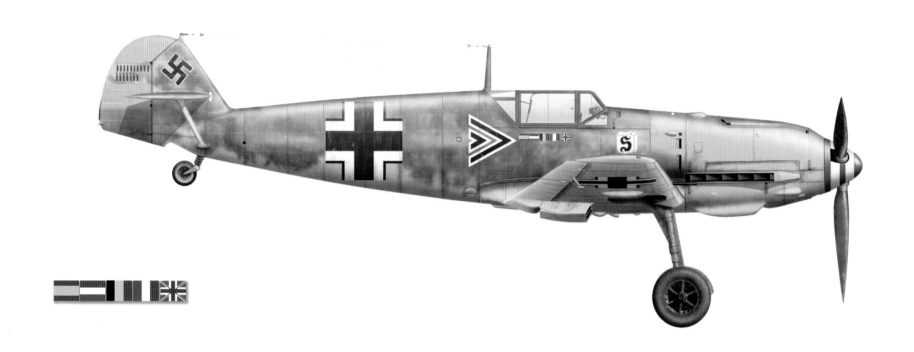

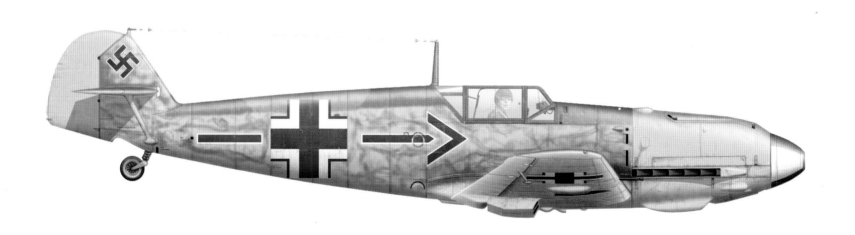

17. Bf 109 E-4

Flown by *Hauptmann* Herbert Ihlefeld, *Stab* I.(J)/LG 2, Radomir/Bulgaria, April 1941.

As Herbert Ihlefeld returned to Germany after the Spanish Civil War, with nine victories he was one of the most successful aces of the Condor Legion. During the Battle of Britain he once again demonstrated his outstanding skills in aerial combat, returning from almost every mission across the Channel with new kills. From August 1940 he commanded I.(J)/LG 2 (later I./JG 77). On February 26, 1941, German fighters claimed six RAF fighters shot down over the Channel. One of them, a Spitfire, was recorded as Ihlefeld's 30th victory. The British pilot, Flight Sergeant Howard Squire of RAF 54 Squadron, force-landed his Spitfire MK II (A/C P7443) near Calais. Squire was brought to the base of I.(J)/LG 2, where he met with and shared a few drinks with Ihlefeld. Before being transferred to a POW camp, Squire asked Ihlefeld to drop a note that he was safe over 54 Squadron's base at Croydon. Ihlefeld did so a few days later, and on the return flight he bagged another Spitfire for his thirty-first victory. Forty-three years later the two men met at the same place again. According to recent research, Herbert Ihlefeld claimed a total of 132 victories during World War II. He passed away on August 8, 1995, and was buried in the Wennigser Waldfriedhof, near Hannover. Note: The small "bump" beneath the belly of the aircraft displayed here is Peil1G IV, a bearing equipment that was tested by I.(J)/LG 2 during this period.

18. Bf 109 F-2

Flown by *Major* Günther *Freiherr* von Maltzahn, *Stab*/JG 53, St. Omer/France, May 1941.

"Henri" Maltzahn served as *Gruppenkommandeur* II./JG 53 when the war broke out. His flight book is indicative to the calm period during the so-called "Phony War" over the Western Front in 1939 and early 1940: von Maltzahn's first fifteen combat sorties led to no contact with the enemy. Only on his sixteenth mission, on September 26, 1939, did he spot any enemy aircraft. The outcome was a French Potez 633 claimed shot down by him. During the Battle of Britain, where von Maltzahn was appointed *Geschwaderkommodore* of JG 53, he emerged as one of the most popular unit commanders in the Luftwaffe. By late November 1940, his personal victory scores stood at eleven kills – compared to the tallies of other Jagdgeschwader commanders, such as *Oberstleutnant* Adolf Galland (57), *Major* Helmut Wick (56), and *Oberstleutnant* Werner Mölders (54). But von Maltzahn was known to have placed a higher emphasis on taking care of his subordinates than to achieve personal successes in air combat, and it was mainly because of his skills as unit commander that he was awarded with the Knight's Cross on December 13, 1940. Von Maltzahn's greatest individual successes in air combat were achieved on the Eastern Front in 1941, where he claimed thirty-three victories. His fortieth victory was achieved against a Soviet 66 ShAP I-153 on July 20, 1941. In October 1943 von Maltzahn had to give up his post as *Geschwaderkommodore* of JG 53 and was appointed *Luftwaffenbefehlshaber Mitte*. Later, when he served as Jafü in Upper Italy, his superiors accused him of not making sufficient demands on the outnumbered Luftwaffe fighter pilots in Italy. Günther *Freiherr* von Maltzahn passed away on June 24, 1953, at the age of forty-two. He was credited with a total of sixty-eight victories.

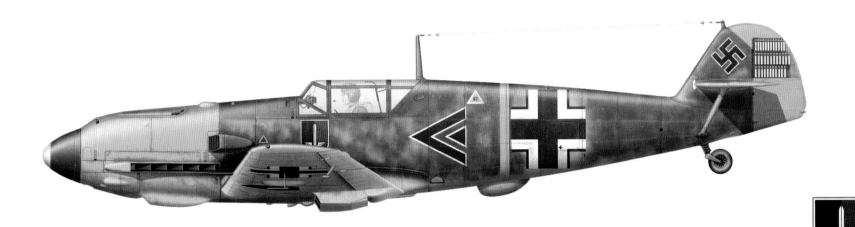

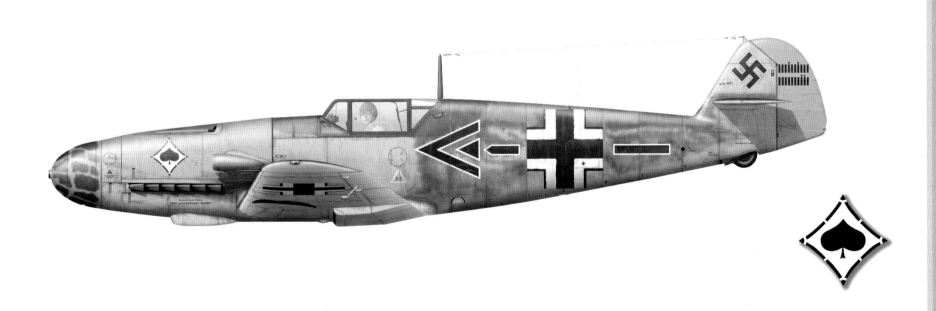

19. Bf 109 F-2

Flown by *Hauptmann* Hermann-Friedrich Joppien, *Stab* I./JG 51, Starawies/Poland, June 1941.

Hermann-Friedrich Joppien was one of the most aggressive fighter pilots of I./JG 51, and scored large successes during the Battle of Britain. He commanded 1./JG 51 from August 5, 1940. During the famous Battle of Britain Day, September 15, 1940, Joppien bagged a Hurricane and a Spitfire for his twentieth and twenty-first victories. Next day he was awarded with the Knight's Cross. One month later he was appointed *Gruppenkommandeur* of I./JG 51. On December 5, 1940, a Spitfire ended up as his thirtieth victory. By that time, Joppien temporarily served with *Major* Werner Mölders's *Geschwaderstab*/JG 51, where Joppien was strongly reproached by Mölders for his alleged habit of strafing civilian targets. When I./JG 51 was transferred to Poland in June 1941 to participate in the invasion of the Soviet Union, Joppien had contributed forty-two to the *Gruppe*'s total of 182 kills. Joppien's most successful day was June 30, 1941, when the Soviets dispatched hundreds of bombers of various types – including very obsolescent models – to destroy the German river crossings at Bobruysk. When the day was over, JG 51 had claimed 113 victories, five of them by *Hauptmann* Joppien. When Joppien was killed in air combat with pilots of VVS-Central Front on August 25, 1941, his seventy victories rendered him a fourth ranking place among the top scorers of the war.

20. Bf 109 F-2

Flown by *Oberleutnant* Werner Pichon-Kalau vom Hofe, *Stab*/JG 54, Lindental/East Prussia, June 1941.

In September 1939, *Leutnant* Werner Pichon-Kalau vom Hofe served as technical officer in I./JG 20 (later III./JG 51), commanded by *Hauptmann* Hannes Trautloft – who would become one of Pichon's closest friends. On July 19, 1940, *Leutnant* Werner Pichon-Kalau vom Hofe achieved his three first victories against Defiant fighters of RAF 141 Squadron. In August 1940, the *Jagdfliegerführer General* von Döring allowed *Hauptmann* Hannes Trautloft – who had recently been appointed *Geschwaderkommodore* of JG 54 – to bring along several of his friends from III./JG 51 to JG 54: His adjutant *Oberleutnant* Otto Kath, Trautloft's First mechanic *Obergefreiter* Pingel, his driver *Obergefreiten* Books, his wingman *Unteroffizier* Deutschmann, and *Oberleutnant* Pichon. On August 30, 1940, Pichon was awarded with the Iron Cross of the First Class. On October 12, 1940, *Oberleutnant* Pichon achieved JG 54's 300th victory by downing a Spitfire. Ten days later, Pichon was less fortunate, as he downed a German Do 17. It proved to be that it was the third time that this Do 17 crew had been brought down by German fighters! On October 25, Pichon claimed his fifth victory against a Spitfire – in reality probably the Hurricane piloted by French pilot Adjutant H. Boquillard of RAF 249 Squadron. In the spring of 1941, Pichon flew combat missions over Yugoslavia, and he participated in the invasion of the Soviet Union in June 1941. On June 25, 1941, he shot down two Soviet SB bombers. On April 26, 1942, Pichon was shot down over Soviet territory, but managed to evade getting captured, and made it back to the German lines after three days. Werner Pichon-Kalau vom Hofe achieved a total of 21 confirmed victories.

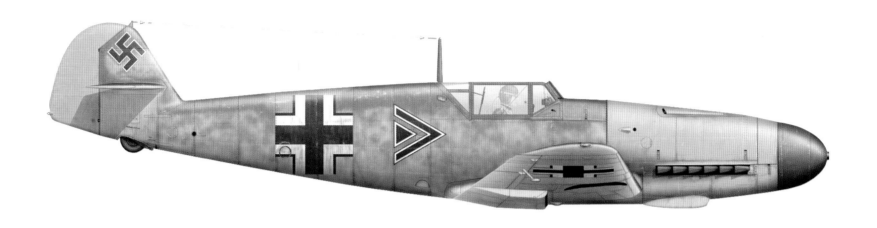

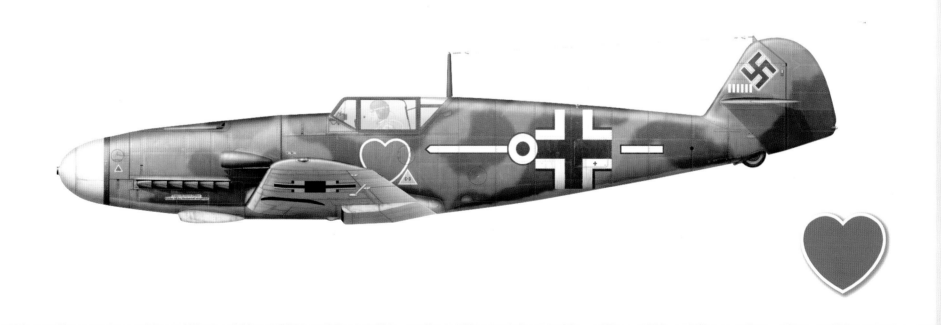

21. Bf 109 F-2
Flown by *Hauptmann* Hans von Hahn, *Stab* I./JG 3, Lutsk/USSR, July 6, 1941.

Hans von Hahn – not to be confused with the famous Oak Leaves holder Hans "Assi" Hahn – was posted to I./JG 3 as this unit's *Gruppenkommandeur* on August 27, 1940. By that time he had amassed eleven victories with JG 53. He served on the Eastern Front from the first day of the attack on the Soviet Union. His first victories on the Eastern Front were all achieved against unescorted bombers or biplane fighters. On July 6, 1941, I./JG 3 caught a formation of DB-3 bombers and shot down eight within ten minutes – two of them by von Hahn, who thus ran up his tally to twenty-four. But when the *Jagdgruppe* ran into the aces of Soviet 88 IAP over Kanev in August 1941, things were different. "All previous air combat had been a children's game compared to what we encountered above the Dnieper Bridge at Kanev," Hans von Hahn wrote. Later in 1941, I./JG 3 was withdrawn from the Eastern Front and transferred to Germany, where it was re-numbered into the new II./JG 1. Following accusations for abuse against subordinates, *Hauptmann* von Hahn was relieved from his command in June 1942. In April 1945, he was appointed commander of the fighter units in Upper Italy. Hans von Hahn, who was credited with a total of 34 victories, died in his home in Frankfurt on November 5, 1957, at the age of forty-three.

22. Bf 109 F-2
Flown by *Leutnant* Hans Beisswenger, 6./JG 54, Sebesya/USSR , July 12, 1941.

II./JG 54, to which Beisswenger belonged, was the most successful *Jagdgruppe* during the opening phase of Hitler's invasion of the USSR. On July 5, 1941, this *Gruppe* surpassed its 300th victory mark, and it scored another two hundred victories until the end of August 1941. On August 24, 1941, *Leutnant* Beisswenger was awarded with the Iron Cross of the First Class for twenty-one victories. October 2, 1941, he achieved his 32nd victory by downing a MiG-3. In 1942, Beisswenger rose to become one of the most successful pilots of the entire *Grünherzgeschwader*. On August 15, 1942, Beisswenger scored his eighty-third victory, and on October 29, 1942, his 100th. His most successful day was December 30, 1942, when he claimed ten kills. But Soviet resistance in the air inevitably grew stronger week by week. On March 6, 1943 – the day after he had reached the 150-victory-mark – *Oberleutnant* Beisswenger and his wingman, twenty-victory-ace *Unteroffizier* Georg Munderloh, were both shot down and killed in combat with Soviet fighters near Staraya Russa. The two LaGG-3s that Beisswenger claimed during his last combat were filed as his 151st and 152d victories. Note: The yellow fuselage band beneath the *Balkenkreuz* on the fuselage side on the aircraft displayed here has been interpreted as "typical for JG 54." In reality, this marking indicated that it was a fighter subordinated to *Luftflotte* 1.

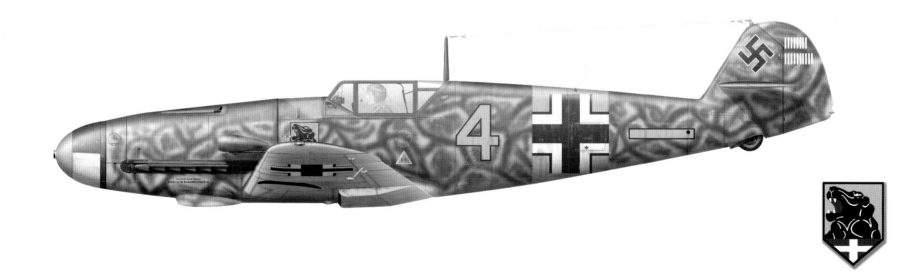

23. Bf 109 E-4/B

Flown by *Oberfeldwebel* Reinhold Schmetzer, 8./JG 77, Balti/USSR, July 20, 1941.

At the outbreak of the war, "Spätzle" Schmetzer served as an *Unteroffizier* with 5.(J)/186. This unit was originally intended to fly sorties from the projected German aircraft carrier *Graf Zeppelin* (a programme which was later disbanded). On May 5, 1940, he scored his first victory against a Blenheim bomber over the German Bight. His second victory was a Dutch Fokker D-XXI on May 10, 1940. At the opening of Operation *Barbarossa*, Hitler's assault on the Soviet Union, Schmetzer served as an *Oberfeldwebel* with III./JG 77, and had five victories on his killboard. On July 20, 1941, Schmetzer took off from Balti Airdrome at 1835 hours for a Stuka escort mission, and when he returned he had scored his twentieth victory against a VVS-Southern Front MiG-3. He achieved another a total of twenty-eight victories on the Eastern Front before he was promoted to *Leutnant* and posted to the new I./JG 4 in the Home Defense in 1943. Intercepting 165 U.S. heavy bombers that went against Osnabrück on May 7, 1944, Schmetzer crippled a U.S. 389th Bomb Group B-24 but was himself shot down and killed by the Liberators' defensive fire, and became the only Luftwaffe casualty in that encounter. The bomber that Schmetzer had hit in his last encounter ditched in the North Sea on return, and two crewmembers were rescued. Schmetzer was one of fourteen combat losses sustained by I./JG 4 in May 1944.

24. Bf 109 E-7

Flown by *Oberleutnant* Erbo Graf von Kageneck, 9./JG 27, Chudovo/USSR, August 20, 1941.

Born on April 2, 1918, Erbo Graf von Kageneck served with I./JG 1 from the beginning of the war. His first two victories were achieved against RAF Blenheims over France on May 12, 1940. With a total of eighty-one victories for thirteen combat losses, I./JG 1 was the one of the most successful *Jagdgruppen* during the Battle of France in May and June 1940. In July 1940, the unit was redesignated as III./JG 27. The following operations over the English Channel proved to be more difficult, and on July 19, 1940, Graf Kageneck had to belly-land his Bf 109 in France after sustaining injuries in combat with RAF 43 Squadron Hurricanes. On September 18, 1940, Graf Kageneck was appointed *Staffelkapitän* of 9./JG 27. By that time his victory total had reached 10. His rise to real fame would come in 1941. In May 1941, when III./JG 27 operated over Malta for a brief period, Graf Kageneck was personally responsible for four of the five RAF 185 and 261 Squadron Hurricanes that were shot down by the *Gruppe*. During III./JG 27's participation in the invasion of the Soviet Union – from June 1941 to October 1941 – Graf Kageneck increased his victory tally from 17 to 65. His greatest success was achieved on August 14, 1941, when he claimed five kills during two separate engagements. On August 20, 1941, he brought down two Soviet fighters and two Il-2s, thus reaching a total tally of fifty-two. In December 1941, III./JG 27 arrived in North Africa to join the *Geschwader*'s I. *Gruppe*. On Christmas Eve, Graf Kageneck was shot down by an RAF Hurricane piloted by either Pilot Officer Thomson or Sergeant Maxwell. Nineteen days later, he died from the wounds sustained. Erbo Graf von Kageneck was credited with a total of 67 victories.

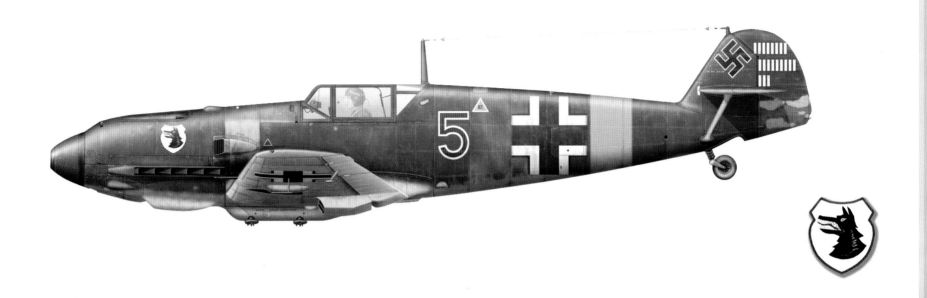

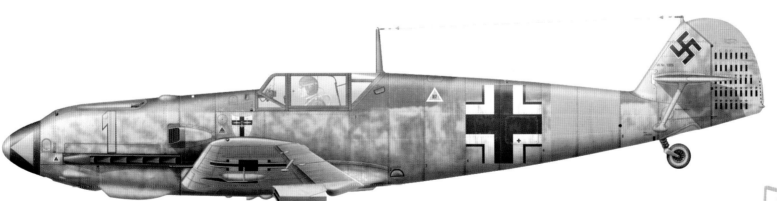

25. Bf 109 E-7 Trop

Flown by *Feldwebel* Günther Steinhausen, 1./JG 27, Ain-El-Gazala/Libya, August 1941.

Günther Steinhausen was known as a gentle and rather shy NCO in I./JG 27. He was one of the first Luftwaffe fighter pilots in North Africa. He was posted to I./JG 27 in the spring of 1941. His rise to fame began in 1942. On January 9, 1942, *Feldwebel* Günther Steinhausen shot down two Hurricanes, one of them piloted by RAF 229 Squadron's commander, Squadron Leader Smith. On June 28, 1942, three I./JG 27 Bf 109 pilots bounced a formation of ten Hurricanes and claimed six shot down without own losses. Five of these claims can be verified with RAF loss files. Stenhausen contributed with four kills, achieved in eight minutes. On July 9, 1942, Steinhausen spotted six Liberator bombers of the U.S. Halverson Detachment in Egypt and shot down one. At 0845 hours on September 6, 1942, *Oberfeldwebel* Steinhausen and seven other I./JG 27 Bf 109 pilots scrambled against twelve Hurribombers, escorted by nineteen South African and British Hurricane fighters. In the ensuing air combat, eight Hurricanes and two Bf 109s were shot down. Counted among five casualties in 7 SAAF Squadron was the unit commander, *Major* Whelehan. *Oberfeldwebel* Günther Steinhausen, who had brought down the first Hurricane in the engagement – his fortieth and last victory – failed to return to base. On November 3, 1942, he was posthumously awarded with the Knight's Cross.

26. Bf 109 F-4 Trop

Flown by *Hauptmann* Wolfgang Lippert, II./JG 27, Ain-El-Gazala/Libya, September 1941.

When II./JG 27 arrived in North Africa during the latter half of September 1941, it had amassed a total of 141 aerial victories over France, the English Channel, the Balkans, and the Soviet Union. The most successful individual pilot was the *Gruppenkommandeur*, *Hauptmann* Wolfgang Lippert, who landed in Libya on September 29, 1941, fifteen days after his twenty-ninth birthday. By that time, his score stood at twenty-five. Lippert was a veteran from the Condor Legion in Spain, where he had scored four victories. When he assumed command of II./JG 27 on September 4, 1940, his score stood at eleven. Twenty days later, *Hauptmann* Lippert was awarded with the Knight's Cross. On October 25, 1940, he bagged two Hurricanes for his nineteenth and twentieth kills. Under Lippert's command, II./JG 27 developed into the most successful JG 27 *Gruppe* during the Battle of Britain, with sixty victories against twenty-five pilot casualties. On November 23, 1941, Lippert was shot down over British-held territory in Libya during a combat with 24 SAAF Squadron Bostons and RAF 229 and 238 squadron Hurricanes. Ten days later, he died from his sustained wounds at General Hospital 119 in Egypt. In total Wolfgang Lippert scored 30 confirmed victories.

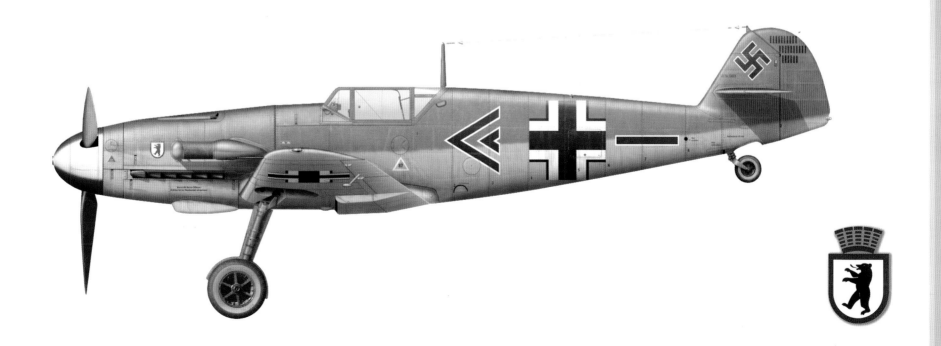

27. Bf 109 F-2
Flown by *Leutnant* Herbert Schramm, 8./JG 53, Ossiyaki/USSR, September 10, 1941.

Herbert Schramm served under *Hauptmann* Werner Mölders's command with III./JG 53 as a *Feldwebel* from the beginning of the war. His first victory was achieved against a French Morane-Saulnier M.S. 406 fighter on May 14, 1940 – when 102 French and British aircraft were shot down (Luftwaffe fighters and AAA claimed 170 victories). The total score for Mölders's III./JG 53 during the Battle of France was approximately ninety-eight victories for only seven combat losses. In June 1941, when Schramm's victory score had reached seven, he participated in the invasion of the Soviet Union. On September 10, 1941, III./JG 53 was assigned to cover *Generaloberst* Heinz Guderian's *Panzergruppe* 2, which was advancing to close the sack behind five Soviet armies in the Kiev area. The battered air forces of Soviet Southwestern and Bryansk fronts did whatever they could to slow down the German attack, but suffered dearly at the hands of the Bf 109 pilots. Herbert Schramm contributed to the day's success by knocking down an I-15 biplane fighter, but was himself shot down in the process. He nevertheless survived. After attaining a total of thirty-nine victories with III./JG 53 – the last one, a Blenheim, over Malta on February 12, 1942 – Schramm was posted to serve as fighter trainer. On August 13, 1943, he was assigned to take command of 5./JG 27 in the Home Defense. Schramm managed to shoot down three U.S. heavy bombers before he was killed in combat with Thunderbolts near Eupen/Belgium on December 1, 1943. He was awarded with the Oak Leaves to his Knight's Cross posthumously on February 1, 1945. Herbert Schramm was credited with a total of forty-two confirmed victories.

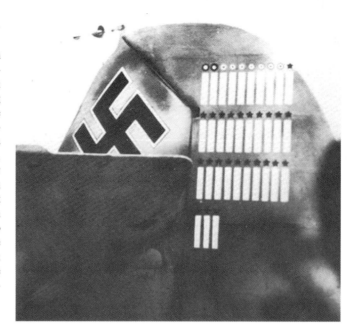

28. Bf 109 F-4
Flown by *Unteroffizier* Alfred Grislawski, 9./JG 52, Poltava/USSR, October 23, 1941.

Alfred Grislawski was born on November 2, 1919. He entered the Luftwaffe and *Flieger-ersatzabteilung* 16 in Schleswig on November 1, 1937. His flight training began in August 1939, and *Gefreiter* Grislawski received his wings at Salzwedel flight school in April 1940. He received fighter pilot training – led by *Feldwebel* Hans Beisswenger – at *Jagdfliegerschule* Stolp-Reitz, and in June 1940 he was posted to the *Ergänzungsjagdgruppe* Merseburg, where he learned to know *Leutnant* Hermann Graf. In August 1940, he was posted to III./JG 52, where he shortly afterward was incorporated into first 7. *Staffel*, later 9. *Staffel*, in Romania. Grislawski flew a large part of his sorties as the wingman of Hermann Graf, who in 1942 would become the first pilot to reach the 200-victory-mark. On October 23, 1941, Grislawski took off from Poltava airdrome, and after only a few minutes, the engine of his Bf 109 F-4 seized. The German pilot had no option but to make a rapid belly-landing. Unfortunately, the wing of his aircraft hit a Russian woman on a field. Grislawski attended to her wounds, and when a German Army truck arrived to pick him up, he insisted that it should bring the Russian woman to hospital. Grislawski went on to become one of the most successful fighter pilots of the war, amassing a total of 132 victories. After the war, Grislawski turned down an offer made by Erich Hartmann to join the *Bundesluftwaffe*. He is still alive.

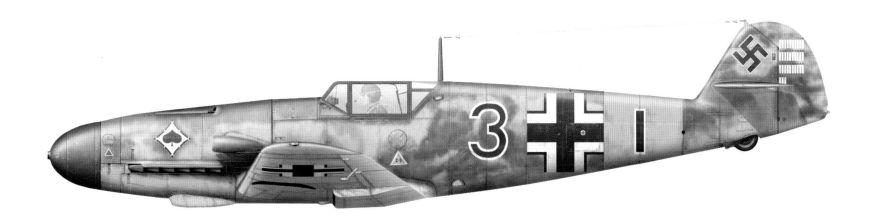

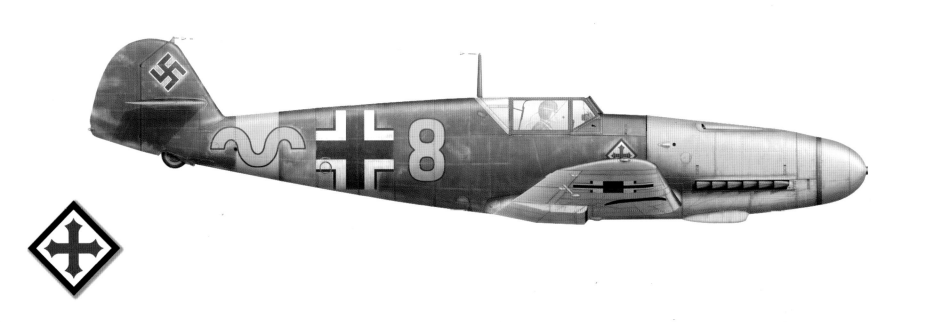

29. Bf 109 F-4

Flown by *Oberst* Werner Mölders, *Nahkampfführer Krim*, Sarabuz/Crimea/USSR, November 1941.

Few fighter aces of World War II are as versatile as Werner Mölders. He was one of the most formidable fighter pilot, a true master in air-to-air combat. During the Spanish Civil War he flew a Bf 109 in the Condor Legion on *Generalissimus* Franco's side, scoring the highest number of victories achieved by any German pilot in that conflict – 14. After his 20th victory in World War II, Mölders was the first fighter pilot to be awarded with the Knight's Cross, on May 29, 1940. Mölders was also a tactical inventor, and the fighter plane's "finger-four formation" was invented by him in Spain. He took great care of all his subordinates, and this earned him his nickname "Vati", "Daddy". Later he was appointed the first inspector of the Luftwaffe's Fighter Arm, and in this position he definitely earned a great respect from the fighter pilots. Werner Mölders was shot down by a French fighter pilot on June 5, 1940 and spent the last weeks of the war with France in captivity. Liberated after the armistice, he was promoted to *Major* and took charge of JG 51. Although Mölders was injured in combat with the South African ace "Sailor" Malan in late July 1940, he remained in first-line service during the entire Battle of Britain. On September 20, 1940, he achieved his fortieth victory as the first pilot in World War II. Under his command, JG 51 was credited with a total of around five hundred victories during Battle of Britain. Participating in the invasion of the USSR, Mölders became the first to reach 100 victories on July 15, 1941. Appointed to the first Inspector of the Luftwaffe's Fighter Air Arm, Mölders flew sorties on the Crimea in November 1941, achieving a number of "unofficial" victories that could be added to his official score 115, including 101 in World War II. Mölders was killed en route to the state funeral of the Inspector of the Luftwaffe, Ernst Udet, on November 22, 1941. JG 51 adopted the honorary name *Mölders*.

30. Bf 109 F-4

Flown by *Oberleutnant* Josef Priller, 1./JG 26, St Omer-Arques/France, November 25, 1941.

By late summer of 1941, Oak Leaves holder *Oberleutnant* Josef Priller had reached the position as the third top scorer in JG 26 Schlageter on the "Kanalfront." On December 6, 1941, when the *Gruppenkommandeur* of III./ JG 26 succeeded *Oberstleutnant* Adolf Galland as *Geschwaderkommodore* of JG 26, Priller was promoted to take command of the IIId *Gruppe*. By that time, Priller's total score had reached fifty-eight. Priller brought his faithful wingman, *Leutnant* Robert Unzeitig, to III./JG 26, and on January 3, 1942, he scored his first victory with this *Gruppe*. During an air combat with RAF Tangmere Wing on April 12, 1942, both Unzeitig and *Major* Schöpfel's wingman were shot down and killed. The two Spitfires claimed shot down by Priller (one of which was confirmed) was a poor consolation. The situation grew worse from the fall of 1942, when the first U.S. heavy bombers appeared. On October 9, 1942, Priller had his first encounter with the American bombers and shot down a 93 BG Liberator. A second B-24, Lieutenant Joe Tate's *Ball of Fire*, sustained three 20mm cannon shell hits from an Fw 190, but managed to return to England for an emergency landing at Northolt. In January 1943, Priller was assigned to command the entire JG 26, and he would lead it through the difficult air battles against RAF and USAAF during more than two years – during which 480 pilots of JG 26 were killed or reported as missing. On June 15, 1944, Priller became one of the few to achieve a total of one hundred victories on the "Western Front." On October 12, 1944 – when JG 26 lost twelve aircraft to U.S. fighters – Priller scored the only JG 26 success of the day, as he shot down a Mustang for his 101st and last victory. On January 28, 1945, Priller left JG 26 to serve as Inspector of Day Fighters (West). Josef Priller survived a total of 307 combat sorties but died from a heart attack on May 20, 1961, at the age of forty-six.

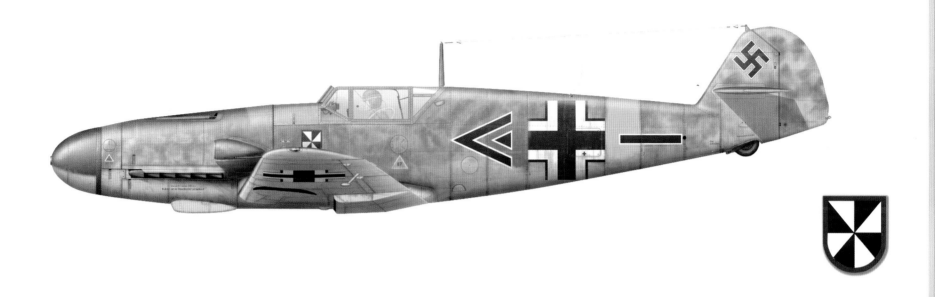

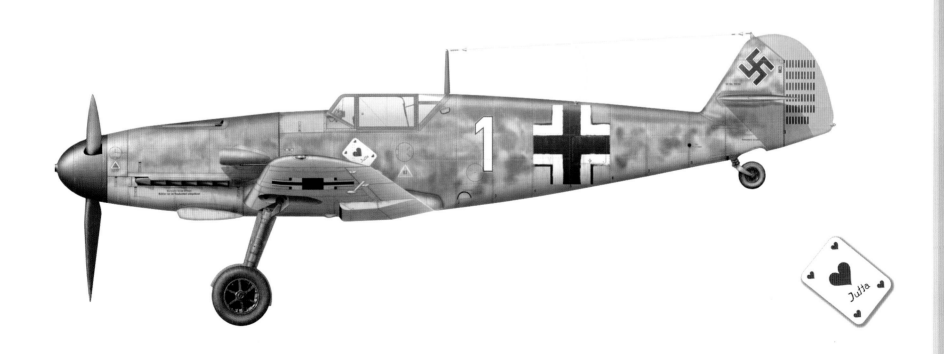

31. Bf 109 F-4

Flown by *Leutnant* Hermann Graf, 9./JG 52, Kharkov/USSR, January 1942.

Born in Engen on October 24, 1912, Hermann Graf graduated as a fighter pilot with the rank of a *Feldwebel* in 1939. As the war broke out, he served with I./JG 51 on the Western Front. After participating in twenty-one combat missions, Graf was posted to the *Ergänzungsjagdgruppe* Merseburg in January 1940 There he served as fighter trainer. Promoted to *Leutnant*, he brought one of his NCO friends, *Gefreiter* Alfred Grislawski, to III./JG 52. During the war against the Soviet Union, Graf and his wingman Grislawski would team to become two of the most successful aces in 9. "*Karayastaffel*"/JG 52, which Graf led from March 1942. On December 8, 1941, Graf and Grislawski attacked twelve R-Z bombers, escorted by two I-16 fighters of VVS-Southern Front, and shot down five – three by Graf and two by Grislawski. Following his forty-fifth victory on January 8, 1942, Graf was awarded the Knight's Cross. Hermann Graf's and Alfred Grislawski's rise to success came in May 1942, when the former achieved thirty-nine and the latter twenty-two victories. With this, Graf had surpassed his 100-victory-mark, for which he was awarded with the Oak Leaves with Swords to his Knight's Cross. Graf broke all previous records in September 1942, when he amassed a total of sixty-two kills in less than five weeks – running up his victory total to 202. His 200th victory – reached as the first fighter pilot of the war – was claimed against an 102 IAD/PVO I-153 on September 26, 1942. Graf was awarded with the Diamonds to the Oak Leaves and was withdrawn from first-line service until the summer of 1943, when he was instructed to form the new JG 50. Graf brought his friend Grislawski from the Eastern Front to this unit. In late 1943 he was appointed *Geschwaderkommodore* JG 11 in the home defense, and he led this until he was injured while ramming a U.S. Mustang on March 29, 1944. He ended the war as *Geschwaderkommodore* JG 52 on the Eastern Front, and spent five years in Soviet captivity. Hermann Graf, credited with 212 confirmed and 40 unconfirmed victories, passed away on November 4, 1988.

32. Bf 109 F-4

Flown by *Major* Hannes Trautloft, *Stab*/JG 54, Siverskaya/USSR, January 1942.

When Hannes Trautloft passed away on January 12, 1996, Germany lost "one of the great educators in the fighter arm," in the words of historian Ernst Obermaier. Trautloft earned great respect for his able command of JG 54 from August 1940 to July 1943. His personal insignia, the "Green heart of Germany" (Thuringia region) was adopted by the entire JG 54, which became famous as *Jagdgeschwader Grünherz*. He achieved eight victories during the Battle of Britain. Following his nineteenth and twentieth victories on July 24, 1941 – two Soviet SB bombers near Soltsy/USSR – *Major* Trautloft was awarded with the Knight's Cross. Under Trautloft's command, JG 54 was credited with 1,200 victories on the Eastern Front through January 2, 1942. *Geschwaderkommodore* Trautloft scored his personal fortieth victory – against a Pe-2 – on May 9, 1942. On July 6, 1943, Trautloft's personal friend, *General der Jagdflieger* Galland, appointed him inspector of the Fighter Air Arm on the Eastern Front. Trautloft ended the war with a total of 53 victories (plus four in the Spanish Civil War) on 560 combat sorties.

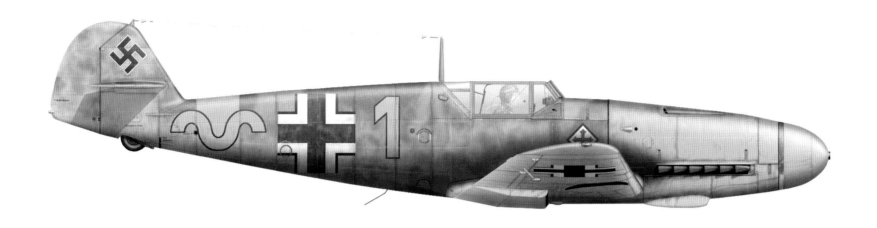

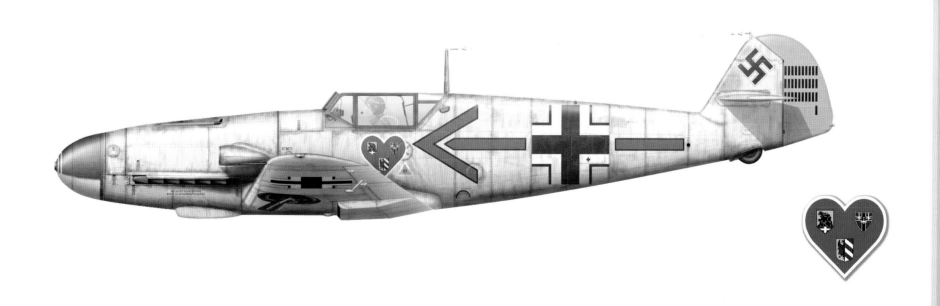

33. Bf 109 F-4
Flown by *Oberfeldwebel* Otto Schulz, *Stab* II./JG 27, Martuba/Libya, February 1942.

Otto Schulz, born on February 11, 1911, served with II./JG 27 from 1940. His first victory was achieved during the Battle of Britain on August 15, 1940. He then scored two more kills over the Balkans in the spring of 1941, and three on the Eastern Front during the following summer. But the bulk of his successes were achieved over North Africa, where he served from the fall of 1941. On October 6, 1941, he carried out his 200th combat sortie and shot down three British fighters over Libya – his seventh through ninth victories. During the next weeks, he stunned his comrades by achieving an impressive victory row, starting with three kills on October 30, 1941. On November 17, 1941, Schulz took off, shot down an RAF 216 Squadron Bombay transport plane, and landed – all within three minutes. For this feat, the men of JG 27 nicknamed him "One-Two-Three-Schulz." He scored three victories again on November 28, and two each on November 30, December 6, and December 20, 1941. Otto Schulz's greatest day was February 15, 1942, when he knocked down five Kittyhawks of RAF 94 and 112 squadrons in ten minutes. Schulz was certain that he had come across a group of British novice pilots, but RAF records reveal that among his victims in that combat was the Allied top scorer in North Africa, Squadron Leader "Imshi" Mason, credited with 17 kills. One week later, Schulz was awarded with the Knight's Cross. By that time, his personal tally had reached forty-four victories. His last victory – No.51 – was attained against a Hurricane on June 17, 1942. Schulz never returned from that sortie and is listed as missing since then.

34. Fw 190 A-2
Flown by *Major* Gerhard Schöpfel, *Stab*/JG 26, Audembert/France, February 1942.

Gerhard Schöpfel's name is intimately linked to the history of the famous JG 26 *Schlageter*, with which he served during more than half the war. Schöpfel, a former police officer, commenced his pilot training in 1936. In June 1938, with the rank of an *Oberleutnant*, he was posted to *Jagdgeschwader Schlageter*, and was assigned as *Staffelkapitän* 9./JG 26 shortly after the outbreak of the war. He succeeded Adolf Galland twice – as *Gruppenkommandeur* of III./JG 26 on August 21, 1940, and as *Geschwaderkommodore* on December 6, 1941. It has been said that Schöpfel not quite was able to assume the role that Galland had played as *Geschwaderkommodore*, but he seems to have been more popular among the NCOs of JG 26 than Galland. On one occasion in May 1942, *Major* Schöpfel hit a Spitfire decisively with a burst from his Fw 190. The Spitfire descended vertically, trailing smoke. Six thousand feet further down, another Fw 190 attacked the doomed Spitfire and took a shot at it. After landing, Schöpfel approached the pilot of this Fw 190, an *Oberfeldwebel*, with the following words: "If I would have been an *Oberfeldwebel* and you were a *Major*, I would have been forced to give you credit for the victory. Because of that, I say that you will have the victory, and I congratulate you." In January 1943, after attaining a total of 45 victories with JG 26, Schöpfel was shifted to the staff of *Jafü Bretagne*. Between June 1943 and November 1943 he served as Fighter Leader Sicily-Italy, and thereafter was appointed *Jafü Norway*. On June 1, 1944 he assumed command of JG 4, but was shortly afterward shot down and injured. He ended the war as *Geschwaderkommodore* JG 6. On August 2, 1945, Schöpfel was arrested in the Soviet occupation zone in Germany and would spend the next four years in Soviet captivity. Gerhard Schöpfel is still alive.

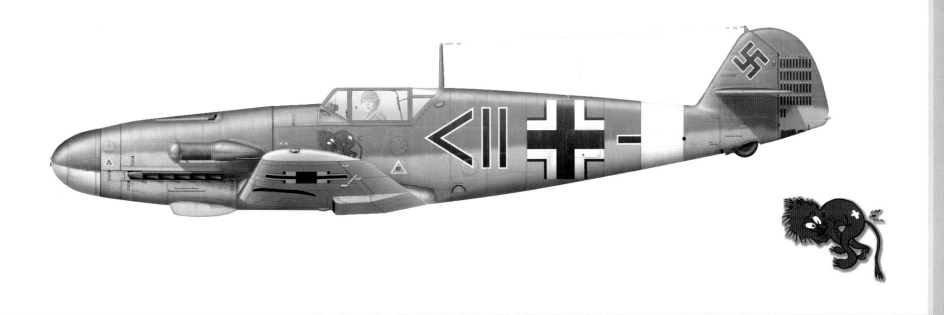

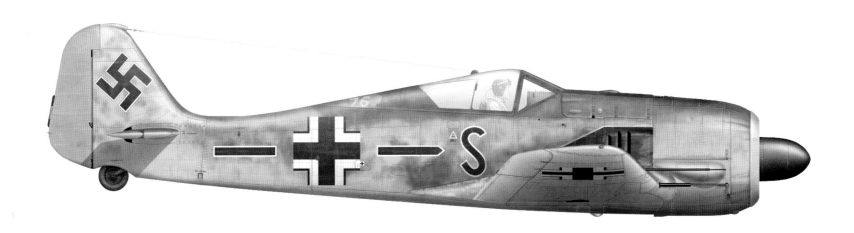

35. Bf 109 F-2
Flown by *Leutnant* Hans Strelow, 5./JG 51, Bryansk/USSR, February 28, 1942.

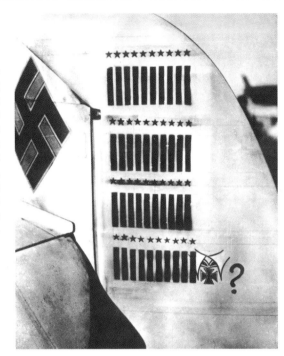

On March 18, 1942, *Leutnant* Hans Strelow of II./JG 51 achieved the largest individual success by any fighter pilot during the Soviet winter offensive, claiming seven victories in one day. The young Strelow developed as a "comet" during the first months of 1942. Having achieved his first victory in June 1941, his total score had reached twenty-seven at the shift of the year. On March 18, 1942, he bagged seven and thus surpassed the fifty-victory-mark. He was awarded with the Knight's Cross on the same day and the Oak Leaves only six days later. Between these two dates, he increased his score with fourteen. Strelow in fact was responsible for more than ten percent of all Soviet aircraft losses in the central combat zone through March 1942. Just having returned from a home leave, Strelow was shot down by a Pe-2 bomber behind the enemy lines on May 22, 1942. Knowing that the Soviet were well aware of his successes, and fearing physical reprisals, Hans Strelow chose to take his own life before Russian troops reached the crash-landed Messerschmitt with the long rows of victory bars painted on the rudder. Hans Strelow was credited with a total of sixty-eight victories.

36. Bf 109 F-4
Flown by *Leutnant* Hermann Neuhoff, 7./JG 53, Catania/Sicily, March 18, 1942.

Born on April 11, 1918, Hermann Neuhoff served as an *Unteroffizier* with III./JG 53 from the beginning of the war. He achieved his first victory on March 2, 1940, when he attacked a formation of RAF Hurricanes over Saarbrücken/Germany together with *Hauptmann* Werner Mölders. At the opening of the German invasion of the Soviet Union in June 1941, he had already amassed ten kills. The first day of the onslaught against the Soviet Union, June 22, 1941, made a strong impact on Neuhoff. "The Russians were caught totally by surprise," he recalls, "and we were able to destroy everything on the ground during our first mission." During his next mission of the day, he had his first encounter with Soviet fighter pilots, and he describes this air combat as extremely hard. Neuhoff describes the Soviet pilots as both skillful and brave, although handicapped by an outdated equipment. In late 1941, III./JG 53 was posted to North Africa, where Neuhoff scored his thirty-second victory against an RAF 94 Squadron Hurricane on December 11, 1941. Shortly afterward, III./JG 53 was shifted to Sicily for operations over Malta, where Neuhoff achieved his fortieth and last kill against a Hurricane on April 9, 1942. Next day, Neuhoff was erroneously shot down by *Leutnant* Werner Schöw of I./JG 53 over Malta and was taken prisoner. On June 16, 1942, Neuhoff was awarded with the Knight's Cross in absentium. He is still alive.

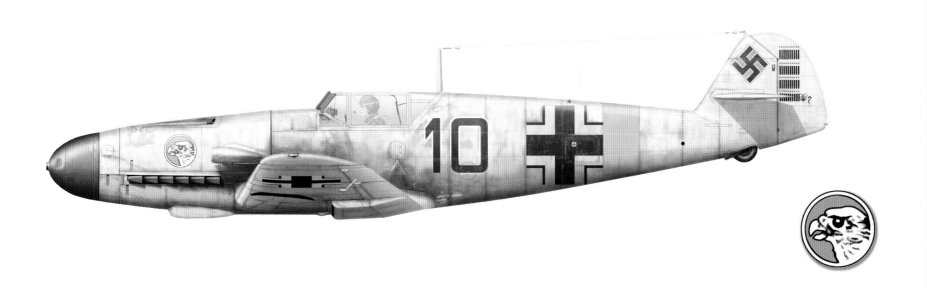

37. Bf 109 F-2

Flown by *Hauptmann* Hans Philipp, *Stab* I./JG 54, Krasnogvardeysk/USSR, March 31, 1942.

Hans Philipp is one of the most famous German fighter pilots of World War II. He developed into one of the best aces of JG 54 already during the Battle of Britain, where he commanded the 4. Staffel. On September 27, 1940 – a day when JG 54 was credited with sixteen RAF fighters shot down for the loss of two Bf 109s – Philipp claimed his twelfth through fifteenth victories. On October 20, 1940, he bagged two Spitfires for his nineteenth and twentieth victories, and was awarded with the Knight's Cross two days later. One year later, on October 2, 1941, Philipp scored his 70th kill, now operating on the Eastern Front since June 1941. In February 1942, he took command of I./JG 54. On March 31, 1942, he achieved his 100th victory as the fourth pilot to do so, and one year later he was the second pilot to reach the 200-victory-mark. In the spring of 1943, Philipp left the Eastern Front and was posted to the Home Defense to assume command of JG 1. On October 8, 1943, his JG 1 was involved in a bitter air battle against U.S. heavy bombers and their escorting Thunderbolts over northwestern Germany and the Netherlands. Philipp shot down a B-17 – registered as his 206th victory, but then his own Fw 190 was hit. Hans Philipp's last words, cried into the R/T, had been a message to his wingman: "Reinhard, attack!" Philipp's 206 victories made him the top-scoring ace by the time of his death.

38. Bf 109 F-4

Flown by *Oberleutnant* Gerhard Homuth, 3./JG 27, Martuba/Libya, April 6, 1942.

On April 6, 1942, *Hauptmann* Gerhard Homuth was returning to base after a stiff encounter with British Boston bombers with strong fighter escort. Suddenly, the twenty-seven-year-old *Hauptmann* spotted a lonely Hurricane. He immediately attacked, and after a prolonged air combat managed to shoot down the enemy plane. The pilot, South African Lieutenant Egner, bailed out and was captured. He was brought to I./JG 27's base, where Egner's first question was: "Who shot me down?" When he learned that his victor was a Knight's Cross holder with more than forty victories to his account, the 4 SAAF pilot was relieved. "I'm glad that it wasn't by any novice pilot," he said. By that time, Gerhard Homuth belonged to the best Luftwaffe fighter pilots in North Africa. He had achieved his fortieth victory (against a 3 RAAF Squadron Kittyhawk piloted by Sergeant Gray) on February 27, 1942. When he was transferred from I./JG 27 in February 1943, his tally stood at sixty-one. In July 1943 he was posted to the Eastern Front as *Gruppenkommandeur* of I./JG 54, but he would not survive many weeks of combat with the considerably reinforced Soviet air force. On August 3, 1943, he was shot down in combat with Yak-9 fighters near Orel. Gerhard Homuth was credited with a total of 63 kills.

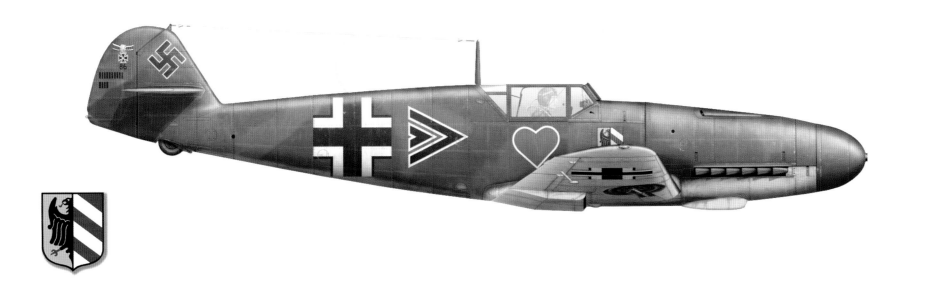

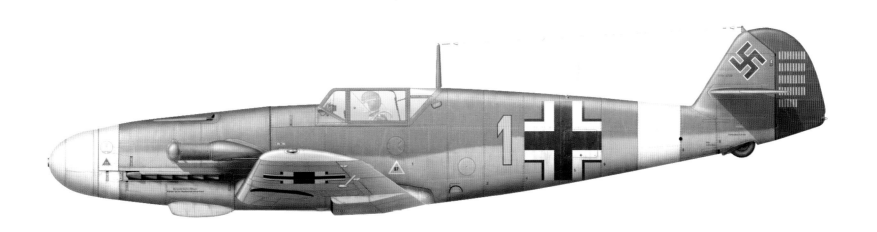

39. Fw 190 A-2
Flown by *Hauptmann* Joachim Müncheberg, *Stab* II./JG 26, Abbéville-Drucat/France, May 1, 1942.

The spring and summer of 1942 is a dismal part of RAF Fighter Command's history. During offensive fighter sweeps over northern France, the Spitfire formations regularly received a heavy beating at the hands of the Fw 190-equipped JG 2 *Richthofen* and JG 26 *Schlageter*. Through April 1942, RAF Fighter Command registered 107 combat losses while no more than twenty-four German aircraft were shot down. Among the most deadly adversaries to the British airmen during this period was the *Gruppenkommandeur* of II./JG 26, *Hauptmann* Joachim Müncheberg. He scored his seventy-fifth victory against an RAF 222 Squadron Spitfire on April 30, 1942. On May 1, 1942, he bagged another – possibly from the same squadron. When Müncheberg was shifted from II./JG 26 to tour all of the *Jagdgeschwader* on the Eastern Front as a preparation for his official assignment as a *Geschwaderkommodore*, he had attained a total of 83 kills. But the air war over the Eastern Front would prove to be not as easy as Müncheberg had expected. During his first four weeks on the Eastern Front, he was shot down twice. On October 1, 1942, Müncheberg was posted as *Geschwaderkommodore* to JG 77, which shortly afterward was transferred to North Africa. On March 23, 1943, Müncheberg and his wingman bounced a formation of U.S. 52nd Fighter Group Spitfires over Tunisia. Müncheberg placed himself behind a Spitfire and opened fire from short distance. The Spitfire exploded but Müncheberg was unable to evade colliding with the debris. Both wings of his Bf 109 were torn off, and the German ace fell to a certain death. Müncheberg was credited with a total of 135 confirmed victories.

40. Bf 109 F-4
Flown by *Oberleutnant* Heinrich Setz, 4./JG 77, Zürichtal/Crimea/USSR, May 9, 1942.

In May 1942, the Soviet élite fighter regiment 6 GIAP of the Black Sea Fleet belonged to the daily adversaries of II./JG 77 in the Crimean skies. The *Staffelkapitän* of 4./JG 77, *Oberleutnant* Heinrich Setz, was one of the most able fighter pilots on the German side during this conflict. 27-years-old Setz had served with II./JG 77 since the summer of 1940. After 45 victories he was awarded with the Knight's Cross on December 31, 1941. In the spring of 1942, Setz participated in the German attack against the Kerch Peninsula in the Crimea. Here, Setz took part in the annihilation of VVS-Crimean Front, and on May 9, 1942 he bagged a MiG-3 and an I-153 for his sixty-sixth and sixty-seventh victories. Following the German seizure of Sevastopol in early July 1942, the airmen of II./JG 77 was dispatched to the Voronezh sector. Here they were encountered with mainly inexperienced Soviet pilots of the new 1st Fighter Aviation Army, and were able to achieve dramatic successes. Setz claimed 27 victories in a three-week period – including his 100th on July 24, 1942. In February 1943, he was transferred to France to assume command of I./JG 27. He was killed in combat over Abbéville on March 13, 1943, after achieving his three last victories against RAF Spitfires. Heinrich Setz's total victory score was 138, achieved on 274 combat missions.

41. Bf 109 F-4
Flown by *Hauptmann* Heinz Bär *Stab* I./JG 77, Kerch/Crimea/USSR, May 19, 1942.

Heinz Bär's rise to fame began with IV./JG 51 on the Eastern Front, where he scored three victories – Nos. 18 through 20 in total – against a MiG-3 and two SBs on June 22, 1941. He achieved five kills on June 30, 1941, and three apiece on July 5, July 23, August 9, and August 19, 1941. Bär was awarded with the Knight's Cross on July 2, 1941, and the Oak Leaves on August 14, 1941. On August 30, 1941, he bagged six, but already on the next day – shortly after reaching his seventy-ninth and eightieth victories against two Pe-2s, Bär was shot down and belly-landed in Soviet-held territory. Bär nevertheless managed to evade capture and made it back to German lines, despite the fact that both his feet had been sprained. On February 16, 1942, he was awarded with the Swords to his Oak Leaves. During this time, he served as *Staffelkapitän* 12./JG 51. The frequently made claim that he served as *Gruppenkommandeur* IV./JG 51 however has proved to be nothing but a long-lasting myth. But Bär soon belonged to the favorites of *Oberst* Adolf Galland, the young Inspector of the Fighter Aviation Arm, and he appointed Bär to command of I./JG 77 in the Crimea in May 1942. Hardly by accident, Galland arrived to inspect Bär's I./JG 77 the same day as Bär achieved his one hundredth victory – by downing an R-5 biplane and five I-16s over the Kerch Peninsula on May 19, 1942. When I./JG 77 was transferred to the Mediterranean area in late June 1942, Bär had reached a total score of 113 aerial victories, which placed him as the top scoring fighter ace by that time.

42. Bf 109 F-4
Flown by *Leutnant* Joachim Marseille, 3./JG 27, Tmimi/Libya, June 1, 1942.

Born of French Huguenot ancestry on December 13 1919, in Berlin-Charlottenburg, Marseille was a real *enfant terrible*. His father, Siegfried Marseille, was a hard officer who later advanced to the rank of *Generalmajor*. But young Hans-Joachim was marked by an unhappy childhood. His parents divorced early in his teens. Brought up by his mother, who led a confused life and obviously failed to discipline the wild teenager boy, "Jochen" finally made it to one of the old Lufthansa flying schools. On November 7, 1939 he joined the Luftwaffe, and was trained as a fighter pilot. Marseille saw his first combat sorties with 4./JG 52 on the Channel front in 1940 before he was sent away by his *Staffelkapitän Oberleutnant* Johannes Steinhoff for "lacking discipline." Steinhoff, who could be a very harsh unit commander, recalls: "Marseille was remarkably handsome. He was gifted pilot and fighter, but he was unreliable. He had girlfriends everywhere, who took up so much of his time that he was often too tired to be allowed to fly. His often irresponsible understanding of duty was the primary reason I sent him packing. But he had irresistible charm." Two years later, on September 30, 1942, Marseille was killed when the engine of his Bf 109 seized over Egypt. He bailed out but his parachute never unfolded. By that time, Marseille had emerged into one of the most outstanding fighter pilots of the entire war, with 158 victories on his killboard.

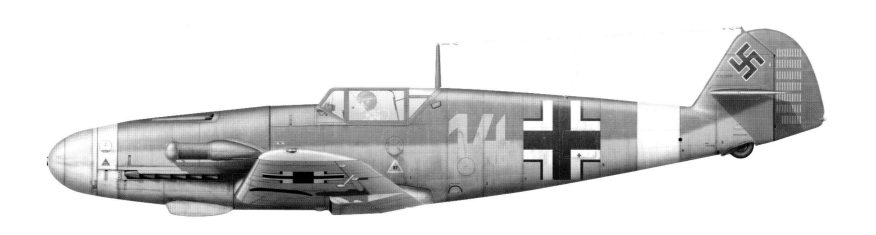

43. Bf 109 F-4
Flown by *Oberleutnant* Erwin Leykauf, *Stab* III./JG 54, Relbitsy/USSR, June 23, 1942.

Erwin Leykauf received his pilot training in 1938 and was posted to JG 26 in May 1940. His first victory was achieved against a Gladiator fighter biplane, when the pilot bailed out immediately following Leykauf's first burst of fire. During the Battle of Britain he was posted to JG 54, where he would achieve the bulk of his success. His second kill was scored against a Spitfire, probably of RAF 610 Squadron, on August 12, 1940. Next, he bagged an RAF fighter each on August 28, August 30, September 2, on September 5, and October 8 or 9, 1940. On the second day of the war against Yugoslavia, April 7, 1941, he knocked down a Hurricane for his seventh victory. Leykauf brought down his first Soviet aircraft – an SB bomber – on July 6, 1941, but was also shot down himself in the process. Between October 1941 and April 1943, Leykauf served as the adjutant of *Hauptmann* Reinhard Seiler, the *Gruppenkommandeur* of III./JG 54. Leykauf's most successful single mission was on the night of June 22//-23, 1942, when he destroyed six Soviet night bombers and transport planes in fifty minutes. He ended the war with Me 262-equipped JG 7, although he never had the opportunity to fly the Me 262 in combat. Erwin Leykauf carried out a total of 525 combat sorties and was credited with 33 aerial victories.

44. Bf 109 F-4
Flown by *Leutnant* Rudolf Sinner 6./JG 27, Tmimi/Libya, June 26, 1942.

"Rudi" Sinner belongs to the few Luftwaffe fighter pilots that achieved fame without ever being awarded with the Knight's Cross. Born in Linz/Austria in 1915, Sinner served as an antiaircraft soldier in the war against Poland in 1939. In 1940 he commenced his pilot training. He was posted to I./JG 27 in North Africa in 1941, where he became known as a gifted pilot. Sinner scored his first victory against a 3 RAAF Tomahawk on October 12, 1941. The pilot, Sergeant Parker, bailed out but was shot dead as he hung in his straps – possibly by a stray bullet. On December 10, 1941, Sinner contributed with one kill to the complete annihilation of a formation of six 24 SAAF Squadron Boston bombers. His victim, the unit commander's, Major Fonnelly, aircraft, belly-landed in Egypt. A week later, Sinner shot down another South African pilot – Lieutenant MacRoberts of Hurricane-equipped 1 SAAF Squadron. On Friday, February 13, 1942, Pilot Officer Week's 274 RAF Squadron Hurricane fell before the guns of Sinner's Bf 109. Although his cannon refused to fire and only one of the 7.92mm machine-guns worked, Sinner managed to shoot down two RAF 450 Squadron Kittyhawks on February 22, 1942, piloted by Flying Officer Thompson and Sergeant McBride. On March 20, 1942, Sinner claimed another doublette. Shortly afterward, Sinner was promoted to *Oberleutnant*. He bagged a Kittyhawk with another encounter with 3 RAAF Squadron on May 30, 1942, and on June 4 was appointed *Staffelkapitän* of 6./JG 27. The thirty-two victories that Sinner achieved in North Africa through December 1942 placed him as the tenth top scorer in this war theater. On June 1, 1943, he was shifted to the new IV./JG 54 on the Eastern Front, where he achieved another three victories. In February 1944, he assumed command over III./JG 54 in the Home Defense. On March 6, 1944, Sinner destroyed a U.S. heavy bomber but got himself shot down and seriously injured. Three months later, Sinner returned to JG 27, where he led I. *Gruppe* from June to August 1944. "Rudi" Sinner flew his last combat missions as *Gruppenkommandeur* of the Me 262-equipped III./JG 7 in 1945.

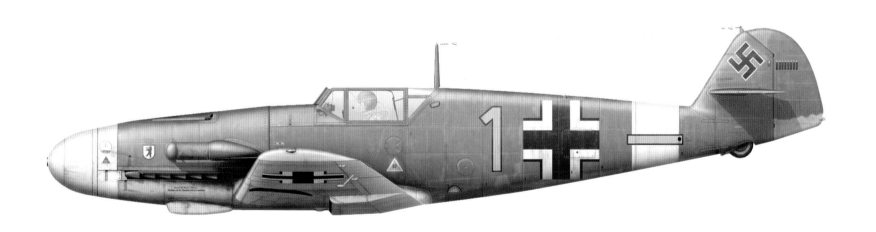

45. Bf 109 F-4
Flown by *Oberleutnant* Viktor Bauer, 9./JG 3, Schshigry/USSR, June 30, 1942.

When III./JG 3 – where the 9. *Staffel* was led by *Oberleutnant* Viktor Bauer – arrived to the Demyansk sector in February 1942, the Soviet air force was massing forces for its onslaught against the German air bridge to the enveloped garrison at Demyansk. On February 18, 1942, *Oberleutnant* Viktor Bauer brought home his 39th and 40th victories – reportedly two MiG-3s, probably misidentifications for VVS-Northwestern Front LaGG-3s. On April 4, 1942, when Bauer scored his fiftieth, the Soviet fighter pilot Leytenant Aleksey Maresyev of 580 IAP was shot down in the same area. Maresyev would survive in the wilderness for nineteen days, eventually saved by a partisan unit that brought him back to the Soviet lines. In 1943, Maresyev would return to combat service, flying with two artificial legs, and ended the war with a total of eleven individual victories. By the time Maresyev entered first-line service again, Bauer was treated for the severe injuries he had sustained when he was shot down in combat with Soviet fighters on August 10, 1942. Viktor Bauer, who was credited with a total of 106 victories – all but four on the Eastern – would never return to first-line duty again.

46. Bf 109 F-2
Flown by *Leutnant* Walter Nowotny 3./JG 54, Krasnogvardeysk/USSR, July 7, 1942.

Walter Nowotny, born in Austria on December 7, 1920, was the most successful fighter pilot of JG 54 *Grünherz*, where he served with I. *Gruppe*. But his career as a fighter pilot had a most unfortunate start. On July 19, 1941, he was shot down by a Soviet fighter over the Gulf of Riga and had to spend three days in a rubber dinghy before he finally reached the Lithuanian shore. He did not overcome the shock from this until his section leader, thirty-two-victory ace *Leutnant* Gerhard Lautenschläger was shot down and killed in front of him by a Soviet Kittyhawk on May 16, 1942. Nowotny blew the Kittyhawk out of the sky, and from then on, the spell was broken. On August 2, 1942, he brought home seven kills- – bringing his total score to fifty-four. On September 4, 1942, he was awarded with the Knight's Cross. Nowotny's most successful year was 1943. On June 5, 1943 he brought his total to ninety-two by bagging another four. Between June 21 and June 24, 1943, Nowotny achieved twenty-four victories, including ten on the latter day alone – Nos. 115 through 124. Shortly afterward, I./JG 54 was shifted to Orel to participate in Operation *Zitadelle*, Germany's last major offensive on the Eastern Front. The next two months, Nowotny would attain almost eighty kills – until he reached No. 200 on September 9, 1943. Since August 21, 1943, he served as *Gruppenkommandeur* I./JG 54. Nowotny brought home forty-five victories during the month of September 1943 alone, and was awarded with both the Oak Leaves and Swords to his Knight's Cross that month. On October 14, 1943 he became the first fighter pilot to reach the 250-victory-mark. Nowotny was then awarded with the Diamonds to his Oak Leaves, and was withdrawn from first-line service. One year later he was assigned to command the first operational Me 262 jet fighter unit, *Kommando Nowotny*, but was shot down and killed on November 8, 1944.

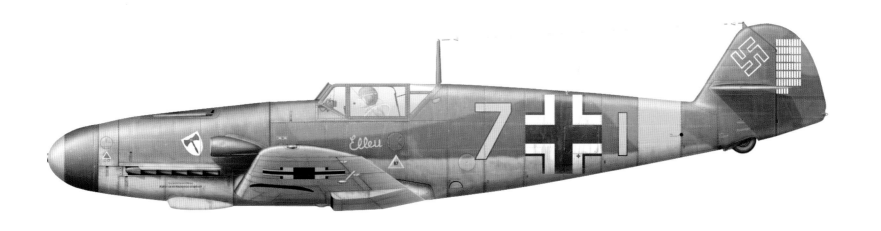

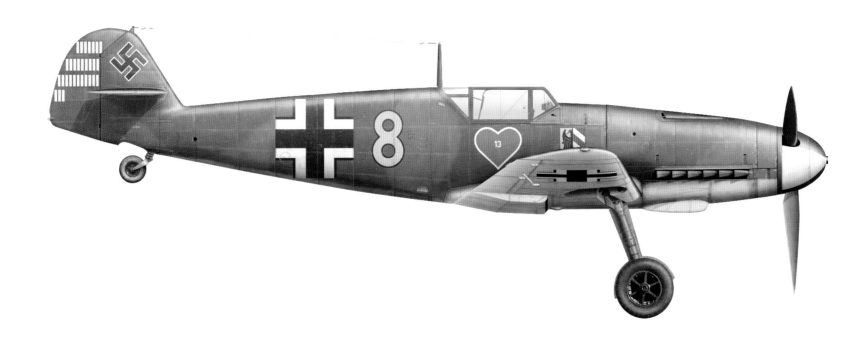

47. Bf 109 F-4
Flown by *Unteroffizier* Johann Halfmann, 7./JG 54, Kotly/Finland, July 1942.

During Operation *Barbarossa*, the German invasion of the USSR in 1941, *Unteroffizier* Johann Halfmann flew as the wingman of 7./JG 54's *Oberfeldwebel* Karl Kempf. On September 13, 1941, Halfmann achieved his first victory against a MiG-3, probably of Soviet 7 IAK-PVO. His second victory was attained, also against a Soviet fighter, on October 11, 1941. On January 2, 1942, *Oberfeldwebel* Kempf and *Unteroffizier* Halfmann carried out a most successful combat mission, resulting in six victories – five by Kempf, and one (an I-16) by Halfmann. On February 16, 1942, Halfmann brought down an I-15bis, and on March 15, 1942 he downed another MiG-3. *Unteroffizier* Halfmann's sixth victory was achieved against a Soviet fighter on May 25, 1942, while *Oberfeldwebel* Kempf brought home his forty-second through forty-fourth victories on the same occasion. On June 10, 1942, Kempf shot down two, and Halfmann one Soviet fighter. On June 23, 1942, Halfmann was awarded with the Iron Cross of the First Class. On August 27, 1942 he shot down his first heavily armored Il-2. On September 1, 1942 he was promoted to *Feldwebel*. In February 1943, III./JG 54 left the Eastern Front and was transferred to France, later to Germany, to participate in the Home Defense against U.S. heavy bombers. On May 19, 1943, *Feldwebel* Halfmann shot down a B-17. On July 27, 1943, he was injured when he force-landed near Katwijk in the Netherlands. Shortly afterward he was promoted to *Oberfeldwebel*. *Oberfeldwebel* Halfmann was killed during a training flight during the conversion to Fw 190s at Ludwigslust Airdrome in Germany on January 23, 1944. By that time, Halfmann had served longer than anyone else in 7./JG 54. He was credited with a total of eleven confirmed victories.

48. Bf 109 F-2
Flown by *Oberfeldwebel* Franz-Josef Beerenbrock, *Stab* IV./JG 51, Dugino/USSR, August 1, 1942.

Franz-Josef Beerenbrock was posted to 10./JG 51 as an *Unteroffizier* and shot down his first enemy aircraft on the Eastern Front on June 24, 1941. During the following seventeen months he took part in the air combats on the Eastern Front with great enthusiasm and was able to achieve considerable successes. Beerenbrock's most favored tactic was to approach an enemy aircraft formation undetected from below, and then he attacked the aircraft one by one. His most successful day was August 1, 1942, when he carried out three combat sorties and brought down nine Soviet planes in the Rzhev area – nine Il-2s, two MiG-3s, and a Pe-2 bomber. Beerenbrock thus surpassed the 100-victory-mark, reaching a total of 102. On August 3, 1942, Beerenbrock was awarded with the Oak Leaves to the Knight's Cross, and was granted a long home leave. When he returned to the Eastern front in October 1942, he had been promoted to the rank of a *Leutnant* and was appointed *Staffelkapitän* 10./ JG 51. On November 9, 1942, Beerenbrock was involved in a stiff combat with Soviet fighters. He managed to shoot down three – his victories Nos. 115 through 117 – but was in turn himself shot down and captured by Red Army troops. Beerenbrock is still alive.

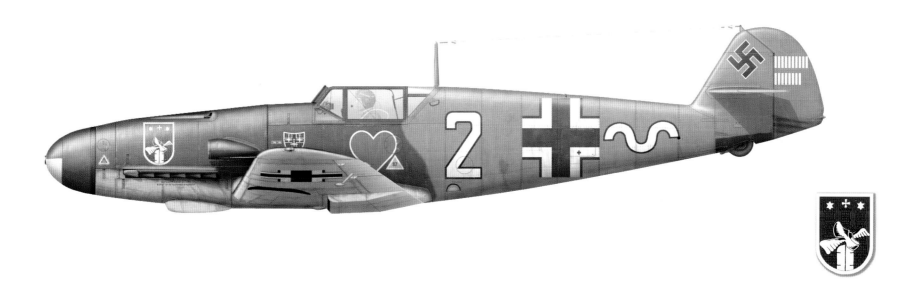

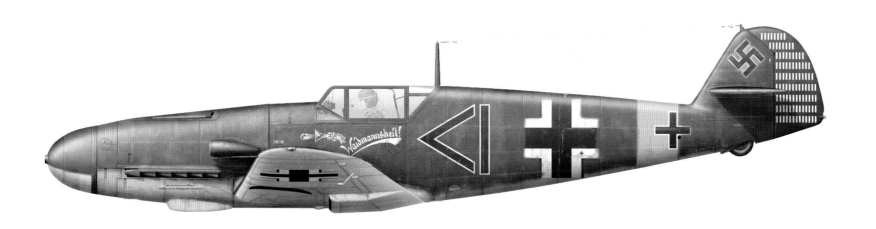

49. Bf 109 F-4
Flown by *Oberleutnant* Helmut Mertens 1./JG 3, Frolov/USSR, August 1, 1942.

Helmut Mertens started his career as a fighter pilot with I.(J)/LG 2 (later I./JG 77) in 1939. He achieved his first victory against an RAF Hurricane over France on May 12, 1940. The bulk of his successes were however achieved with JG 3, with which he served since late 1941. He achieved his twentieth victory with III./JG 3 against a Soviet SB bomber on August 11, 1941. In July 1942 he was posted to I./JG 3, also on the Eastern Front, where he attained his fortieth kill against a LaGG-3 on July 20, 1942. On August 1, 1942, he bagged a Yak-1 for his fiftieth kill, and for this Mertens was awarded with the Knight's Cross on September 4, 1942. In September 1943, when his victory total had reached fifty-three, *Oberleutnant* Mertens was found to be totally exhausted and was relieved from first-line service to command the replacement unit 1./JGr Ost in France. In April 1944, he returned to I./JG 3 as its *Gruppenkommandeur*, but it soon proved that he had not recovered from his battle fatigue, and after only two months he was posted to the Staff of *General der Jagdflieger*. From September 1944 he commanded another replacement unit, *Jagdgruppe Süd* (later III./EJG 1). His final score is not known, at least fifty-three – according to another source, ninety-seven.

50. Bf 109 F-4
Flown by *Hauptmann* Horst Carganico II./JG 5, Petsamo/Finland, August 12, 1942.

Teaming with *Oberfeldwebel* Hugo Dahmer, *Oberleutnant* Horst Carganico became one of the most successful German fighter aces on the far northern sector of the Eastern Front in 1941-1942. On September 25, 1941, Carganico was awarded the Knight's Cross for 27 victories. But one year later, when Carganico commanded II./JG 5, the Soviet resistance in the air had grown considerably stiffer. On July 22, 1942, *Hauptmann* Carganico had to belly-land his Bf 109 F-4 near Zimnaya Motovka due to engine trouble. After a difficult walk in the wilderness in no-man's land, he returned to the Finnish-German front-line three days later. On August 12, 1942, Carganico took off with his II./JG 5 on a fighter sweep toward Murmansk. The Germans encountered a formation of MiG-3s, but the only success scored was a single MiG-3 claimed, while a Soviet fighter pilot – possibly of 767 IAP – made Carganico take a second long walk through the wild landscape, reaching the German front-line the next day. His belly-landed Bf 109 F-4 was seized by the Soviets and put on display in Murmansk. After the war, it was restored into flight condition and was used in a Soviet war movie. In recent years, it has been sold abroad and is currently on display in Canada.

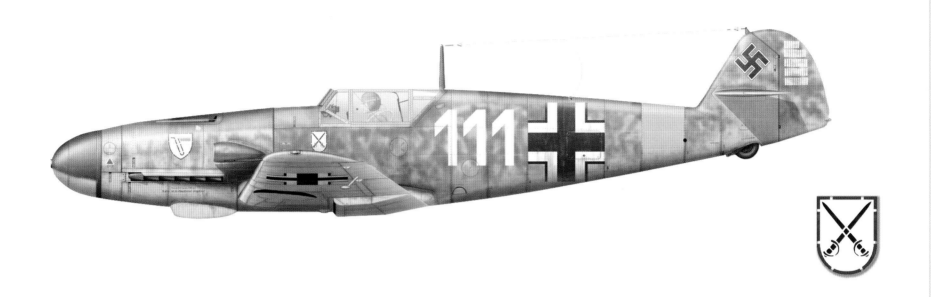

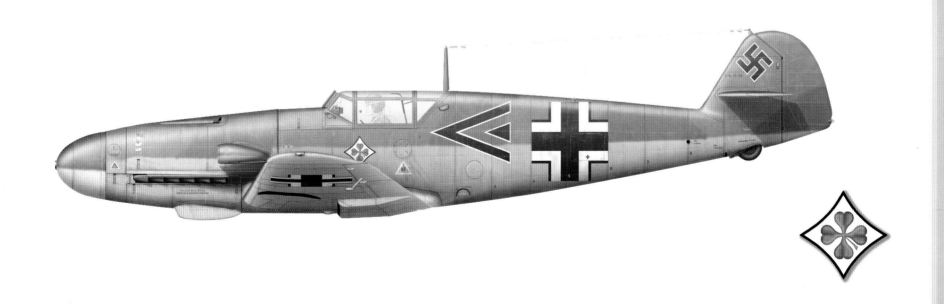

51. Bf 109 F-4
Flown by *Feldwebel* Fritz Gromotka 6./JG 27, Quotaifiya/Egypt, August 1942.

Fritz Gromotka was born in Kronschkow/Poland on June 2, 1915. He joined JG 27 as an *Unteroffizier* early in the war and would remain with this *Geschwader* until the end of the war. During the German attack on Greece in the spring of 1941, he participated in the air battle on April 10, 1941, when 6./JG 27 wiped out an entire formation of six RAF Blenheims. Counted among the victims of this carnage was the commander of the RAF force in Greece, d'Albiac. One of the Blenheims that were shot down ended up on Gromotka's tally. During II./JG 27's brief participation in the war against the Soviet Union in June-July 1941, Gromotka would add another two kills to his score. He was later posted to III./JG 27, where he achieved the bulk of his victories. His tenth and eleventh victories were attained against two Spitfires over the Greek island of Kos on September 27, 1943. A Beaufighter that fell into the sea west of the island of Karpathos on November 10, 1943 marked his fifteenth. In March 1944, III./JG 27 was posted to Vienna to provide the Austrian industrial areas with air cover against the increasing attacks from 15th USAAF heavy bombers. On March 19, 1944, III./JG 27 caught seventy-six unescorted Liberators that had raided Graz, and shot down twelve within less than a half hour. One of them was filed as *Oberfeldwebel* Gromotka's twentieth victory. Fighting against the Allied air forces during the invasion of Normandy in the summer of 1944, Gromotka was shot down on July 2, 1944. But he was soon back in action again, and contributed with one to the five RAF Typhoons that were bagged in a single engagement by III./JG 27 on August 17. On February 1, 1945, *Leutnant* Gromotka was appointed *Staffelkapitän* 9./JG 27, and he led this unit until the end of the war. He was awarded with the Knight's Cross on February 20, 1945.

52. Bf 109 F-4
Flown by *Hauptmann* Anton Mader, *Stab* II./JG 77, Staryy Oskol/USSR, September 1942.

Croatian-born Anton Mader earned great popularity for his caring of his subordinates in various unit command positions. In June 1941 he was posted from JG 2 *Richthofen* in France to Romania, where he assumed command of II./JG 77. Under Mader's leadership, this *Jagdgruppe* would develop into one of the best German fighter units on the Eastern Front. During the opening phase of the Battle of Odessa in August 1941, II./JG 77 managed to suppress the Soviet fighter opposition in this sector. Only when II./JG 77 was shifted to another sector did the Soviet fighter pilots, commanded by the famous ace Lev Shestakov, manage to seize control in the air over Odessa. The losses suffered by the Romanian Air Force in this area compelled the Romanian leadership to withdraw the majority of its aviation units from first-line service. During most of the summer and fall of 1942, Mader's II./JG 77 was the only *Jagdgruppe* operating against three Soviet air armies in the Voronezh sector, to the north of Stalingrad. Between July 5 and 31, 1942, II./JG 77 was credited with 364 victories in this sector – for eleven own combat losses. Soviet 2 VA alone lost more than three hundred aircraft at Voronezh between June 28 and July 31, 1942. On September 8, when his *Gruppe* claimed twenty-six victories in a single engagement, Mader increased his personal score to sixty-five by bringing down four Soviet aircraft. Anton Mader headed II./JG 77 until March 1943, and shortly afterwards he took charge of the new JG 11 in the Home Defense. Later he commanded JG 54. He survived the war with a total score of 86 victories.

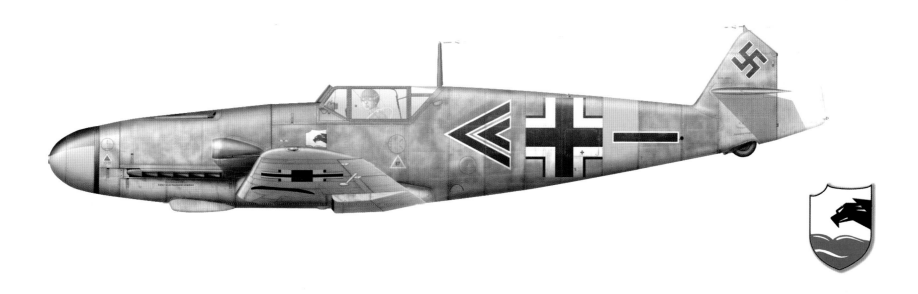

53. Bf 109 F-4

Flown by *Oberleutnant* Anton Hackl, 5./JG 77, Kastornoye/USSR, September 19, 1942.

"Toni" Hackl belongs to the most successful pilots of JG 77. On May 27, 1942 he was awarded with the Knight's Cross for forty-eight victories. During the Battle of Sevastopol in June 1942, Hackl emerged as the most successful German fighter pilot. On the Soviet side, the ace Kapitan Mikhail Avdeyev of 6 GIAP/VVS-ChF dedicated the following lines to Hackl in his post-war memoirs: "[He] appeared every day, always with his back protected by other fighters. Usually, he picked his victims carefully, and only rarely were his attacks without success. More than once, I tried to pursue [him], but this proved to be a most difficult undertaking. It was clear that [he] was an outstanding pilot. He deprived us of our sleep and never left us in peace. It was as if he jeered at us. A hundred times I examined my mind to find out different ways of attacking him – from above, from below, from the clouds or from the sun. But these fine theories always were shattered by the realities. [He] wasn't someone whom you could lure into a trap, or who could be made to lose his nerves through a frontal attack. He was a worthy opponent, and he definitely gave us a lot of headache." Operating in the Voronezh sector on the Eastern Front, Hackl increased his tally from 63 to 118 victories between July 2 and September 19, 1942. His last victory in this sector was attained against a LaGG-3 on September 19, 1942.

54. Bf 109 G-2

Flown *Hauptmann* Reinhard Seiler, *Stab* III./JG 54, Lissino/USSR, September 1942.

Born on August 30, 1909, Reinhard "Seppl" Seiler joined the *Reichswehr* on September 30, 1929. In 1935 he received his pilot training, was selected as a fighter pilot and volunteered to fight against the Republican government in Spain. There he became one of the most successful German fighter pilots, with nine victories. When World War II broke out, he served with I./JG 54, and was appointed *Staffelkapitän* 1./JG 54 in December 1939. His first victory with JG 54 was achieved against a French Potez 633 bomber on January 10, 1940. On August 4, 1940 he was shot down and bailed out over the English Channel. He was picked up from the cold water, unconscious, with a severely burned face and a broken arm. But this did not deter Seiler. As soon as he had recovered, he was back in action again. When he was appointed *Gruppenkommandeur* of III./JG 54 on the Eastern Front on September 30, 1941, his victory tally had reached 33. On March 19, 1942, Seiler, was again shot down, this time by a Soviet fighter. Once again he survived and soon was back in action. In the summer of 1942, he carried out night fighter sorties and shot down sixteen Soviet aircraft in this way. In May 1943 he was appointed *Gruppenkommandeur* I./JG 54, which shortly afterward was shifted south to participate in Operation *Zitadelle* – Hitler's last major offensive on the Eastern Front. On July 6, 1943, the second day of the offensive, Seiler was shot down by a Yak-9 and bailed out. He was sent to hospital with several bullet wounds. This time he never was able to return to first-line service. Reinhard Seiler was credited with 109 victories, including 100 in World War II.

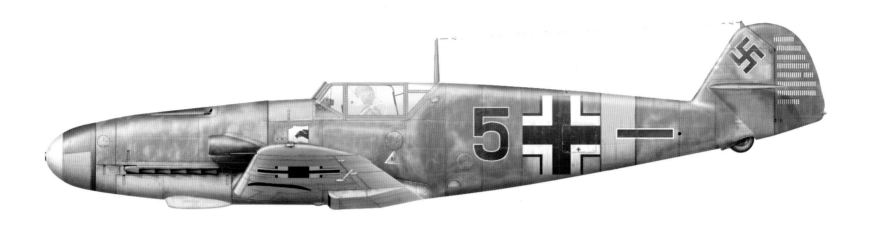

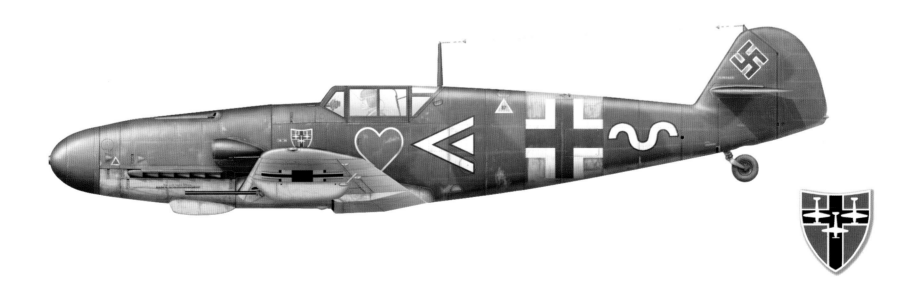

55. Bf 109 G-2
Flown by *Hauptmann* Kurt Ubben, *Stab* III./JG 77, Nikolskoye/USSR, September 20, 1942.

In September 1942, *Hauptmann* Kurt Ubben's III./JG 77 was shifted to *Luftflotte* 1 in the Leningrad area. Operating from Nikolskoye Airdrome, Ubben bagged a Soviet Kittyhawk and a LaGG-3 for his eighty-seventh and eighty-eighth victories on September 20, 1942. Two days later, he brought home his ninetieth kill. In October 1942, III./JG 77 was shifted to North Africa. Here the combination of the British offensive at El Alamein and the Allied landings in Morocco and Algeria soon put III./JG 77 under heavy pressure. With one of the twelve Curtiss P-40 fighters claimed by JG 77 and the Italian Macchi MC 202s of 3 Stormo over Tunisia on January 14, 1943, Ubben scored his 100th kill. Promoted to *Major*, Ubben took charge of JG 2 in March 1944. On April 23, 1944, 356th Fighter Group of U.S. VIII FC lost three pilots, including their commander Colonel Einar Malmstrom, during a sortie over Germany. Four days later, the Thunderbolt-pilots of this fighter group paid back by shooting down four Fw 190s of JG 2 near Chateau-Thierry in France. With one of them, *Major* Kurt Ubben was killed. His final score was 110. Kurt Ubben was credited with a total of 110 aerial victories, plus another twenty-six aircraft destroyed on the ground. Note that the aircraft displayed here carries the typical yellow fuselage band beneath the *Balkenkreuz*, indicating that it was a fighter subordinated to *Luftflotte* 1.

56. Bf 109 G-2
Flown by *Oberfeldwebel* Wilhelm Schilling, 9./JG 54, Siverskaya/USSR, September 1942.

Wilhelm Schilling, born on January 30, 1915, served with *Oberleutnant* Hans-Ekkehard Bob's 3./JG 21 (later 9./JG 54) as an *Unteroffizier* since 1939, and achieved his first victories during the Battle of Britain. On March 19, 1942, when III./JG 54 surpassed its 500-victory-mark, Schilling had contributed twenty to this total. On August 31, 1942, Schilling carried out his 500th combat sortie and achieved his 35th victory – which also was 9./JG 54's 200th. On Wednesday, September 2, 1942, eight Soviet Hurricanes of the crack fighter unit 3 GIAP/KBF intercepted a formation of Bf 109s of III./JG 54 and Ju 87s of III./StG 1 near Leningrad. During a combat that lasted for almost an hour, the Soviets claimed four enemy aircraft destroyed, but in return five Hurricanes were shot down; two were total losses and a further three made emergency landings. One pilot, Starshiy Leytenant Aleksey Yevgrafov, was killed. Among the victorious German pilots was Schilling, who scored his 40th victory in this combat. On September 13, 1942 he was awarded with the German Cross in Gold. After shooting down an Il-2 – his forty-sixth victory – three days later, Schilling was shot down and was seriously injured. On October 10, 1942, Schilling received the Knight's Cross. When he returned to his unit after recovering from his injuries, it had been posted to Germany for Home Defense tasks. On February 14, 1944, Schilling was shot down and severely wounded a second time, this time in combat with U.S. heavy bombers. Wilhelm Schilling carried out a total of 538 combat sorties and was credited with 63 victories.

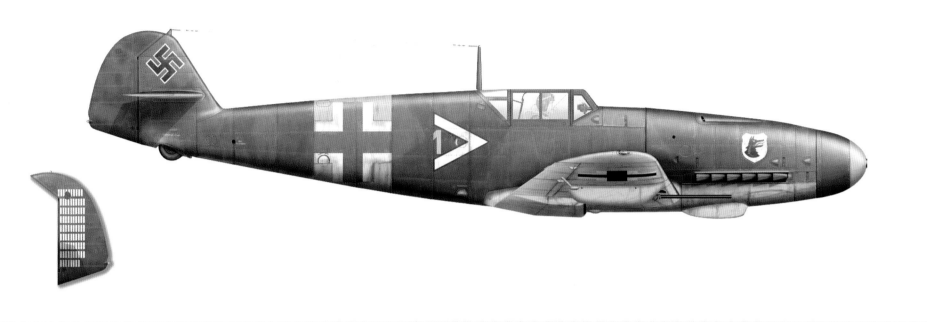

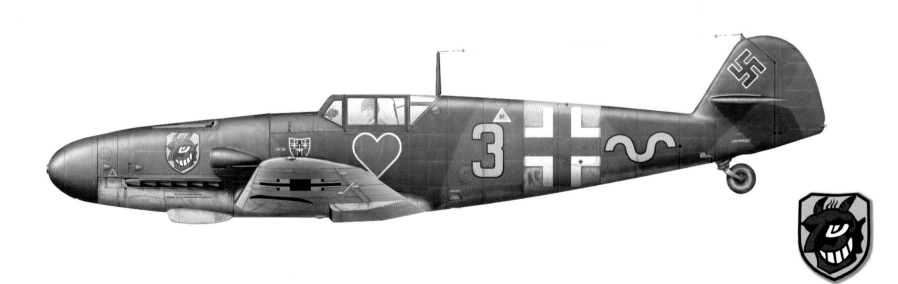

57. Fw 190 A-3
Flown by *Hauptmann* Heinrich Krafft, *Stab* I./JG 51, Orel/USSR, September 1942.

Heinrich "Gaudi" Krafft was one of the most popular officers in JG 51. He was posted to I./JG 51 in 1940. On May 21 that year he scored his first victory over France. Another three would follow during the Battle of Britain. His real successes would follow during the invasion of the USSR. On April 7, 1942, JG 51 became the first *Jagdgeschwader* to surpass its 3,000-victory mark. By that time, Gaudi Krafft's personal score stood at 50, and he had been awarded with the Knight's Cross on March 18, 1942. In May 1942 he assumed command of I./JG 51, which flew fighter cover missions for the Ju 52 airlift to the Demyansk pocket. The Soviet air force in this area – VVS-Northwestern Front – had managed to achieve considerable success against the Ju 52s that flew supplies to Demyansk in February and March 1942, but in doing so, it almost bled white. The scores of inadequately trained airmen that arrived as replacements for the badly mauled units of VVS-Northwestern Front enabled the German fighter units in the area – I./JG 51 and II./JG 54 – to achieve a number of "easy victories." Through May 1942, VVS-Northwestern Front registered fifty aircraft missing or shot down in air combat and eighteen lost to ground fire, while I./JG 51 and II./JG 54 lost only four fighters. But after the summer of 1942, improved Soviet tactics and equipment started to challenge the German air superiority. In early September 1942, fierce air fighting developed in the Leningrad area as the Soviets attempted to break the iron ring around the besieged city. Among the Luftwaffe fighter units brought in to this sector was "Gaudi" Krafft's I./JG 51, which recently had been equipped with Fw 190s – thus introducing the Fw 190s in combat on the Eastern Front. On December 14, 1942, shortly after achieving his seventy-eighth victory, Gaudi Krafft was shot down over enemy territory. He was seized by infuriated Soviet soldiers and beaten to death.

58. Bf 109 G-2
Flown by *Oberfeldwebel* Karl-Heinz Kempf, 7./JG 54, Siverskaya/USSR, October 1942.

Karl-Heinz Kempf joined 3./JG 21 (later 9./JG 54) as a *Gefreiter* in 1940. His first victory was achieved against a Hurricane near Wavre on May 12, 1940, but his real success would begin with 7./JG 54 on the Eastern Front, where he knocked down his first Soviet aircraft on June 22, 1941. Four days later he claimed four SB bombers. On September 27, 1941, *Feldwebel* Kempf brought home five victories – Nos. nineteen through twenty-three. His most famous mission was carried out on January 2, 1942. During a fighter sweep south of Lake Ladoga, he spotted a group of VVS-KBF "I-18s" above Novaya Ladoga Airdrome – probably LaGG-3s of 5 IAP/VVS-KBF. *Oberfeldwebel* Kempf made a high-side attack and claimed two of the Soviet fighters shot down. Later during the same mission, he became entangled with I-16s (apparently from VVS-Volkhov Front), resulting in Kempf claiming two, and his wingman, *Unteroffizier* Hans Halfmann, one. At the same time, the Soviets sent five Pe-2s, escorted by eight I-16s, against JG 54's base at Siverskaya. There the Soviets succeeded in taking out six Bf 109s, four Ju 88s, and twenty trucks. One soldier was killed and ten injured. Returning from their mission over Lake Ladoga, Kempf arrived over the airfield just as the Soviets were unloading their bombs. Seeking revenge, Kempf blew one of the Pe-2s out of the sky with his last rounds of ammunition. Thus, he had again achieved five kills in a single sortie, bringing his total victory score to forty-one. Two days later he was awarded with the Knight's Cross. After serving as a fighter instructor for more than a year, Kempf was posted to 2./JG 26 as *Staffelkapitän* in May 1944. On September 3, 1944, he was shot down and killed by a U.S. 55th Fighter Group Mustang during take-off from Grimbergen Airdrome in Belgium. Karl-Heinz Kempf was credited with a total of 65 victories on 445 combat sorties.

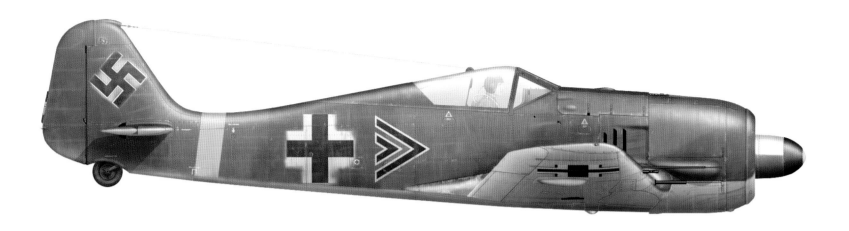

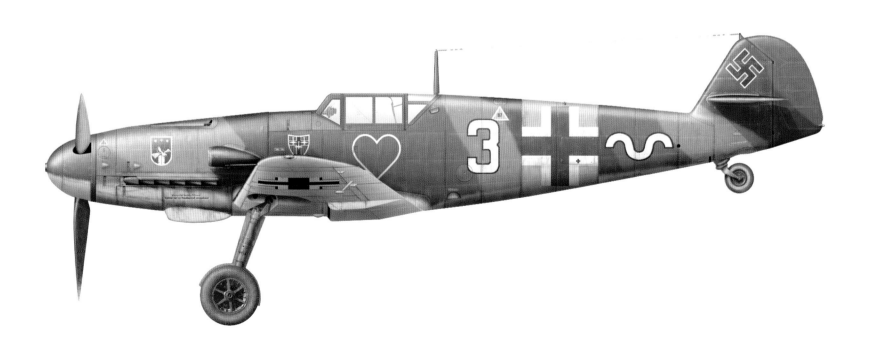

59. Bf 109 G-2

Flown by *Oberfeldwebel* Herbert Rollwage, 5./JG 53, Comiso/Sicily, October 1942.

Herbert Rollwage served with II./JG 53 as an *Unteroffizier* from 1941 and shot down his first enemy aircraft, a Soviet SB bomber, on June 22, 1941. In October and November 1942, II./JG 53 was assigned to provide fighter escort to the last air offensive against Malta. But by this time, the RAF fighter defense of the island had been considerably reinforced. The Luftwaffe's 196 bombers and 73 fighters – to which three Italian MC-202 Gruppi were added – stood against 130 operational Spitfires, supported by radar observations. On October 12, 1942 six German bombers and two escort fighters were shot down. Another six Ju 88s were lost five days later. Having lost thirty-eight aircraft in only ten days, the air offensive against Malta was canceled on October 19, 1942. Three days later, Rollwage scored his thirtieth victory by downing a Spitfire during a free hunting sortie over the island. But on November 10, 1942 another Spitfire pilot paid back by shooting up Rollwage's Bf 109. The German pilot barely managed to reach the island of Koufonisi, where he carried out a belly-landing. Rollwage's total number of victories is uncertain. He was credited with at least seventy-five, but according to unconfirmed sources, his total was 102 – including forty-four during the last twelve months of the war. All but eleven were achieved against the RAF and the USAAF.

60. Bf 109 G-2

Flown by *Hauptmann* Wolf-Dietrich Huy, 7./JG 77, Tanyet Harun/Egypt, October 29, 1942.

Wolf-Dietrich Huy served with III./JG 77 from the outbreak of the war, and would remain with this unit. In 1941, he became one of the top scorers of this *Gruppe*. Nevertheless, on January 23, 1942, he was shot down by one of the best aces in Soviet 32 IAP/VVS-ChF, Starshiy Leytenant Mikhail Avdeyev. "Everything happened very quickly", recalls Huy. "Before I had time to place myself in a firing position, another Russian took a shot at me and hit my engine, which stopped abruptly and then started to emit smoke." On March 11, 1942, Huy achieved his thirty-eight victory, but was mistakenly shot down by German ground fire. He returned to his unit after recovering from his sustained wounds in August 1942, and shortly afterward, this unit was transferred to North Africa. During most of the air war over North Africa, the German fighter pilots took advantage of the inferior equipment in the fighter units of their enemy. The three most successful "desert aces", JG 27's Marseille, Schroer and Stahlschmidt scored 151, 61 and 59 victories respectively in 1942 – most of them against Curtiss P-40s or Hurricanes. Things started to change when the Spitfires arrived in Egypt. From August 1942, the Spitfires of Nos. 145 and 601 Squadron were in regular activity over North Africa. On September 1, 1942, when Marseille scored 17 victories against Hurricanes and P-40s, the Spitfires of RAF 601 Squadron brought down *Oberfeldwebel* Herbert Krenz, an ace in JG 27 with 11 victories. One week later, *Oberleutnant* Hans-Arnold Stahlschmidt was killed in combat with the same Spitfires. On October 29, 601 Squadron's Pilot Officer Nicholls brought down yet another German ace, *Hauptmann* Wolf-Dietrich Huy of III./JG 77. Huy had recently arrived from the Eastern Front. In service with III./JG 77 since the outbreak of the war, he had amassed 40 aerial victories. He would spend the remainder of the war in British captivity.

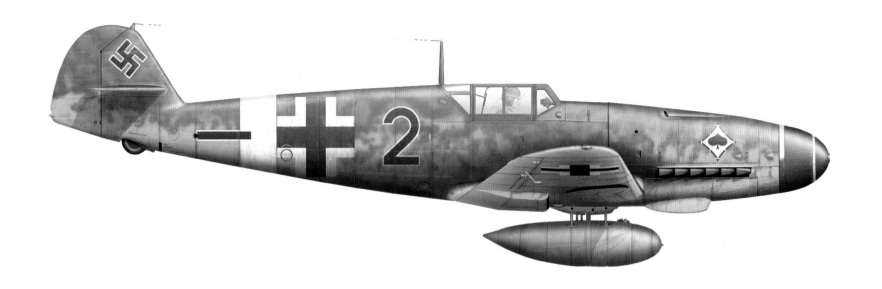

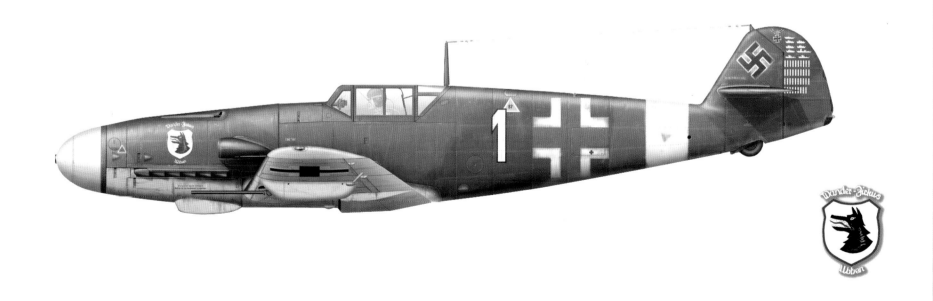

61. Fw 190 A-4

Flown by *Oberleutnant* Kurt Bühligen, 4./JG 2, Kairouan/Tunisia, November 1942.

Kurt Bühlingen belongs to the most experienced fighter pilots of World War II. He was in almost uninterrupted combat service from July 1940 until 1945, constantly with JG 2 *Richthofen*. During this period, he advanced from *Unteroffizier* and wingman to *Oberstleutnant* and his unit's last *Geschwaderkommodore*. Born on December 13, 1917, he joined the Luftwaffe in 1936 as a mechanic. This inspired him to apply for flight training. In 1940, shortly after he had achieved his "wings", he was posted to JG 2 as a fighter pilot. *Unteroffizier* Bühlingen achieved his first victory against a Hurricane on September 4, 1940. One year later, he had surpassed the 20-victory-mark and was awarded with the Knight's Cross. In mid-November 1942, following the Allied landings in Morocco and Algeria, II./JG 2 was hastily rushed to Tunisia to participate in the German build-up in this previously unoccupied country. The air war over Tunisia would lead to Bühlingen's most successful period as a fighter pilot. Between December 1942 and the spring of 1943 he teamed with the famous *Hauptmann* Erich Rudorffer and scored a total of forty individual victories. On February 3, 1943 – when five out of a formation of six U.S. 33rd Fighter Group Warhawk fighters were shot down by Luftwaffe fighters on one mission over Tunisia, and another four went lost on a second mission – Bühlingen achieved his fiftieth kill. Following this, 33rd Fighter Group was left with only thirteen Warhawks remaining (out of originally 71), and was pulled out of combat. Bühlingen added another forty-six kills to his tally until March 1944, and on March 2, 1944, he was awarded with the Oak Leaves for ninety-six aerial victories – all of which had been achieved against the RAF and the USAAF.

62. Bf 109 G-2

Flown by *Feldwebel* Anton Hafner, 4./JG 51, El Aouina/Tunisia, December 1942.

The summer of 1942 had opened fortuitous to the fighter pilots of JG 51 *Mölders* on the Eastern Front, and 6./JG 51's *Feldwebel* Anton Hafner bagged seven kills on July 5, 1942 alone, including his fortieth total. But only a few weeks later, it stood clear to the Luftwaffe men on the Eastern Front that the Soviet Air Force had resurged from its heavy losses during the first twelve months of the war. When August 1942 ended, it had been the severest month in the history of JG 51 *Mölders*, the most successful *Jagdgeschwader* during Operation *Barbarossa*. Through August 1942, JG 51 recorded 101 Bf 109s destroyed or severely damaged to all causes – including seventy-five (thirty-four total losses) to enemy action. Seventeen JG 51 pilots were killed, missing, or injured in August 1942. Hafner nevertheless was lucky to survive, and in the fall of 1942, he followed II./JG 51 when it left the Eastern Front and was transferred to Tunisia. He became II./JG 51's most successful pilot during the air war in this theater, shooting down twenty U.S. and RAF aircraft in slightly more than a month. U.S. fighter pilot Rocky Byrne, who served as a 2nd Lieutenant with the Warhawk-equipped 64th Fighter Group in Tunisia, wrote: "We were facing some of the Luftwaffe's elite pilots ... The top gun in *Jagdgeschwader* 51 was *Leutnant* Anton Hafner." On December 26, 1942, Hafner brought home his eightieth victory against a Lightning. In the summer of 1943 he returned to the Eastern Front with III./JG 51, and amassed a total of 124 victories in fifteen months – including five apiece on June 24, 1944 and July 16, 1944, and seven on August 8, 1944. When he achieved his 199th through 203rd victories on October 15, 1944, *Feldwebel* Anton Hafner was the top scoring ace of JG 51 *Mölders*. Two days later, shortly after he had brought down his 204th enemy aircraft, Hafner was shot down and killed by a Soviet Yak-9 pilot.

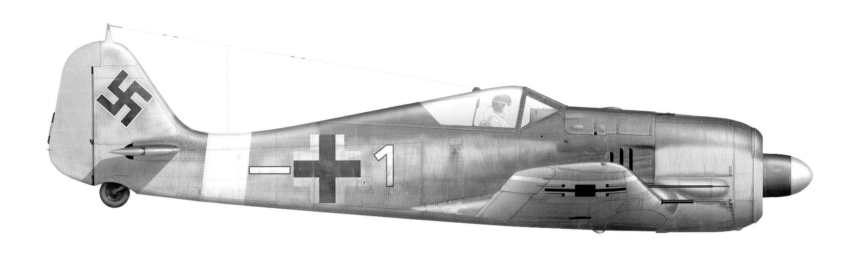

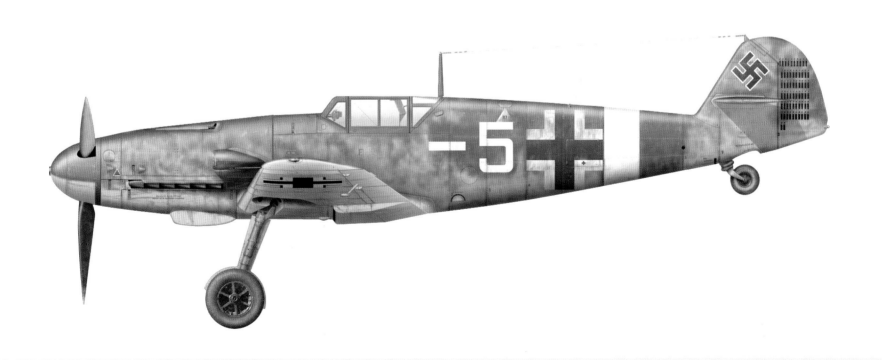

63. Bf 109 F-4

Flown by *Feldwebel* Walter Schuck, 9./JG 5, Petsamo/Finland, January 1943.

Walter Schuck flew with JG 5 in northern Finland and Norway from 1941. On May 15, 1942 he achieved his first victory against the Soviets. On June 5, 1942, he knocked down four Soviet Hurricanes near Murmansk. His thirtieth through thirty-fourth victories were achieved on April 14, 1943, and during the next six weeks, another ten Soviet aircraft would fall before his guns. But Schuck's main successes came later in the war, when the table had turned and the Soviets were an equal opponent to most German fighter pilots. On April 7, 1944, he attained his victories Nos. 80 through 84, and the next day he was awarded with the Knight's Cross. During the following twelve months he would amass another 112 kills – including six (Nos 96-101) on June 15, twelve on June 17, 1944, and seven on July 17, 1944. Soviet unit statistics however indicate that the claims made by JG 5 during this period of the war were highly inflated. Thus, on July 17, 1944, when JG 5 reported thirty-seven Soviet planes shot down, only five Soviet aircraft losses can be found in this area. On August 23, 1944 Schuck surpassed the 150-victory-mark by downing two Soviet fighters. On September 30, 1944, *Leutnant* Walter Schuck was awarded with the Oak Leaves for 171 victories. In March 1945 he was posted to JG 7 and shot down his last eight enemy planes (including four heavy bombers on April 10, whereby he got himself shot down) while flying a Me 262 jet fighter. Walter Schuck survived the war with the rank of an *Oberleutnant* and 206 confirmed and 30 unconfirmed victories on his tally.

64. Bf 109 G-2

Flown by *Oberfeldwebel* Ernst-Wilhelm Reinert, 4./JG 77, Castell Benito/Libya, January 1943.

When *Feldwebel* Ernst-Wilhelm Reinert of 4./JG 77 was injured in combat with a Pe-2 on the Eastern Front on July 23, 1942, he ended a remarkable victory tally. Twenty-eight Soviet aircraft had been brought down by him in slightly more than a fortnight. Half a year later, he would repeat this feat against the western allies over Tunisia. Reinert opened his score in the Tunisian war zone by downing a Curtiss P-40 on January 2, 1943. On January 11, 1943 he bagged four Spitfires, and on February 26, another four Allied fighters fell before his guns. His most successful days over Tunisia were March 13, and April 1, 1943, when he brought home five kills each day. On April 19, 1943, Reinert brought home his 150th victory, achieved against a Spitfire. With forty-nine kills from January through April 1943, Reinert was the most successful fighter ace during the Battle of Tunisia. In August 1943 he was appointed *Staffelkapitän* 1./JG 77, and in 1945 he assumed command of IV./JG 27. One month later, Reinert was awarded with the Swords to the Knight's Cross with Oak Leaves. Reinert carried out more than seven hundred combat sorties between June 1941 and May 1945. He was credited with 174 victories (103 on the Eastern Front), plus 16 aircraft and 10 tanks destroyed on the ground.

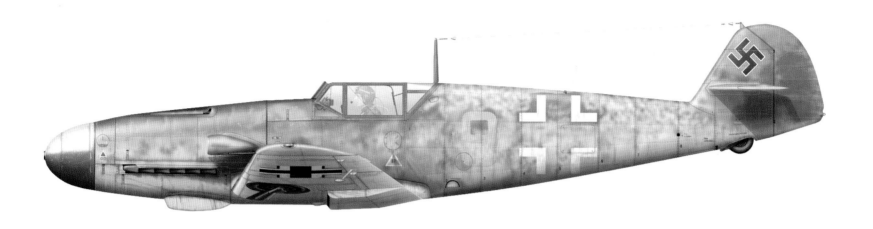

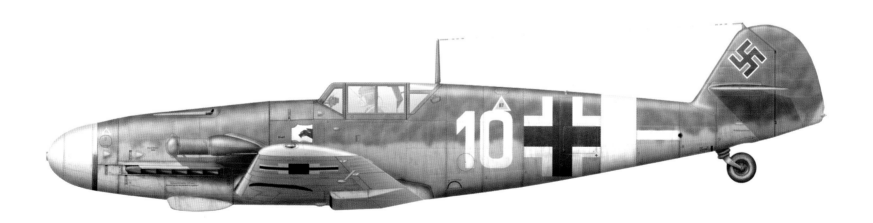

65. Fw 190 A-4

Flown by *Oberleutnant* Erich Rudorffer, 6./JG 2, Kairouan/Tunisia, February 9, 1943.

Erich Rudorffer served with 2./JG 2 as an *Oberfeldwebel* from 1940, and soon developed into one of the most notable aces of that *Staffel*. He scored his first victory against a French Curtiss Hawk 75 on May 14, 1940, and on May 26, 1940, his fifth and sixth kills were achieved against two Spitfires over Dunkirk. During the extensive air fighting over the Paris area on June 6, 1940 – when JG 2 claimed twenty-two victories – Rudorffer achieved his first triple kill. On May 1, 1940 – following nineteen victories – *Leutnant* Rudorffer was awarded the Knight's Cross, and next month he was appointed *Staffelkapitän* of 6./JG 2. Erich Rudorffer became famous for the serial victories that he claimed against British, American, and Soviet opponents. On February 9, 1943, he claimed eight victories in only seven minutes over Tunisia. Six days later, he brought home another seven. In July 1943, he took charge of IV./JG 54 on the Eastern Front. By that time, Rudorffer had amassed a total of seventy-four victories and had been shot down himself nine times. Between August 1943 and February 1945 he led II./JG 54, and scored 136 victories with this unit. On August 24, 1943, he reported five Soviet aircraft shot down on the day's first mission, then another three on the second mission. On November 6, 1943, he was credited with thirteen Soviet aircraft shot down between 1300 hours and 1317 hours. Again, on October 28, 1944, he claimed eleven victories in a single day's fighting. The last months of the war saw him as *Gruppenkommandeur* of Me 262-equipped II./JG 7. On March 19, 1945, Rudorffer was responsible for two of the five Mustangs lost by U.S. 78th Fighter Group to Me 262s on that day. Erich Rudorffer survived a total of 950 combat sorties, during which he was shot down sixteen times, and was credited with 222 victories – including 136 on the Eastern Front and twelve with Me 262.

66. Fw 190 A-4

Flown by *Hauptmann* Wilhelm-Ferdinand Galland, *Stab* II./JG 26, Vitry-en-Artois/France, February 3, 1943.

Wilhelm-Ferdinand and Paul Galland were Adolf Galland's two younger brothers who both served in JG 26. All three developed into aces, but only one of them would survive the war. Wilhelm-Ferdinand, known as "Wutz," started the war as an anti-aircraft soldier. Shortly afterward he applied for pilot training, and on June 27, 1941 was posted to his elder brother's JG 26 *Schlageter* in France. *Leutnant* Paul Galland achieved his first victory on July 6, 1941, but Wilhelm-Fredinand's first victory claim, a Spitfire on July 23, 1941, was not confirmed. In May 1942, Wilhelm-Ferdinand was appointed *Staffelkapitän* 5./JG 26. During the air battle over the invasion beach at Dieppe on August 19, 1942, Wilhelm-Fredinand and Paul each shot down a Spitfire, reaching their victory totals fourteen and fifteen respectively. On October 31, 1942, *Leutnant* Paul Galland, was killed during a fighter-bomber raid against Canterbury when his Fw 190 was shot down by an RAF 91 Squadron Spitfire. Paul Galland's victor may have been the South African ace Squadron Leader Johannes "Chris" LeRoux, who destroyed two Fw 190s on this occasion. (Incidentally, LeRoux was the pilot who strafed and injured *Generalfeldmarschall* Erwin Rommel in Normandy on July 17, 1944.). By the shift of the year 1941/1942, "Wutz's" tally had reached twenty-one. On February 3, 1943, he contributed a Ventura bomber and two Spitfires to JG 26's total for the day of seventeen victories against only one loss to their own. On August 17, 1943, *Major* Wilhelm-Ferdinand Galland – now commanding III./JG 26 – was shot down and killed, possibly as Captain Walker Mahurin's (U.S. 56th FG) first victory. Wilhelm-Ferdinand Galland was credited with a total of fifty-five victories on 186 combat sorties.

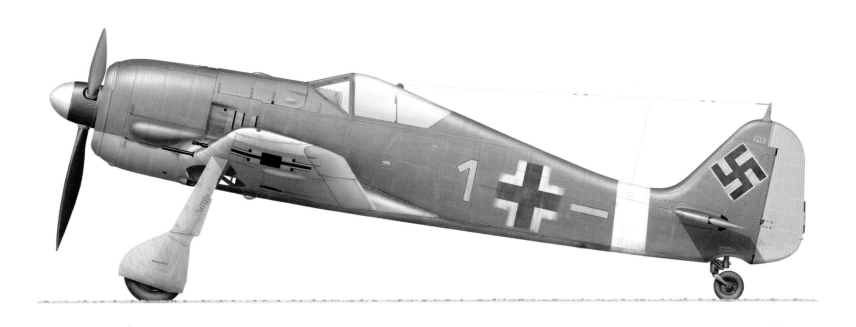

67. Bf 109 G-2

Flown by *Hauptmann* Werner Schroer, 8./JG 27, Rhodes/Greece, February 1943.

Werner Schroer, born on February 12, 1918, joined I./JG 27 in August 1940. His name is associated with the air war over North Africa, where he scored his first victory and eventually rose to become the second-ranking German ace after Hans-Joachim Marseille. Schroer's rise to fame began after he was appointed to *Staffelkapitän* 8./JG 27 on July 1, 1942. By that time his victory tally stood at fourteen. He then achieved three victories each on July 3, and July 13, 1942. On September 15, 1942, he claimed six British fighters over El Alamein – the last, a Spitfire, was registered as his fortieth victory. On October 20, 1942, Schroer was awarded with the Knight's Cross. Another doublette three days later brought his total score to fifty. On November 4, 1942, he caught nine American Liberators that had raided the Libyan port of Benghazi, and shot down one – Schroer's sixtieth victory. With a tally of sixty-one victories in North Africa, Schroer followed III./JG 27 to Greece and – later the island of Rhodes – in November 1942. There, two RAF Beauforts went down as Schroer's sixty-second and sixty-third kills on February 11, 1943. Two months later he was appointed *Gruppenkommandeur* II./JG 27, and led this unit in the Mediterranean area and the Home Defense. On March 7, 1944 he was assumed command of III./JG 54, also in the Home Defense, and scored his 100th victory on May 24, 1944. Between July 1944 and February 1945 he served in a unit commander's school. During the last months of the war, Schroer commanded JG 3 on the Eastern Front, where he achieved his last twelve victories in March and April 1945. Werner Schroer was credited with 114 victories – including 112 against the RAF and USAAF – on 197 combat sorties. He passed away on February 10, 1985.

68. Bf 109 G-2

Flown by *Feldwebel* Rudolf Müller, 6./JG 5, Salmijärvi/Finland, April 19, 1943.

Rudolf Müller was one of the first German top aces in the Far North combat zone – the Russo-German front in the Murmansk area. Posted to the "*Expertenstaffel*" 6./JG 5 as a young *Unteroffizier*, Müller claimed his first victory against a Soviet I-16 on September 12, 1941. During the following twelve months, another sixty-nine victories would follow. A comparison between German and Soviet records show that "Rudi" Müller frequently had dramatic encounters with 72 GSAP/VVS-SF (later renamed into 2 GSAP and 2 GIAP), where the most famous character was the Soviet top ace by that time, Podpolkovnik Boris Safonov (20 individual and six shared victories). During an escort mission for seven I./St.G. 5 Ju 87s and four KG 30 Ju 88s against Vayenga Airdrome near Murmansk at noon on April 23, 1942, Müller shot down the 2 GSAP/VVS-SF Hurricanes piloted by Serzhants Anatoliy Semyonov and N. F. Yepanov. On the subsequent return flight, Müller spotted a formation of SB bombers escorted by Hurricanes. When the fight was over, 20 GIAP's Starshiy Leytenant I. Ya. But and Serzhant A. I. Chibisov, and the SB piloted by 137 SBAP's Mladshiy Leytenant Golovanov had been shot down – all of them by "Rudi" Müller. Five days later, 2 GSAP/VVS-SF once again came across "Rudi" Müller, and lost another four Hurricanes to this formidable ace. The claim that appears in various sources that Müller shot down the ace Safonov on May 30, 1942 however can not be verified. Again on June 2, 1942, Müller bagged two 2 GSAP/VVS-SF Hurricanes. One year later, April 19, 1943, Müller had his last encounter in the air with 2 GIAP/VVS-SF, when he was shot down by one of its aces. "Rudi" Müller, credited with 94 aerial victories, was captured and was brought to a Soviet airbase where he had the opportunity to meet with and talk to the pilots of 2 GIAP/VVS-SF. His final fate is unclear.

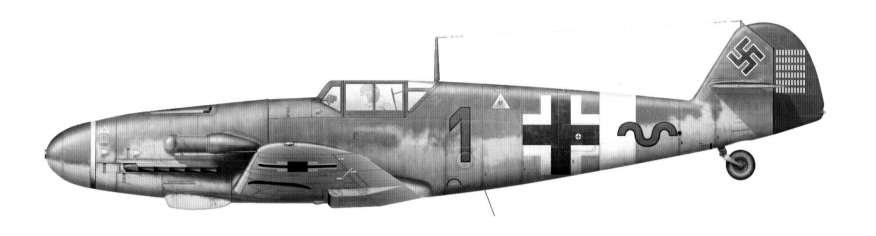

69. Fw 190 A-5Y

Flown by *Major* Fritz Losigkeit, *Stab* I./JG 1, Deelen/Netherlands, April 1943.

Born in Berlin on November 17, 1913, Fritz Losigkeit began his career as fighter pilot already in 1936. Two year later Losigkeit went to Spain and flew with J. 88 in the Condor Legion before he was shot down and captured on February 10, 1939. With Francisco Franco's victory, Losigkeit was released from captivity and returned to Germany. The outbreak of World War II saw Losigkeit serving as *Staffelkapitän* 2./JG 26. He flew over France and the English Channel until May 1941. Then he was posted to several diplomatic missions abroad, serving as a military attaché. Once again having returned to Germany he assumed command of IV./JG 1 (later I./JG 1) in the Home Defense in May 1942. Following a controversy with the commander of Jagddivision 3 who accused the fighter pilots of the Home Defense of cowardice, Losigkeit was released from his command and sent to the Eastern Front to take charge of III./JG 51 on June 26, 1943. He ended the war as a Knight's Cross holder and *Geschwaderkommodore* of JG 77, with a total of sixty-eight victories to his credit.

70. Bf 109 G-4

Flown by *Leutnant* Erich Hartmann, 7./JG 52, Taman/USSR, May 1943.

Piloting this Bf 109, *Leutnant* Erich Hartmann flew as a *Rottenführer* in 7./JG 52 over the Kuban in northwestern Caucasus during the spring of 1943. When Hartmann had arrived at III./JG 52 on the Eastern Front in October 1942, it showed that he lacked combat discipline. All of this was brought out of him by his harsh fighter trainer in first-line service, *Oberfeldwebel* Alfred Grislawski – one of the toughest pilots in JG 52. It was Grislawski who gave Hartmann his nickname "Bubi" (Little Boy) – originally intended as a derogatory nickname. Hartmann learned much from Grislawski, and was able to claim seventeen victories through May 1943. But the air combats over the Kuban bridge-head in northwestern Caucasus put a terrible strain on the German pilots. After his fifth force-landing on May 25, 1943, Hartmann was but a nervous wreck and was sent on home leave by his commander. His plane was repaired and taken over by *Unteroffizier* Herbert Meissler. On May 28, 1943 Meissler went missing over Kuban in his first sortie in Hartmann's plane. According to Soviet sources he was forced to land on a Soviet airfield by the Soviet fighter ace Kapitan Pavel Tarasov (24 victories). This Soviet claim however was refuted by Meissler after the war, who claims that he simply made an erroneous navigation.

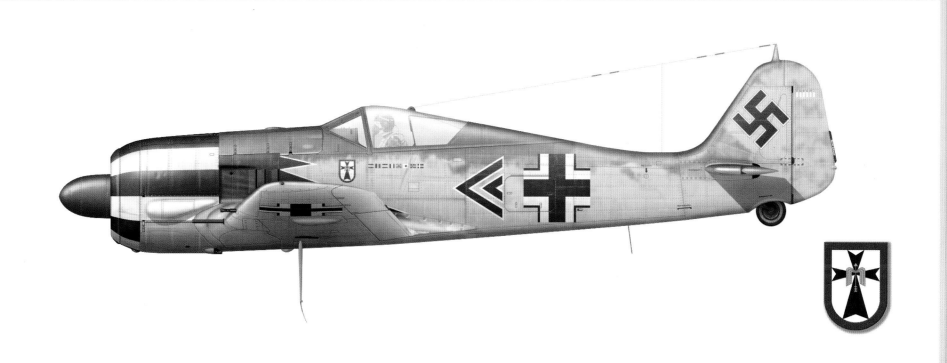

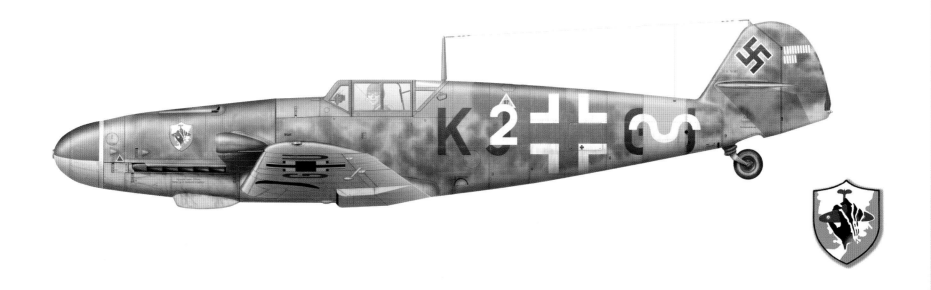

71. Fw 190 A-5

Flown by *Hauptmann* Egon Mayer, *Stab* III./JG 2, Beaumont le Roger/France, June 1943.

Egon Mayer served with JG 2 *Richthofen* since December 1939, and achieved his first victory during the German invasion of France in 1940. One year later, his score stood at twenty. In the summer of 1942, he bagged sixteen RAF fighters in a sixteen-day-period, and achieved his fiftieth kill during the battle of Dieppe on August 19, 1942. From November 1942, he headed III./JG 2, and developed the tactic of attacking the U.S. heavy bombers head on. "In those days Egon Mayer's group perfected the twelve o'clock pass and created a great deal of havoc for our Flying Fortresses," recalls Edgar C. Burford, who participated in the air war over Europe as a U.S. 305 BG B-17 gunner. Burford describes the JG 2 aces that 305 Bomb Group met over western France in 1943 as "well trained veterans, well defended by capable wingmen, extremely good marksmen, and capable leaders of anybody's respect." He wrote: "When it came to aerial fighting, the Germans were the professionals and we were amateurs with a great deal to learn." On April 16, 1943, Mayer was awarded with the Knight's Cross. On July 1, 1943, Mayer was appointed *Geschwaderkommodore* JG 2. On September 6, 1943, he claimed to have knocked down three heavy bombers in nineteen minutes. Mayer had been credited with a total of 102 victories, including twenty-five four-engine bombers, when he was killed in combat with Thunderbolts near Montmedy on March 2, 1944. He was awarded with the Swords to the Knight's Cross with Oak Leaves the same day.

72. Bf 109 G-6

Flown by *Hauptmann* Heinrich Ehrler, *Stab* III./JG 5, Petsamo/Finland, June 1943.

Heinrich Ehrler came from the antiaircraft artillery to a flight training school, and was posted to *Jagdgruppe Kirkenes* (later II./JG 5), with which he flew against the Soviets in the Far North from 1941. The resistance from the Soviet airmen in this area was considerably stronger than in other sectors of the Eastern Front. On February 19, 1942, three 4./JG 5 Bf 109s met six Soviet LaGG-3s, whereby Ehrler shot down one while the German pilot *Obergefrieter* Gerhard Seibt was lost. On May 17, 1942, Ehrler participated when II./JG 5 met the Soviet Hurricanes of 760 IAP. While *Unteroffizier* Karl Heinz Wellner was shot down, *Oberleutnant* Ehrler knocked down the Hurricane flown by Serzhant Bazarov. As the doomed Hurricane went down, it tore straight into a Bf 109 piloted by *Unteroffizier* Helmut Schattschneider. The unfortunate German managed to nurse his badly crippled plane down to the ground and made a forced landing far behind Soviet lines. Fifteen days later, a totally exhausted Schattschneider reached the German lines by foot. Ehrler claimed the bulk of his successes between November 1942 and November 1944, when he increased his victory tally from forty-four to 199. However, corresponding Soviet loss statistics can not substantiate a large share of the victories claimed by JG 5 during this period. Thus, on August 18, 1943, only four of the twenty-one Soviet aircraft claimed shot down by JG 5 (including two fighters as Ehrler's 114th and 115th victories) can be found in Soviet loss statistics. By late August 1943, a Finnish report noted that "the initiative in the air war in the Far North seems to be totally in Russian hands." Ehrler, who commanded JG 5 since June 1943, was held responsible for the loss of the battleship *Tirpitz* in November 1944, and was court-martialed. He was nevertheless allowed to serve with Me 262-equipped JG 7, where he got killed in action on April 4, 1945. He was credited with a total of 205 victories.

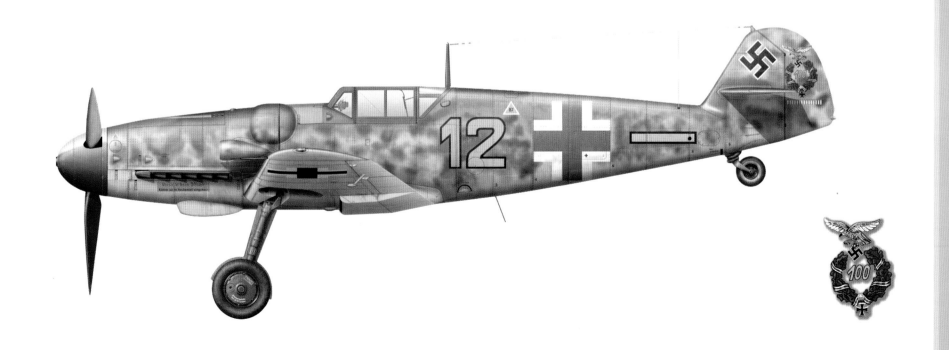

73. Fw 190 A-5

Flown by *Unteroffizier* Walter Köhne, 1./JG 1, Deelen/Netherlands, July 1943.

Köhne started his career as fighter pilot with 4./JG 52 in late 1940. On June 22, 1941, he was seriously injured when his Bf 109 was shot down by ground fire during a low-level attack against Soviet tanks. He returned to his unit in April 1942, and achieved a total of twelve victories on the Eastern Front before he was shifted to 11./JG 1 (later 2./JG 1) in the Home Defense. On June 22, 1943, he knocked down his first American heavy bomber, a B-17. On February 20, 1944, another B-17 fell before his guns as his twentieth victory, and on May 12, 1944, a B-24 became his twenty-ninth kill. On July 14, 1944 *Leutnant* Köhne was appointed *Staffelkapitän* 6./JG 11. On October 6, 1944, he survived being shot down by a Thunderbolt. He paid back by destroying a Thunderbolt as his thirtieth victory during Operation *Bodenplatte* on January 1, 1945. In April 1945, Köhne was posted to III./EJG 2 to receive training on the Me 262 jet fighter. Walter Köhne was credited with a total of thirty confirmed victories, including twelve on the Eastern Front.

74. Bf 109 G-6

Flown by *Hauptmann* Wilhelm Lemke, 9./JG 3, Bad Wörishofen/Germany, August 1943.

Wilhelm Lemke joined III./JG 3 in November 1940 and would rise to one of the most successful pilots of this unit on the Eastern Front, where he scored his first victory on June 26, 1941. On August 11, 1942, he was appointed *Staffelkapitän* 8./JG 3 *Udet*. His fiftieth victory was attained against an Il-2 on August 25, 1942. Shortly afterward he received the Knight's Cross. During the subsequent Battle of Stalingrad, Lemke claimed forty-three victories. On October 21, 1942, he achieved his seventieth victory by downing a LaGG-3 – possibly piloted by the commander of 512 IAP, Batalyonnyy Komissar Ivan Mamykin, who was killed. Recalling the air battle over Stalingrad in 1942, Mayor Boris Yeryomin of 296 IAP said: "The German hunters from the 'Udet Wing' taught us many bitter lessons." While supporting the German counter-strike that led to the re-conquest of Kharkov on March 16, 1943, Lemke became the thirty-fourth German fighter pilot to attain his 100th victory – against a La-5. Wilhelm Lemke had amassed a total of 125 victories on the Eastern Front when III./JG 3 *Udet* was transferred to Home Defense duties in August 1943. On August 17, 1943, he knocked down a U.S. 56th Fighter Group Thunderbolt. III./JG 3 would become the most successful *Jagdgruppe* in the Home Defense during the fall of 1943, and chalked up fifty victories – all but three against American heavy bombers – against only eight combat losses from August through December 1943. But Lemke, who was posted to II./JG 3 as *Gruppenkommandeur*, was killed in combat with Thunderbolts over the Netherlands on December 4, 1943. Wilhelm Lemke was credited with a total of 131 victories on approximately 700 combat sorties.

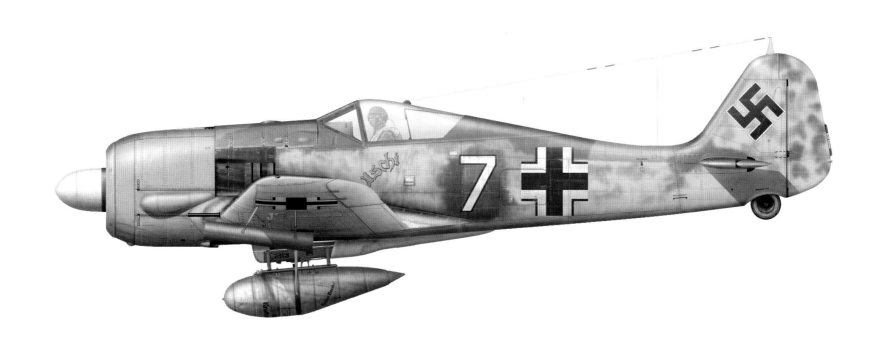

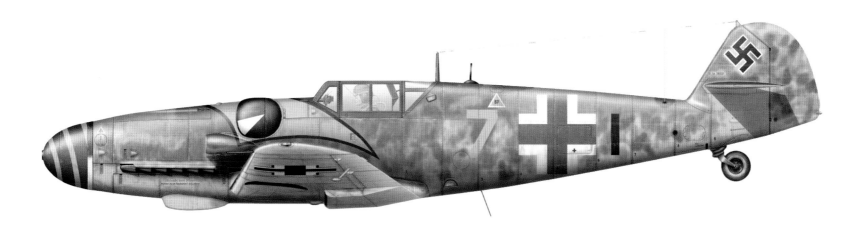

75. Bf 109 G-6
Flown by *Oberleutnant* Rudolf Trenkel, 2./JG 52, Kuteinikovo/USSR, August 19, 1943.

Rudolf Trenkel started his career as a fighter pilot with JG 77 in February 1942. Four months later he was posted to 2./JG 52, which by that time had just returned from a long period of rest and recuperation in Germany. Trenkel carried out many sorties as a wingman during the German summer offensive against Caucasus in the summer of 1942. In August 1942, I./JG 52 was posted to the central combat zone of the Eastern Front to help out JG 51, which was in deep trouble against superior Soviet air forces. This was Trenkel's learning period, and from 1943 on he achieved considerable personal successes. On April 16, 1943, he reached a total tally of fifty victories by downing five Soviet aircraft. In May 1943, Trenkel's unit was posted to the Kuban area, where he frequently had encounters with aces such as Aleksandr Pokryshkin and Grigoriy Rechkalov of Airacobra-equipped 16 GIAP. Trenkel became known as an almost fearless pilot with an incredible luck. On August 19, 1943, he was awarded with the Knight's Cross for 76 victories. But after achieving his ninety-first and ninety-second kills against two Il-2s on October 23, 1943, he was shot down and seriously injured in combat with Yak-9s and Il-2s on November 1, 1943. Back in action again, he reached his 100-victory-mark on July 14, 1944. By that time, the Soviet airmen had gained considerable skills, and in October 1944, they shot down Trenkel five times within ten days. But Trenkel was always lucky to survive. On March 15, 1945, he carried out his final combat sortie; he was shot down by ground fire and was injured. Two months later, victorious Red Army troops found the 138-victory ace in a hospital and confined him for many years. Rudolf Trenkel passed away on April 26, 2001.

76. Bf 109 G-6
Flown by *Major* Horst Carganico, *Stab* II./JG 5, Alakurtti/Finland, September 1943.

According a statement made by a JG 5 ace, the incident on August 12, 1942, when Carganico was shot down behind Soviet lines and walked back to the German lines through the wilderness, turned Carganico into a most cautious pilot. Carganico had scored his fiftieth kill in June 1942, and ten months later, his tally stood at fifty-two. In March 1944, Major Carganico was posted to the home defense to assume command of I./JG 5. On May 27, 1944, Carganico was instructed to scramble his *Jagdgruppe* in bad weather against 930 U.S. heavy bombers and 590 medium bombers, escorted by 1,135 fighters, that flew against marshalling yards in the border area between Germany and France. No more than 90 German fighters were brought up against this huge attack force, and Carganico's unit was in the forefront of the interception. Every third participating German fighter was shot down – twenty-three were claimed by U.S. 357th Fighter Group alone. Counted among seven killed pilots in I./JG 5 was *Major* Horst Carganico, who was shot down by a Mustang near Saint Dizier/France. Horst Carganico was credited with a total of 60 victories.

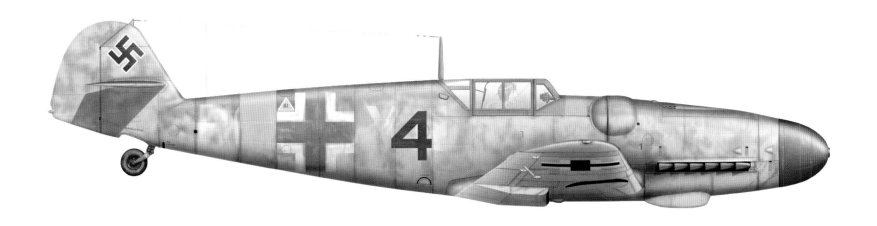

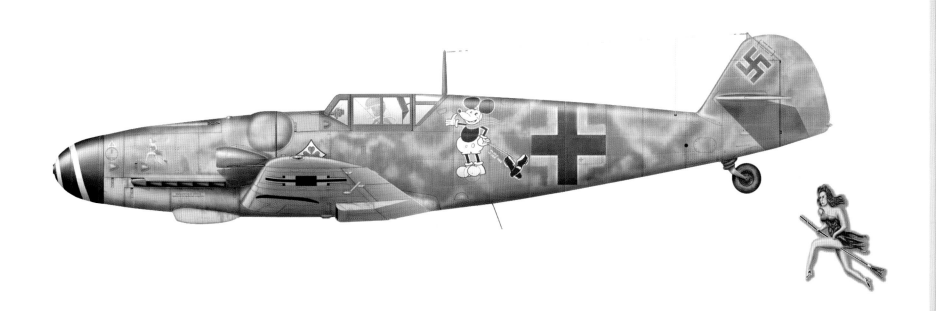

77. Fw 190 A-4
Flown by *Oberfeldwebel* Kurt Knappe, 7./JG 2, Poix/France, September 1943.

Born on June 2, 1918 in Berlin, Kurt Knappe belonged to the most able NCO pilots of JG 51, where he achieved the bulk of his victories on the Eastern Front. Knappe brought home his first air kill in June 1941. JG 51, where Knappe served as an *Unteroffizier* in II. *Gruppe*, was the most successful German fighter unit during the first stage of the war. At the opening of the German invasion of the Soviet Union on June 22, 1941, it had been credited with a total of 691 aerial victories. It would chalk up another 1,820 kills until the end of 1941. On April 7, 1942, JG 51 surpassed the 3,000-victory-mark. On October 4, 1942, Knappe, still with the rank of an *Unteroffizier*, scored his fiftieth victory. On November 3, 1942, he was awarded with the Knight's Cross. A few days later, II./JG 51 left the Eastern Front and was shifted to Tunisia. By that time, Knappe's score stood at fifty-one. He was promoted to *Feldwebel* and, in the summer of 1943, was brought to 7./JG 2 Richthofen in France. On September 3, 1943, when U.S. 8th Air Force and RAF dispatched a large-scale operation against airfields and aircraft factories across northern France, the Fw 190s of JG 2 intercepted U.S. 4th Bomber Wing near Paris, without any success. In the ensuing combat, Kurt Knappe was shot down and killed by a Spitfire pilot, probably from RAF 421 Squadron. Knappe was credited with a total of 56 victories – 51 on the Eastern Front, and one four-engine U.S. bomber.

78. Fw 190 A-6
Flown by *Oberfeldwebel* Anton-Rudolf Piffer, 2./JG 1, Deelen/Netherlands, October 4, 1943.

On October 4, 1943, 8th USAAF dispatched about three hundred heavy bombers, the bulk of which were directed against the city of Frankfurt. The German Home Defense mounted most of JG 1, JG 3, JG 11, JG 27 and ZG 76 against the attack force, but still managed to knock down no more than sixteen bombers for the loss of sixteen fighters. The authorities in Frankfurt had all reason to complain over the meager achievement by the defense forces, and three days later, *Reichsmarschall* Göring summoned the *Geschwaderkommodore* of the Home Defense and accused them of cowardice. On October 9, 1943, the Inspector of the Fighter Arm, *Generalmajor* Adolf Galland, was airborne to inspect how the German fighter attacks against the heavy bombers' Box formations were carried out. To his dismay, he saw how most of his fighter pilots attacked "in an unorganized manner, disengaging while still at too large distance." The frontal attacks against the closed formations of heavily armed B-17s and B-24s was similar to the bloody head-on assaults on the Western Front in World War I, and it took much nerves to carry out such attacks to the limit. The German fighter pilots that managed to cope with such attacks either were killed after a short while, or were lucky to survive and developed into famous "Four-engine killers." One of the latter was 2./JG 1's *Oberfeldwebel* Anton-Rudolf Piffer, who destroyed one B-17 on each of the U.S. major raids against Germany on October 4, October 8, October 9, October 10, and October 14, 1943. On January 30, 1944, Piffer even managed to knock down two B-17s. Among Piffer's total record of thirty-five victories were twenty-six four-engine bombers. On June 17, 1944, Piffer was shot down and killed in combat with RAF Mustangs over Normandy. He was posthumously awarded with the Knight's Cross.

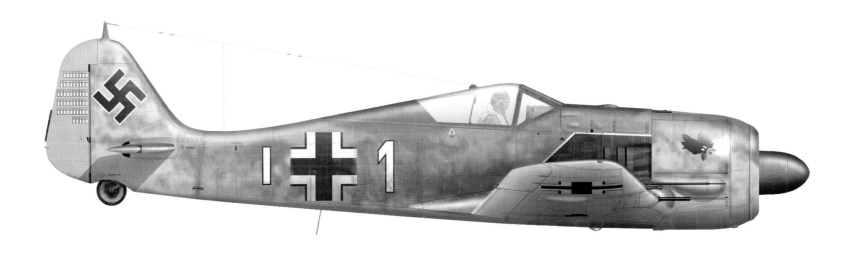

79. Fw 190 A-5/U12

Flown by *Leutnant* Erich Hondt, 2./JG 11, Husum/Germany, October 8, 1943.

On October 8, 1943 U.S. Eighth Air Force dispatched a large-scale raid against northwestern Germany. Four days previously, the American bombers had wrought devastation in Frankfurt. The civilian authorities in this city expressed severe criticism toward the fighter defense for "lacking protection. Hermann Göring summoned all the unit commanders of the Home Defense on October 7 and threatened them to be court-martialed if the fighters did carry home their attacks with more determination. "I know what I have to do," *Oberstleutnant* Hans Philipp, the *Geschwaderkommodore* of JG 1, said prior to take-off on this October 8. In violent clashes between 300 heavy bombers, almost as many escort fighters and 566 German fighters, twenty-seven American bombers, three Thunderbolts and twenty-four German fighters were shot down. Among the killed airmen was Hans Philipp. *Oberleutnant* Erich Hondt survived with severe burns.

80. Bf 109 G-6

Flown by *Major* Kurt Brändle, *Stab* II./JG 3, Schiphol/Netherlands, November 3, 1943.

On November 3, 1943, the 378 U.S. fighters providing fighter escort for 566 heavy bombers that went against Wilhelmshaven, for the forst time abandoned their previous close escort tactic, flying in free hunting over the Low Countries and northwestern Germany. The result was an immediate success. Most German fighters were tied up in fighter combat and were unable to break through to the bombers, who lost only seven planes. II./JG 3 clashed with the Thunderbolts of U.S. 4th Fighter Group over the North Sea coast. *Major* Kurt Brändle, *Gruppenkommandeur* II./JG 3, claimed two P-47s (his 171st and 172nd victories), while on the American side Lt. Robert S. Johnson claimed a Bf 109 as his 6th victory. Later that day, sixty-five B-26 Marauders of U.S. 9th Air Force were dispatched against *Major* Brändle's base at Amsterdam/Schiphol. The scrambling Bf 109s were bounced on by escorting RAF Spitfires before they had time to assemble, and in the ensuing dogfight, six Bf 109s were shot down. Among the lost pilots was the Oak Leaves holder and veteran from the first day of the war, *Major* Kurt Brändle. Kurt Brändle was credited with a total of 172 victories.

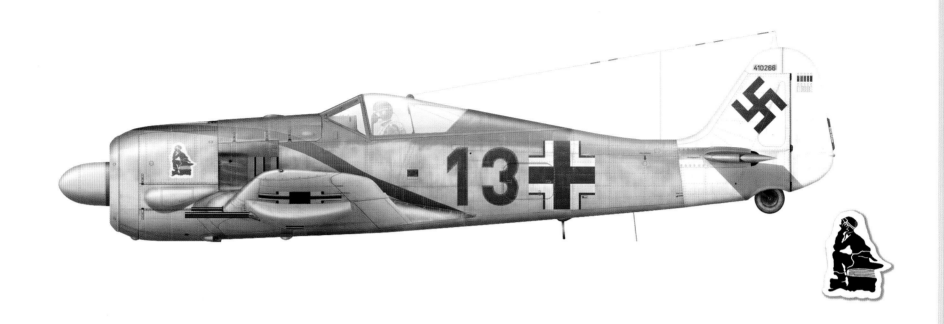

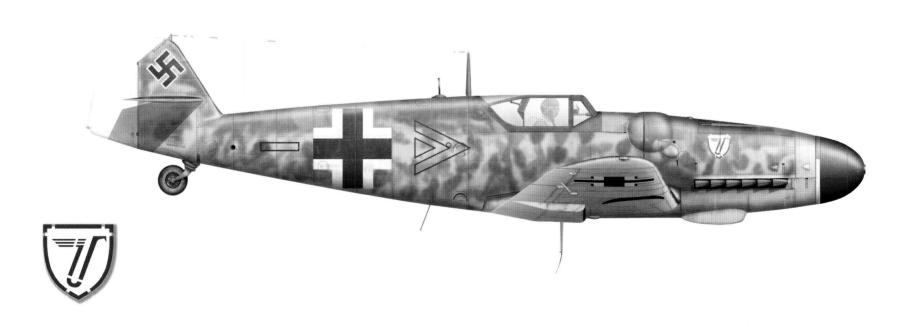

81. Bf 109 G-6

Flown by *Oberleutnant* Heinrich Klöpper, 7./JG 1, Leeuwarden/Netherlands, November 13, 1943.

Heinrich Klöpper was born on January 9, 1918. He served with I./JG 77 (later IV./JG 51) from the onset of the war. After achieving his eighth victory on the Eastern Front, Klöpper was shot down on July 26, 1941, but survived. His most successful day was August 4, 1942, when he was credited with the destruction of three Il-2s, a Pe-2, and a MiG-3 during three separate engagements in the Rzhev area. That day, JG 51 brought home forty-two victories. But this also was the most difficult period in JG 51's history – the Battle of Britain included. During the first four days of August 1942 alone, the heavy air battle over Rzhev on the Eastern Front cost *Jagdgeschwader Mölders* twenty-two Bf 109s shot down. Men with Klöpper's experience were badly needed to ward off the operations carried out by increasingly aggressive and skillful Soviet fliers. On September 4, 1942, Klöpper was awarded with the Knight's Cross for sixty-five kills. With eighty-two marks on his killboard, Klöpper was posted to I./JG 2 *Richthofen* in France in the spring of 1943, and to the Home Defense to assume command over 7./JG 1 in May 1943. Here he scored his ninetieth kill against a U.S. B-17 on November 3, 1943. Ten days later, Klöpper contributed with one to the seven losses sustained by Lighting-equipped U.S. 55th Fighter Group. However, Klöpper's own Bf 109 also was damaged and he had to belly-land. On November 29, 1943, 55th Fighter Group once again lost seven Lightnings – one of them filed as *Oberleutnant* Klöpper's ninety-fourth kill. But during the return flight, all three Bf 109s of Klöpper's Kette crashed due to low could ceiling. The remains of Heinrich Klöpper were found in his destroyed aircraft.

82. Bf 109 G-6

Flown by *Major* Günther Rall, *Stab* III./JG 52, Apostolovo/USSR, November 28, 1943.

Günther Rall was the third top scoring ace of World War II. He was appointed *Staffelkapitän* 8./JG 52 in July 1940. By that time his total tally was a single aerial victory claim – against a French Hawk 75 during a melee with GC 2/4 on May 18, 1940. His next airkill was scored against a Soviet bomber over Romania in June 1941. He amassed another thirty-four victories over the Eastern Front until he was shot down and seriously injured by a VVS-Southern Front Yak-1 on November 28, 1941. After recovering from his wounds, he returned to his *Staffel* in August 1942, and already by the end of that month he had increased his victory tally to sixty-two – for which he was awarded with the Knight's Cross on September 3. However, the bulk of Rall's successes were achieved in 1943. On April 20, 1943, Rall achieved his personal 116th and JG 52's five thousandth victory. On July 6, 1943, he was appointed *Gruppenkommandeur* of III./JG 52. Two days later he achieved four victories, and again four on July 28, 1943. He continued with another five kills on August 23, 1943. Six days later, he reached the 200-victory-mark, as the third pilot to do so – the second in III./JG 52 (after Hermann Graf)! Following this, Rall was awarded with the Swords to the Knight's Cross with Oak Leaves on September 23, 1943. Back in action after a brief home leave, Rall brought home four victories on October 9, 1943, and five the next day. On November 28, 1943, he became the second fighter pilot to reach the 250-victory-mark. On April 18, 1944, Rall was transferred to command II./JG 11 the Home Defense. After bringing down a U.S. Thunderbolt on May 12, 1944 – his 275th and last victory – Rall was himself shot down and sustained severe injuries. From November 1944 until the end of the war, Günther Rall served in the Staff of *General der Jagdflieger*. Günther Rall is still alive.

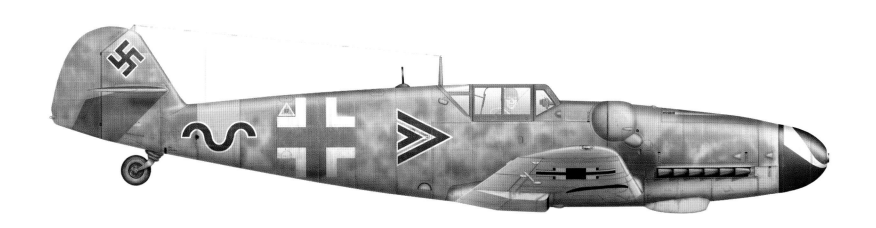

83. Fw 190 A-6
Flown by *Oberleutnant* Joachim Brendel, 1./JG 51, Orel/USSR, December 1943.

Joachim Brendel was posted as a *Leutnant* to JG 51 shortly before the invasion of the USSR. During the first two years he was picked to fly mainly close-support missions against Soviet ground targets. During one of these sorties, on February 6, 1942, he was severely injured as he belly-landed and the unreleased bomb exploded. Returning to JG 51 after recovering from his wounds, Brendel was relieved from the hazardous fighter-bomber missions and started to fly regular fighter sorties. From then on, his rise to fame began. On January 6 and January 18, 1943 he achieved triple victories. Again, on March 18, 1943, he destroyed three Il-2s. In early June 1943, Brendel participated in the large-scale air battles when Soviet aviation attacked Orel and Bryansk airdromes with large forces. During these encounters, JG 51 claimed sixty-one victories on June 10, 1943 – three of them by Brendel. By downing six Soviet aircraft on November 22, 1943, Brendel reached his 100-victory-mark. The majority of these kills were achieved since the spring of 1943. As *Gruppenkommandeur* of III./JG 51, Brendel was one of the most successful German pilots during the final stage of World War II. On February 20 and March 18, 1945, Brendel claimed triples over East Prussia. His 189th and last victory was attained on April 25, 1945.

84. Fw 190 A-6
Flown by *Hauptmann* Heinz Lange, 3./JG 51, Minsk/USSR, December 1943.

Heinz Lange, born on October 2, 1917 in Cologne, served as a fighter pilot from the first day until the very end of the war. When the war started he was a *Leutnant* in I./JG 21 (later III./JG 54). His first victory was attained against an RAF Blenheim on October 30, 1939. From June 1941, Lange served on the Eastern Front. When he was posted to JG 51 to assume command of its 3. Staffel on November 6, 1942, his victory tally had risen to twenty. Piloting the Fw 190 with I/JG 51 – the first unit to be equipped with this fighter on the Eastern Front – Lange developed into one of the most successful "Shturmovik killers." The heavy armored Il-2 Shturmovik was dubbed the "Cement Bomber" by the German fighter pilots, but Lange succeeded in shooting down twenty-four of this type. "The Il-2 was a dangerous opponent because it was equipped with a rear gunner," says Lange. "I always tried to get in position slightly below the Il-2s, from where I could hit its vulnerable radiator." On December 4 and December 17, 1942 he achieved double victories – all against Il-2s.On his 500th combat sortie on January 17, 1943, Lange achieved his twenty-sixth victory. During the remainder of the war, he carried out another 138 combat sorties, during which he increased his victory tally to 72. On May 8, 1944, he was appointed *Gruppenkommandeur* of IV./JG 51, which attained a total of 2,370 victories against 134 pilot casualties during the war. On April 12, 1945 Lange became JG 51's last *Geschwaderkommodore*. His final aerial combat was fought against four La-7s over Neubrandenburg on April 29, 1945. After the war, Lange passed the exam as a juridical doctor, and today he lives a quiet life in Bergisch Gladbach.

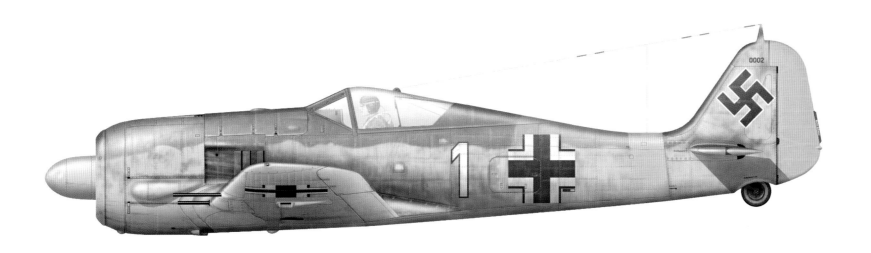

85. Mc 205 V

Flown by *Oberleutnant* Joachim Deicke, 6./JG 77, Lagnasco/Italy, December 28, 1943.

Following the Italian armistice in September 1943, one of the German *Jagdgruppen* in this country – *Hauptmann* Siegfried Freytag's II./JG 77 – was outfitted with Italian Macchi MC 205 fighters. This formidable fighter was highly esteemed by *Hauptmann* Freytag and his pilots, and only maintenance difficulties limited its service with the Luftwaffe. The first Luftwaffe sortie with MC 205s was carried out against U.S. heavy bombers over Italy on November 8, 1943. Already on the following day, *Oberleutnant* Franz Hrdlicka claimed the first victory while flying an MC 205, against a P-38 Lightning of the U.S. 82nd Fighter Group. Two days later, an MC 205 of II./JG 77 was responsible for the only loss sustained by thirty-one 15th USAAF Liberators on a long-range mission against a target in France. With the foundation of the new Fascist Italian Air Force, the MC 205s were handed over to the Italian 1 Gruppo Caccia on the last day of 1943. During almost two months of service with the Luftwaffe, not a single MC 205 was lost due to enemy action. Joachim Deicke, who flew this MC 205 late in 1943, carried out a total of 661 sorties during World War II and scored 16 victories.

86. Fw 190 A-6/R11 Neptun

Flown by *Oberleutnant* Fritz Krause, 1./NJGr. 10, Werneuchen/Germany, January 1944.

The British twin-engine high-speed Mosquito bombers, which roamed the skies above Germany day and night from 1942 onward, constituted a constant headache to the commanders of Germany's home defense. It was particularly annoying to the Luftwaffe's C-in-C, *Reichsmarschall* Hermann Göring, who once had boasted that no enemy aircraft would be able to penetrate German airspace. In 1943, Göring ordered the formation of two daytime fighter units with the main task of hunting down Mosquitoes, JG 25 and JG 50. Both units however failed to fulfill their task and were disbanded in late 1943. Then Göring formed a night fighter unit with the same task. *Nachtjagdgruppe* 10 was formed on January 1, 1944, commanded by 56-victory night fighter ace *Major* Rudolf Schoenert. It was thought that NJGr. 10's Fw 190 A-6/R11s and Bf 109 G-6s, which were able to fly considerably faster than the regular twin-engine night fighters, would be able to out-run and catch the Mosquitoes. In order to increase speed further, the single-engine night fighters received an extra polishing. To locate the Mosquitoes in the darkness, NJGr. 10 became first night fighter unit to operate single-engine night-fighters equipped with radar. The idea of equipping single-engine fighters with radar was launched by *Jagdfliegerführer Oberst* Gordon Gollob in late 1943. The new *Rüstsatz* (equipment) 11 – FuG 217 Neptun J – also allowed the fighter pilots to track down enemy aircraft in the darkness. But in reality, NJGr. 10 was met with only limited success. In the decisive moment of air combat – when they were about to attack – the single-engine night fighter pilots found that the staring at their radar screens for several minutes while tracking down their opponent, had deprived their eyes of their ability to see in the darkness. In fact, only one Mosquito was shot down by NJGr. 10 – west of Berlin on the night of July 7//-8, 1944. The victorious pilot was *Oberleutnant* Fritz Krause.

87. Fw 190 A-7

Flown by *Hauptmann* Alfred Grislawski, 1./JG 1, Dortmund/Germany, January 11, 1944.

Of Alfred Grislawski's achievements during World War II, he is most proud over the fact that he managed to bring home his wingman safely on every single combat mission. Alfred Grislawski carried out a total of 800 combat missions and was credited with 132 aerial victories. Among the novice pilots that learned air combat tactics from Alfred Grislawski was Erich Hartmann, and Hartmann earned his famous nick-name "Bubi" ("Little Boy") from Grislawski. Counted among the 109 Soviet pilots that were shot down by Grislawski on the Eastern Front between September 1941 and June 1943 are a number of the VVS top aces. On August 5, 1943, Grislawski's friend *Major* Hermann Graf brought him to JG 50 in Wiesbaden, where Grislawski was appointed *Staffelkapitän* of 1. *Staffel*. During the American bomber mission against Schweinfurt and Regensburg on August 17, 1943, Grislawski knocked down two B-17s – registered as his 110th and 111th victories. Promoted to *Hauptmann* on recommendation by Graf on October 1, 1943, Grislawski was later posted to JG 1, where he took command of 1. *Staffel*. On January 24, 1944, he shot down a U.S. B-17 over Baske/Belgium, but was also himself shot down and injured. Grislawski met a surviving crew of the shot down B-17 at hospital. It proved that his fighter attack had came so sudden that the American was certain that he had been shot down by heavy AAA fire. The siderudder of one of Grislawski's last Bf 109s is currently on display at Luftfahrtmuseum Langehagen at Hannover/Germany.

88. Fw 190 A-6 *Sturmjäger*

Flown by *Major* Erwin Bacsila, Sturmstaffel 1, Dortmund/Germany, January 30, 1944.

Born on January 27, 1910 in Budapest, Erwin Bacsila served with the Austrain Air Force in the 1930s. He joined the Luftwaffe's I./JG 333 (later II./ZG 1) after his country's *Anschluss* to the Third Reich in 1938. In 1939, he flew a Bf 109 E as *Gruppenadjutant* in II./ZG 1 against Poland. Shortly afterward, he was appointed *Staffelkapitän* of the Bf 109 D-equipped night fighter unit 11.(N)/JG 2. On July 25, 1940, when the *Staffelkapitän* of 7./JG 52, *Oberleutnant* Wilhelm Keidel, was shot down and killed – by RAF 610 Squadron's Flight Lieutenants D. S. Wilson and J. Ellis – over the English Channel, Bacsila took charge of 7./JG 52. Bacsila led this unit in France and in Romania – where he served as a fighter instructor to Romanian pilots – until July 11, 1941. Thereafter he served in various staff positions until he was posted to *Stab*/JG 77 in September 1942, where he flew as *Major* Joachim Müncheberg's wingman. In early 1944, Bacsila volunteered to *Major* Horst-Günther von Kornatzki's new *Sturmstaffel* 1, which was subordinated to I./JG 1 in the home defense. Equipped with heavily armored Fw 190s, the task of *Sturmstaffel* 1's pilots was to approach the U.S. heavy bombers from astern in close formation. The so-called *Sturmjäger* then positioned themselves close behind the B-17s, firing against their target until it was destroyed. The thick armor of their Fw 190s generally gave a good protection against the machine-gun fore from the B-17s and B-24s, but they stood little chance against U.S. escort fighters. On January 30, 1944, *Sturmstaffel* 1 claimed two B-24s and a B-17 shot down but had fifteen Fw 190s destroyed or damaged. Based on the experience of *Sturmstaffel* 1, a row of *Sturmgruppen* was later formed. Later in 1944, Bacsila was shifted to Ekdo 16 and, in the fall of 1944, JG 301. Between January 15, 1945 and February 17, 1945, he commanded IV./JG 3, which was used in the ground-attack role on the Eastern Front. During the last months of the war, Bacsila served with Me 163-equipped JG 400. He passed away in 1982. His total number of victories are unknown some sources quote it as high as 34, but he achieved at least two kills, including one with *Sturmstaffel* 1.

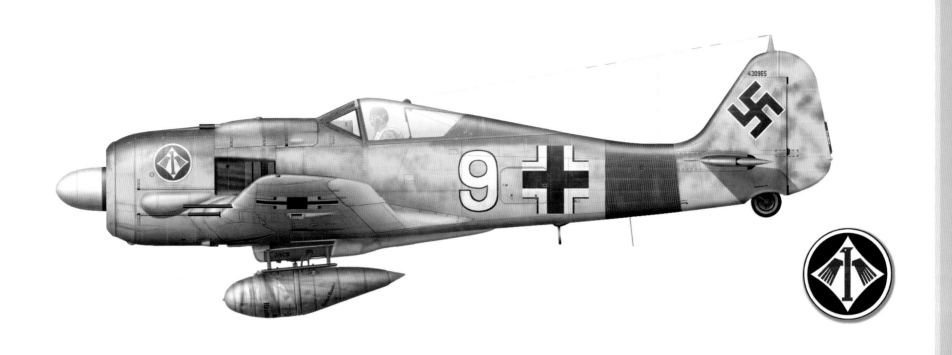

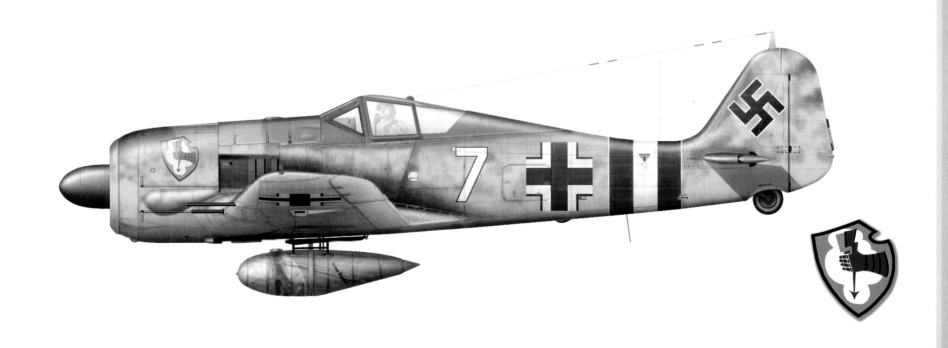

89. Fw 190 A-7
Flown by *Hauptmann* Rolf Hermichen, *Stab* I./JG 11, Rothenburg/Germany, March 8, 1944.

Rolf Hermichen undoubtedly was one of the toughest German airmen in World War II. First he served as a *Zerstörer* pilot with II./ZG 1 (previously II./SKG 210), and scored his first eleven aerial victories with a Bf 110. From November 1941 to October 1943, he served with JG 26 – most of the time as *Staffelkapitän* of 3. Staffel – and attained another thirty-one kills with this unit. In October 1943, Hermichen was appointed *Gruppenkommandeur* I./JG 11 in the Home Defense and rapidly developed into one of the most successful "Four-engine killers." On February 20, 1944, Hermichen attacked the heavy bombers of U.S. 2nd Bomb Division as they returned from their raid against Brunswick, and destroyed four Liberators in eighteen minutes. On March 6, 1944, he led a massive formation of more than one hundred German fighters in a concentrated attack against eighty B-17s and eight P-47s – resulting in the destruction of twenty U.S. bombers and three Thunderbolts for the loss of ten German fighters. Two days later, Hermichen shot down four heavy bombers in twenty-one minutes – his victories Nos. fifty-seven through sixty. He was shot down by Mustangs on March 29, 1944 and bailed out unhurt. On April 2, 1944, *Generaloberst* Hans-Jürgen Stumpff, the C-in-C of *Luftflotte Reich*, awarded Hermichen with the Knight's Cross. On April 15, 1944, Hermichen contributed two to the total of eleven U.S. Lightnings that were claimed by JG 11 (actual American losses in fact were eleven). Hermichen's sixty-fourth victory was scored against a Mustang on April 24, 1944. He was shot down a second time on May 12, 1944, and following this, Hermichen was withdrawn from first-line service. He was posted to the staff of 2. *Jagddivision*, and ended the war commanding the training unit II./JG 104. On February 19, 1945, Hermichen was awarded with the Oak Leaves in recognition for his achievements during the Home Defense. Rolf Hermichen was credited with a total of 64 victories (including 26 heavy bombers) on 629 combat sorties.

90. Bf 109 G-6
Flown by *Leutnant* Walter Wolfrum, 5./JG 52, Grammatikovo/USSR, March 1944.

Walter Wolfrum was posted to 5./JG 52 on the Eastern Front in February 1943. On May 10, 1943, his Bf 109 was badly shot up by a Soviet fighter. Shortly after his 20th birthday, Wolfrum scored his first airkill on May 23, 1943, and another five would follow during the next two months. From 1943 on, the air war on the Eastern Front grew increasingly difficult to the Luftwaffe. 5./JG 52 sustained thirteen combat losses – more than the normal outfit of a Staffel – during slightly more than five months from late October 1943 to early April 1944. During the same period it was credited with 250 victories. On April 9, 1944, Wolfrum, promoted to *Leutnant*, achieved his fifty-eighth and fifty-ninth kills by downing two Yak-7s near Karanki. But six days later he was shot down and seriously injured by an Il-2. After recovering from his wounds, he was appointed *Staffelführer* in 1./JG 52. During the Battle of Iasi on the Romanian border on May 30, 1944, Wolfrum shot down eleven Soviet fighters – his victories eighty-two through ninety-two. On July 16, 1944 – when the Germans claimed eighty-eight Soviet aircraft shot down on the Eastern Front – Wolfrum claimed ten victories (numbers 117 through 126) before he was shot down by a Soviet Airacobra, but again he survived. Wolfrum returned to first-line service in February 1945, and scored another eleven victories during the final weeks of the war, amassing a total of 137 confirmed victories on 423 combat sorties. After the war, Wolfrum became involved with aerobatics, and 1962 he was appointed aerobatics master in Germany. Between 1967 and 1982 he served as the trainer of the German national aerobatics team.

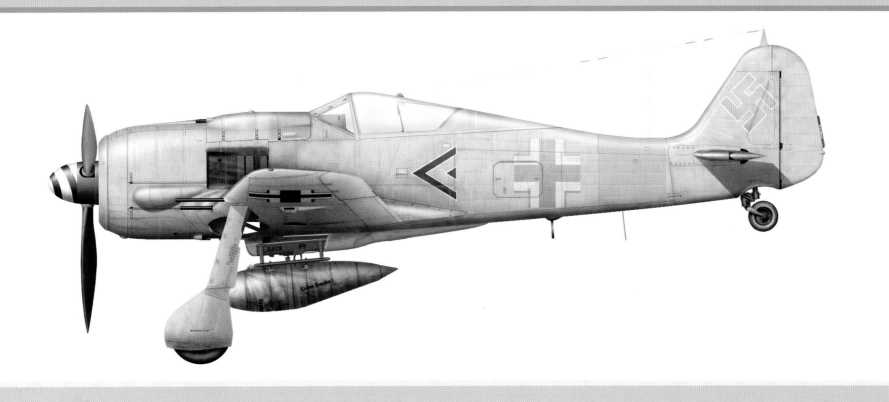

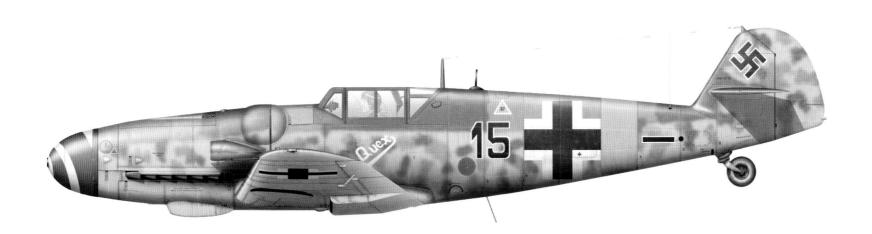

91. Fw 190 A-6
Flown by *Oberfeldwebel* Fritz Tegtmeier, 3./JG 54, Wesenberg/Estonia, March 1944.

Born on July 30, 1917, Fritz Tegtmeier was posted to 1./JG 54 as an *Unteroffizier* in October 1940, shortly after the unit had been withdrawn from offensive operations over the English Channel. On November 17, 1940, Tegtmeier was seriously injured in a flight accident at Jever. After he recovered from his injuries, he joined 2./JG 54 and saw action against the USSR. He scored his first victory already on June 22, 1941. In late spring 1943, when he had developed into one of the most successful NCOs of I./JG 54 *Grünherz*, he was placed as a fighter instructor for a period. After the summer of 1943, he returned to I./JG 54 for a third operational tour, this time with 3. *Staffel*. Tegtmeier scored his 75th victory in the fall of 1943. On February 7, 1944, Tegtmeier brought home five victories. Eleven days later, I./JG 54 was shifted to Wesenberg/Estonia, to help counter the Soviet offensive in this area. Operating from this base, Tegtmeier reached his 100-victory-mark in May 1944, and was promoted to *Leutnant* and appointed *Staffelkapitän* 3./JG 54 three months later. By that time, I./JG 54 operated in the so-called Courland pocket in northern Latvia, and it was here that the *Geschwader* achieved its 8,000th victory on August 15, 1944. Another 1,000 Soviet aircraft would fall before the guns of the JG 54 aircraft during the next four months. In March 1945, *Leutnant* Tegtmeier was instructed to fly out of the Courland pocket to join Me 262-equipped JG 7. Fritz Tegtmeier ended the war with a total of 146 victories, all on the Eastern Front, on 700 combat missions.

92. Fw 190 A-7
Flown by *Oberfeldwebel* Siegfried Zick, 7./JG 11, Oldenburg/Germany, March 23, 1944.

Although Siegfried Zick achieved a total of thirty-one confirmed victories – the majority of them during the late stage of the war – he was never awarded with the Knight's Cross. Siegfried Zick was specialized in hunting down U.S. Lightning escort fighters, and several of the casualties in 8th USAAF's 20th Fighter Group and 55th Fighter Group were due to him. Zick was posted to *Jagdstaffel Münster-Loddenheide* (later 2./JG 1) in the Netherlands in June 1941. His first victory was achieved against an RAF Blenheim on August 12, 1941. During 8th USAAF's first raid against Germany on January 27, 1943, Zick managed to knock down a 44 BG Liberator. On November 13, 1943, when JG 1 and JG 11 shot down seven U.S. 55th Fighter Group Lightnings without any loss to themselves, Zick scored his eighth victory. On January 5, 1944, U.S. 20th and 55th Fighter Groups lost seven Lightnings again, and one of them ended up on Zick's killboard as his number twelve. On March 23, 1944, a Liberator fell before his guns as Zick's twentieth confirmed victory. Zick's victories must be seen against the background of the immense suffering brought upon the Luftwaffe units in the Home Defense during this period. JG 11 suffered heavier losses than any other Luftwaffe unit through March 1944 – it registered sixty-two fighters lost, with forty-seven pilot casualties. Zick's next two victories were achieved against Lightnings from U.S. 20th Fighter Group and 55th Fighter Group on April 13, 1944. Another 20th Fighter Group Lightning was shot down by Zick on May 22, 1944.

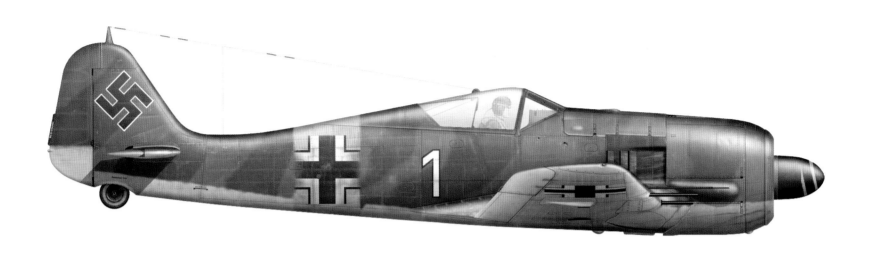

93. Bf 109 G-5/AS

Flown by *Major* Günther Specht, *Stab* II./JG 11, Ludwigslust/Germany, April 9, 1944.

Günther Specht started his combat career as a *Zerstörer* pilot with I./ZG 26. On September 29, 1939, when eleven RAF 83 Squadron Handley-Page Hampden bombers attacked two German destroyers near Helgoland, Specht was responsible for two of the five that were shot down. However, on December 3, 1939, when 24 Wellington bombers attacked Helgoland, Specht was himself shot down and lost the sight on his left eye. He nevertheless returned to first-line service and achieved another four kills before the severe pain in his injured eye rendered him unfit for combat duty. In late 1942 he was then posted to 10./JG 1, where he achieved his seventh victory against a U.S. 8th Air Force 1st Bomb Wing B-17 on February 26, 1943. In March 1943 he was appointed *Staffelkapitän* 7./JG 1, and due to his proven leadership talent, he was promoted to command II./JG 11. "I have never met an officer who made such a strong impression on me as Specht," wrote *Leutnant* Heinz Knoke, who served under his command in II./JG 11: "Specht is a typical, conscientious Prussian soldier. He is Spartanic demanding toward himself, and he is just as demanding toward his subordinates." On April 8, 1944, Specht was awarded the Knight's Cross, and twenty days later he was appointed *Geschwaderkommodore* JG 11. *Oberstleutnant* Günther Specht failed to return from the fateful Operation *Bodenplatte* on January 1, 1945, when a massive fighter-bomber attack was launched against Allied air bases in Belgium and France. He was credited with a total of 34 aerial victories.

94. Fw 190 A-6

Flown by *Major* Anton Hackl, *Stab* III./JG 11, Oldenburg/Germany, April 11, 1944.

Anton Hackl was credited with 118 victories and awarded with the Knight's Cross with Oak Leaves when his 5./JG 77 was transferred from the Eastern Front to North Africa in the fall of 1942. He would attain another five victories in this combat zone before he was shot down and injured in combat with U.S. B-17s over Tunisia on February 4, 1943. In early summer of 1943, Hackl was posted to *Stab*/JG 11 in the Home Defense, and on October 1, 1943 he assumed command over III./JG 11. On April 11, 1944, Hackl brought down a Liberator as his 141st victory. Following his 150th victory he was awarded with the Swords to the Knight's Cross with Oak Leaves on July 13, 1944. In August 1944, Hackl was assigned to lead the new JG 76 (formed on the basis of parts of ZG 1 and ZG 76). He then took command of II./JG 26 in October 1944. On December 23, 1944, when he carried out his first sortie with an Fw 190 D-9, Hackl downed a Mustang, a Lancaster, and a Mosquito in four minutes. During Operation *Hermann/Bodenplatte* – the disastrous large-scale attack against Allied airbases in France and Belgium on New Year's Day 1945 – Hackl brought home his 173d victory by bagging a Spitfire. Two weeks later, a 366th Fighter Group Thunderbolt and a 78th Fighter Group Mustang ended up as his 174th and 175th victories. Shortly afterward he was appointed *Geschwaderkommodore* of JG 300 – where his last great success was achieved when he, on February 3, 1945, led JG 300 against a large formation of U.S. heavy bombers, resulting in the claim for thirty-six bombers and nine escort fighters shot down. On February 20, 1945, Hackl returned to JG 11, which he would command until the end of the war. Anton Hackl carried out more than one thousand combat sorties from 1939 to 1945, he was shot down eight times, and was credited with 192 confirmed and 24 unconfirmed victories. He passed away in 1984.

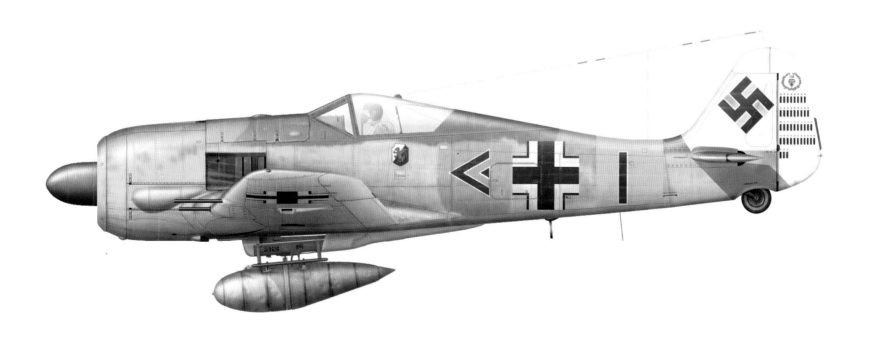

95. Bf 109 G-6
Flown by *Major* Klaus Mietusch, *Stab* III./JG 26, Lille-Nord/France, April 1944.

Klaus Mietusch served with JG 26 from 1938 until 1944. JG 26 historian Don Caldwell characterized him as "a wild man in the air" who paid "no apparent heed to his own personal safety or that of his pilots." Mietusch was shot down himself at least ten times. But it was only after he, in September 1941, had succeeded *Oberleutnant* Joachim Müncheberg as *Staffelkapitän* 7./JG 26 that Mietusch was able to overcome his feeling of lacking competence as fighter pilot. In 1942, Mietusch became one of the first German pilots to score victories against U.S. airmen; his fifteenth victory was achieved against an American Spitfire pilot of RAF 71 (Eagle) Squadron on April 12, 1942, and another two American pilots serving with the RAF fell before his guns on August 19, 1942. On October 9, 1942, Mietusch was credited with the destruction of two four-engine bombers during the first really effective Luftwaffe interception of a formation of U.S. heavy bombers. In early 1943, 7./JG 26 was posted to the Eastern Front, where Mietusch was injured on March 20, 1943. Back in action, he claimed four Soviet aircraft shot down on May 21 (his victories Nos 31 through 33), and five (Nos 38 through 42) on June 18, 1943. Shortly afterward he was sent back West to assume command of III./JG 26. On July 17, 1944, after he had downed a Spitfire for his seventy-first kill, Mietusch was shot down and injured by a 411 RCAF Spitfire. On September 17, 1944, Mietusch finally ran out of luck. During a dogfight over the Dutch-German border, he was out-turned and shot down by Lt. William R. Beyer, a Mustang pilot in the 361st U.S. Fighter Group's 376th Squadron. Mietusch had no chance to bail out, and followed the crippled Bf 109 down to a certain death. He had scored his 75th victory – against another 361st Fighter Group Mustang – on his 452d and last combat sortie only minutes earlier. Lieutenant Beyer would return to the States with a tally of nine confirmed kills on 87 combat missions.

96. Bf 109 G-6/ASy
Flown by *Hauptmann* Ludwig-Wilhelm Burkhardt, 7./JG 1, Paderborn/Germany, April 1944.

Ludwig-Wilhelm Burkhardt came from the antiaircraft artillery to flight training. In 1941 he was posted to ErgGr/JG 77 in Romania, and in April 1942 joined II./JG 77 in the Crimea on the Eastern Front. His first victory was achieved against an I-153 biplane of Soviet 214 ShAP on May 3, 1942. In early July 1942, II./JG 77 was posted to the Voronezh area, where this Gruppe soon stood as the only German *Jagdgruppe* against two Soviet air armies. But the inexperienced and poorly trained pilots and commanders of General-Major Yevgeniy Beletskiy's Soviet 1st Fighter Aviation Army (1 IA) proved to be easy victims to the experts of II./JG 77. Between July 5 and July 11, 1942, 1 IA registered ninety-three aircraft missing in combat, plus twenty-three that force-landed in Soviet-controlled territory. II./JG 77's main task however was to combat the large numbers of Il-2 ground-attack planes that dealt bloody losses to the German ground troops, and for this they developed a special tactic – they aimed at shooting the tailfins of the heavily armored Il-2s to pieces. While II./JG 77 aces such as *Oberleutnants* Heinrich Setz and Erwin Clausen, and *Feldwebel* Ernst-Wilhelm Reinert bagged four, five or even more Soviet aircraft at a time, Burkhardt increased his tally to twenty on July 19 and thirty on July 26, 1942. When II./JG 77 brought home thirty-five victories for six own Bf 109s shot down on August 12, Burkhardt achieved his fortieth through forty-second victories. On September 22, 1942, he was awarded with the Knight's Cross for 53 victories. In the fall of 1942, II./JG 77 was posted to North Africa, where Burkhardt was injured by a grenade explosion on the ground. He returned to JG 77 to assume command of I./JG 77 in August 1943. Following a controversy with a superior officer, he was relieved from his command and posted to 1./*Jagdgruppe Süd* – later to JG 1, where he assumed command of 7. *Staffel*. In July 1944 a severe bout with malaria left Burkhardt unfit for frontline service. He ended the war training on Me 262s with III./EJG 2. Burkhardt was credited with a total of 68 confirmed victories.

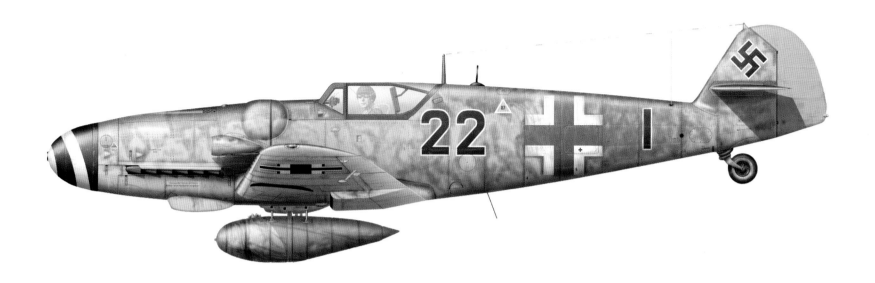

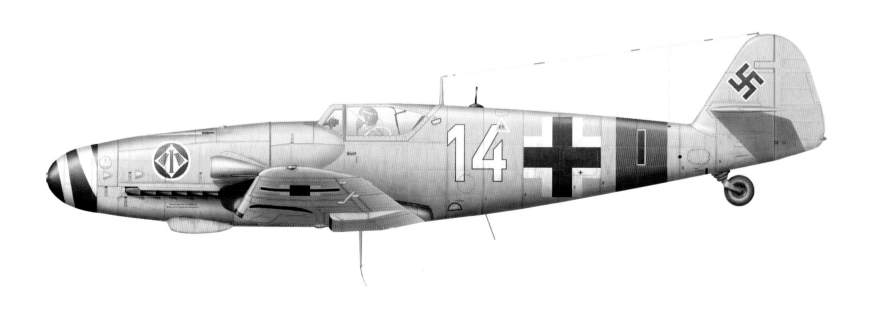

97. Fw 190 A-7
Flown by *Major* Heinz Bär, *Stab* II./JG 1, Störmende/Germany, April 22, 1944.

When I./JG 77 arrived to Sicily in early July 1942 to participate in the air offensive against Malta, this *Jagdgruppe* was commanded by the most successful fighter pilot by that time – *Hauptmann* Heinz Bär, credited with 113 victories. Four British aircraft fell before Bär's guns over Malta before the unit was shifted to North Africa in October 1942. On November 3, 1942, the day when the Battle of El Alamein was decided, Bär knocked down five Kittyhawk fighters, increasing his tally to 123. During the combats over Tunisia between January and April 1943, Bär increased his tally from 139 to 177. But the combat strain inevitably wore down Bär's physical and mental strength, and in the summer of 1943 he was released from his command under humiliating forms. Later he was posted to JG 1 as a *Staffelkapitän*, in order to "rehabilitate" himself. Heinz Bär was not the only ace to be sent away by *Oberstleutnant* Johannes Steinhoff, the *Geschwaderkommodore* of JG 77; he shared this fate with Hans-Joachim Marseille, Ernst-Wilhelm Reinert, Ludwig-Wilhelm Burkhardt, and others. In JG 1, Bär once again proved that there were few who could compete with him regarding skills as a fighter pilot. At 2008 hours on April 22, 1944, Heinz Bär destroyed a B-17 for his two hundredth victory. In late 1944 he was trained to fly the Me 262 jet fighter, and in 1945 he succeeded *Generalleutnant* Adolf Galland as the last commander of JV 44. Heinz Bär, who carried out about 1,000 combat sorties and was credited with 220 victories, including 96 against Soviet aircraft, died in a light plane crash on April 28, 1957.

98. Bf 109 G-6
Flown by *Oberfeldwebel* Dieter Rusche, 2./JG 302, Helsinki-Malmi/Finland, May 1944.

In early 1944, Josef Stalin personally instructed the Soviet strategic bomber fleet, the ADD, to initiate a concentrated night bomber offensive against the Finnish capital of Helsinki. The intention was to exert pressure on Finland's government to break its ties with Germany. When two hundred ADD aircraft opened the bombings on the night of February 6/7, Hitler grew greatly concerned. The Luftwaffe was instructed to immediately dispatch the radar ship To*go* plus fifteen single-engine Bf 109 night fighters of I./JG 302, which was based at Helsinki-Malmi Airdrome. When 420 Soviet bombers were sent out against Helsinki on the night of February 16/17, the Bf 109 fighters intercepted and claimed two shot down. During the third raid, in which more than six hundred Il-4s, B-25s, Li-2s and TB-3s participated, I./JG 302 brought down four Soviet aircraft. In recognition for these feats, six I./JG 302 pilots – including *Oberfeldwebel* Dieter Rusche – were awarded with the Finnish Aviator's Award. Through a combination of the night fighters' psychological impact and a highly effective Finnish anti-aircraft system, the raids against Helsinki failed to cause any considerable damage. Instead, the ADD was able to carry out a successful attack against the Estonian capital of Tallinn on the night of March 9/10, wrecking more than half the city's houses and killing more than one thousand people. However, during the ADD's effort against Tallinn on the night of March 22/23, the German defense was alert. Together with AAA artillery, twin-engine fighters of 4./NJG 100 and 1./NJG 200, and possibly also the Bf 109s of I./JG 302, filed a total of twenty-three victory claims during this operation. In the spring of 1944, I./JG 302 was transferred to Hungary, where *Oberfeldwebel* Dieter Rusche's first aerial victory was granted to him on June 9, 1944 when he managed to damage a Liberator so severely that it was forced to leave its combat formation. Three minutes later, in his next attack, he destroyed another Liberator near Regensburg. During the month of July, he knocked down another three Liberators over Hungary and Austria.

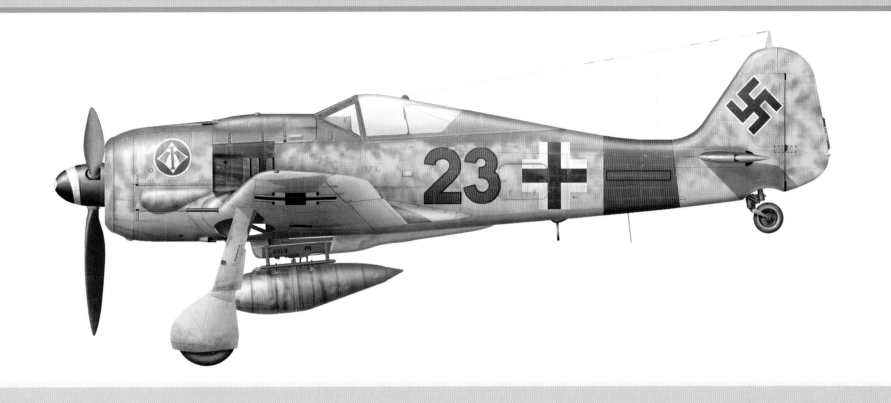

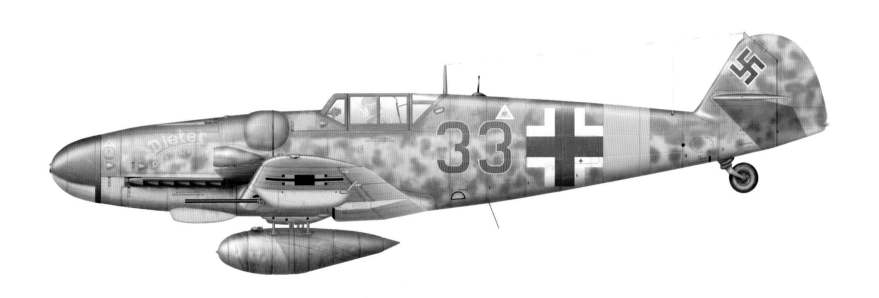

99. Fw 190 A-8
Flown by *Major* Kurt Bühligen, *Stab*/JG 2, France, June 9, 1944.

Following the death of *Major* Kurt Ubben on April 27, 1944, *Major* Kurt Bühlingen assumed command of JG 2 *Richthofen*, which he would lead until the end of the war. This was the period of the downfall of the Luftwaffe. JG 2 alone lost fifty-two aircraft and twenty-five pilots through April 1944. In the summer of 1944, Bühlingen led his *Geschwader* during the difficult air fighting over the Normandy landing beaches, which cost his JG 2 a loss of seventy-nine fighters in June 1944 alone. On June 7, 1944, two Thunderbolts were chalked up as Bühlingen's 100th and 101st victories. He thus became one of the first fighter pilots to reach the 100-victory-mark in the western combat theatre. On August 14, 1944, when Bühlingen's victory tally stood at 104, he was awarded with the Swords to the Knight's Cross with Oak Leaves. Bühlingen survived the war with a total of 112 victories, all against the RAF and the USAAF, on 700 combat sorties. He was shot down three times. In May 1945, Bühlingen ended up in Soviet captivity and would not be released until five years later. Kurt Bühlingen passed away in 1985, at the age of sixty-seven.

100. Fw 190 A-7
Flown by *Oberleutnant* Otto Kittel, 3./JG 54, Riga-Skulte/Latvia, June 23, 1944.

Otto Kittel was a quiet and calm young pilot, and still developed into one of the top scoring fighter aces of World War II. In the fall of 1941 the short-in-growth 24-year-old *Unteroffizier* Otto Kittel had just received his "wings" and was posted to 2./JG 54 on the northern sector of the Eastern Front. Intercepting large formations of Il-2s in the Leningrad sector on February 19, 1943, JG 54 *Grünherz* claimed thirty Soviet aircraft shot down. With one of the last kills on that day, *Feldwebel* Kittel scored his thirty-ninth and the 4,000th victory of the *Geschwader*. The recognition that Kittel – or "Bruno," as he was called – received from this opened the gates to his outstanding row of success in the next two years. Eight months later he reached his 100-victory-mark. On October 29, 1943, *Oberfeldwebel* Kittel was awarded with the Knight's Cross. Following his 150th victory on April 8, 1944, he was promoted to *Leutnant* and put in charge of the new 2./JG 54 on the Eastern Front. At 1206 hours on February 16, 1945 four Fw 190 A-8s led by *Oberleutnant* Otto Kittel of 2./JG 54 took off from an airbase in the Kurland pocket. The mission was free hunting over the frontline area near Dzukste. After only seven minutes the German fighters spotted fourteen Il-2s that were bombing and shooting rockets at German ground troops from an altitude of 450 feet. *Oberleutnant* Kittel radioed an attack order. The Il-2 Shturmoviks were flying in a row, one after another, and Kittel attacked from the right hand side. His wingman *Oberfähnrich* Renner wrote: "Flying at a distance of about 300 feet from *Oblt*. Kittel I saw him dive beneath and behind an Il-2 and attack it. Behind us two other Il-2s pulled up sharply. In the next moment an explosion was seen in his cockpit and the aircraft started to descend." Kittel's Fw 190 tore into the ground with its starboard wing, caught fire, and then exploded. Otto Kittel, victor in 267 aerial combats and the highest scoring fighter pilot to fall prey to the enemy, had no chance whatsoever of surviving.

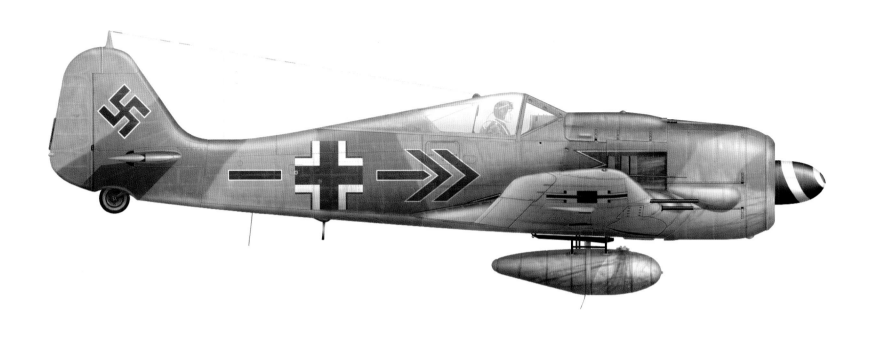

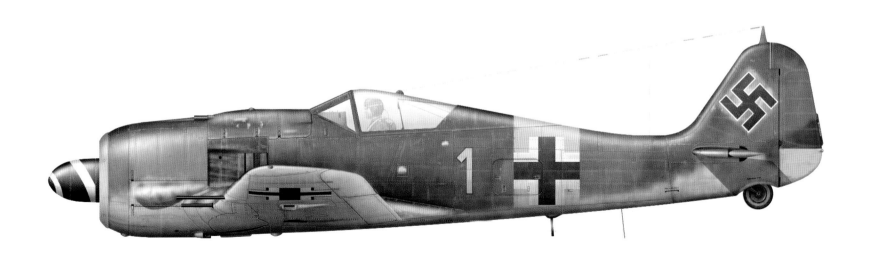

101. Fw 190 A-8

Flown by *Leutnant* Hans Dortenmann, 2./JG 54, Villacoublay/France, June 26, 1944.

Born on December 11, 1921, Hans Dortenmann was drafted into the *Wehrmacht* as an infantry soldier in 1941. Shortly afterward, he applied for pilot training, and was trained as a fighter pilot. With the rank of a *Leutnant*, he arrived to I./JG 54 on the central combat zone of the Eastern Front in the fall of 1943. Following severe battles with a reinforced Soviet air force throughout 1943, I./JG 54 was hurriedly shifted to Estonia in early 1944 to meet the new Soviet offensive in this sector. During these battles, *Leutnant* Dortenmann shot down sixteen Soviet aircraft. In the spring of 1944, 2./JG 54, to which Dortenmann belonged, was surprisingly transferred to the home defense, and it was in this area that Dortenmann would score the bulk of his success. In June 1944, 2./JG 54 was among the first Luftwaffe units to counter the Allied invasion at Normandy. The air fighting against an overwhelmingly numerical superiority in the air over Normandy resulted in very heavy Luftwaffe losses. During June and July 1944, 2./JG 54 alone sustained fourteen pilot casualties, including fifty-eight-victory ace *Leutnant* Horst Forbig. As one of the few survivors of 2./JG 54, Dortenmann was later posted to III./JG 54, where he learned to fly the new Fw 190 D. He ended the war as *Staffelkapitän* of 3./JG 26, with 38 victories to his credit – achieved on only 150 combat sorties.

102. Fw 190 A-8/R2

Flown by *Leutnant* Hans Weik, 10. (*Sturm*)/JG 3, Memmingen/Germany, July 7, 1944.

The *Sturmgruppe* IV./JG 3 was one of the nineteen Jagdgruppen that were rushed to France to counter the Allied invasion at Normandy in June 1944. Eight of these *Jagdgruppen*, including IV./JG 3, were assigned to carry out hazardous fighter-bombing missions against the landing beaches. After only a week, the costly fighter-bomber missions were abandoned and IV./JG 3 returned to the home defense. The first major operation after the *Sturmgruppe*'s return to Memmingen Airdrome in Germany was directed against the formations of 8 USAAF heavies that flew against oil industry targets on July 7, 1944. At 0940 hours, IV./JG 3 caught the Liberators of 492nd Bomb Group without fighter escort, and shot down twelve in a single strike. Shortly afterward, the battered 492d was disbanded, after no more than three months of operations. *Leutnant* Hans Weik contributed to the deathblow against this Bomber Group by knocking down a Liberator as his 35th kill on July 7, 1944. Weik had achieved his first eleven victories with *Stab*/JG 3 on the Eastern Front in March and April 1943. In early 1944, he was posted to the new IV.(*Sturm*)/JG 3 in the home defense, and immediately became one of that unit's most successful "Four-engine killers." Eleven days after the famous battle against 492nd Bomb Group, Weik was shot down and seriously injured in combat against U.S. B-17s near Kempten/Germany. Recovering from his wounds, he received transitional training for Me 262 at Lechfeld, but never saw first-line action again. He was credited with a total of 36 victories, achieved on approximately 100 combat sorties, and was awarded with the Knight's Cross. Hans Weik passed away on June 5, 2001.

103. Fw 190 A-8/R2

Flown by *Hauptmann* Wilhelm Moritz, *Stab* IV.*Sturm*/JG 3, Memmingen/Germany, July 18, 1944.

Wilhelm Moritz was a *Zerstörer* pilot with II./ZG 1 as the war broke out, and served as *Staffelkapitän* of 6./JG 77 with the rank of an *Oberleutnant* between November 1940 and January 1941, in both Norway and on the English Channel. After leading the operational Staffel of *Jagdfliegerschule* 4 more than a year, he led the formation of the new 11./JG 1 in March 1942. On September 10, 1942, he was posted to the Eastern Front, where he assumed command of 12./JG 51. The veterans of *Geschwader Mölders* received the new *Staffelkapitän* who had not scored any victories with skepticism. Moritz earned respect for the great care that he took for his subordinates, but his thirteen months on the Eastern Front did not result in any remarkable individual success in air combat. On most missions, 12./JG 51 was commanded in the air by a more skillful veteran, *Leutnant* Rudolf Wagner, who scored eighty-one victories before he was killed in action in December 1943. Moritz's rise to fame began in the home defense. In April 1944, he was appointed commander of IV.(*Sturm*)/ JG 3, and returned from almost every engagement with U.S. heavy bombers with new victories. During the battle against U.S. 492nd Bomb Group on July 7, 1944, Moritz achieved his fortieth victory. On July 18, 1944, he was awarded with the Knight's Cross. Under Moritz's command, IV./ JG 3 developed into the most successful *Jagdgruppe* of the home defense. On December 5, 1944, Moritz was removed from first-line service due to a complete mental and physical exhaustion. In April 1945, he returned to combat service as *Gruppenkommandeur* of II./JG 4. Wilhelm Moritz carried out more than 500 combat missions and was credited with 44 aerial victories.

104. Fw 190 A-6

Flown by *Hauptmann* Horst Ademeit, *Stab* I./JG 54, Daugavpils/Latvia, July 1944.

Horst Ademeit was born on February 8, 1912 in Breslau. After completing his fighter pilot training he was posted – with the rank of an *Unteroffizier* – to 1./JG 54 at the English Channel in the summer of 1940. Ademeit soon demonstrated to be both courageous and dutiful. During an escort mission for II./LG 2 fighter-bombers against London's Tilbury Docks on September 18, 1940, Ademeit was shot down by a Hurricane into the English Channel. He nevertheless survived and was rescued by the *Seenotkommando*. Since Ademeit mainly served in the role of a wingman, he did not achieve more than one victory during the Battle of Britain. His second kill was obtained on the Eastern Front in 1941, where he first served with II./JG 54. Until May 1942, his victory tally had reached twenty-one. His rise to fame came in 1943, when he was promoted to the rank of a *Leutnant*. On April 16, 1943, when he had reached a score of fifty-three victories, he became JG 54's thirtieth Knight's Cross holder. In early 1944, he succeeded *Hauptmann* Walter Nowotny as I./JG 54's *Gruppenkommandeur*, and he led this unit during the difficult retreat to the Courland pocket later that year. He was awarded the Oak Leaves for approximately 120 victories on March 2, 1944. On August 8, 1944 Ademeit took off at 1445 hours to lead four Fw 190s on a free hunting sortie in the Kreuzberg area/Courland. At 1517, they intercepted ten Il-2s and Yak-9s. Three minutes later, Ademeit attacked an Il-2 from astern without being able to score any result. He was next seen to pursue another Il-2. The last thing his wingman, *Gefreiter* Biebrichter, saw was the Il-2 and Ademeit's Fw 190 disappearing into a thick smoke cloud from fire on the ground. A few minutes later, Ademeit's Fw 190 crashed, hit by machine-gun bullets from the ground, killing the pilot on impact. Horst Ademeit was credited with a total of 166 aerial victories, all but one on the Eastern Front.

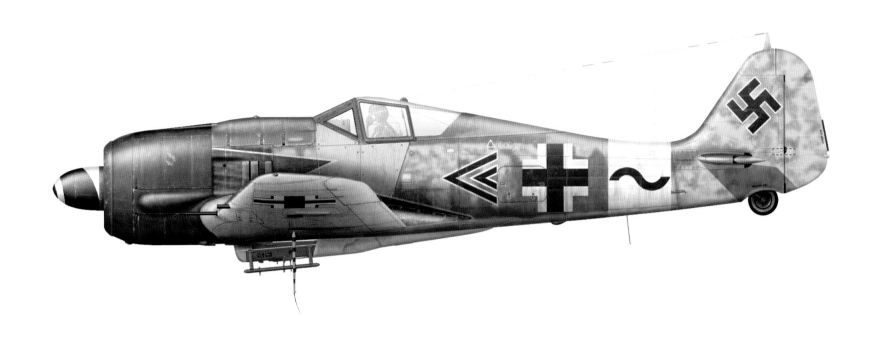

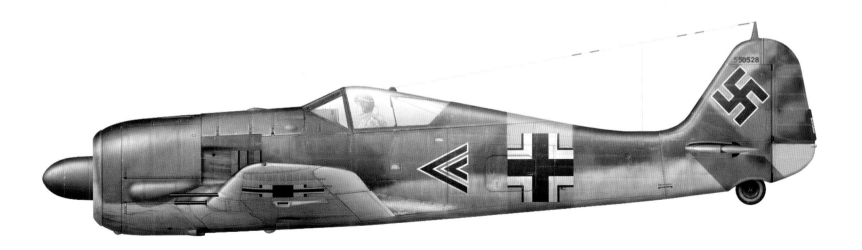

105. Me 262 A-1a

Flown by *Oberfeldwebel* Helmut Lennartz, *Erprobungskommando* 262, Lechfeld/Germany, August 15, 1944.

Helmut Lennartz flew with 5./JG 11 in the Home Defense as an *Unteroffizier* at least from the spring of 1943. On May 14, 1943, he followed the example of his *Staffelkapitän*, *Leutnant* Heinz Knoke, and destroyed a B-17 by dropping a bomb against a formation of heavy bombers over the German Bight. During take-off from Marx Airdrome in Germany on October 18, 1943, Lennartz crashed into another parked Bf 109 and was only lucky to survive. Three months later, Lennartz was posted to *Hauptmann* Werner Thierfelder's *Erprobungskommando* 262, the first Me 262-equipped Luftwaffe unit, although non-operational. The jet aircraft training however was severely hampered through an acute lack of aircraft. On July 18, 1944, Thierfelder was killed in a flight acci-dent. On August 15, 1944, Lennartz became the first Me 262 pilot to shoot down a U.S. heavy bomber – a 303rd Bomb Group B-17, which was added to the six aircraft this unit had lost to IV./JG 3 one hour earlier. Shortly afterward, *Ekdo.* 262 was officially made operational, and at least eight more kills were achieved during the next four weeks. Later in September 1944, the famous *Major* Walter Nowotny arrived to assume command of the unit, which from then became known as *Kommando Nowotny*. Lennartz's next victory was achieved against a 44 BG Liberator on October 7, 1944. Five days later, he blew an U.S. 364th Fighter Group Mustang out of the sky. Following Major Nowotny's death on November 8, 1944, *Kommando Nowotny* was redesignated into III./JG 7. On March 3, 1945, Lennartz shot down an U.S. 3rd Air Division B-17 near Brunswick. Sixteen days later, he bagged one of the three 45 BW B-17s that went lost to III./JG 7. On April 10, 1945, *Oberfeldwebel* Lennartz contributed with a Mustang to the sixteen U.S. aircraft claimed shot down by JG 7. But this was a Pyrrhic victory, with JG 7 losing twenty-seven Me 262s and nineteen pilots. Helmut Lennartz ended the war with a total of 14 confirmed victories.

106. Bf 109 G-14/AS

Flown by *Oberleutnant* Ernst Scheufele, 14./JG 4, Reinersdorf/Germany, October 1944.

Ernst Scheufele joined I./JG 5 in April 1942. After flying fighter cover over the Norwegian western coast for eighteen months, without seeing much combat, he was transferred to II./JG 5 on the "Murmansk front" as a Leutnant in October 1943. *Oberleutnant* Theodor Weissenberger, the formi-dable ace heading 6./JG 5, adopted the experienced *Leutnant* as wingman. By that time, Weissenberger had amassed 114 victories. Shortly afterward, II./JG 5 left the Far North and was transferred to the Leningrad sector, where the Soviets had opened a powerful offensive. Scheufele told the authors that with Weissenberger in the air, the German fighter pilots still in the beginning of 1944 felt superior toward the Soviets. Escorting a formation of Ju 87s against Dno on February 1, 1944, the pilots of II./JG 5 got entangled in a combat with thirty La-5s. While Weissenberger bagged five La-5s within eight minutes, Scheufele was able to shoot down one for his fourth personal victory. In October 1944, the *Gruppe* was renamed IV./JG 4 in the Home Defense. During a close-support mission against U.S. troops in the Aachen area on December 3, 1944, JG 4 lost sixteen pilots. One of them was the *Staffelkapitän* of 14./JG 4, *Oberleutnant* Ernst Scheufele, who nevertheless was lucky to survive and was captured. Scheufele was credited with a total of 18 confirmed victories.

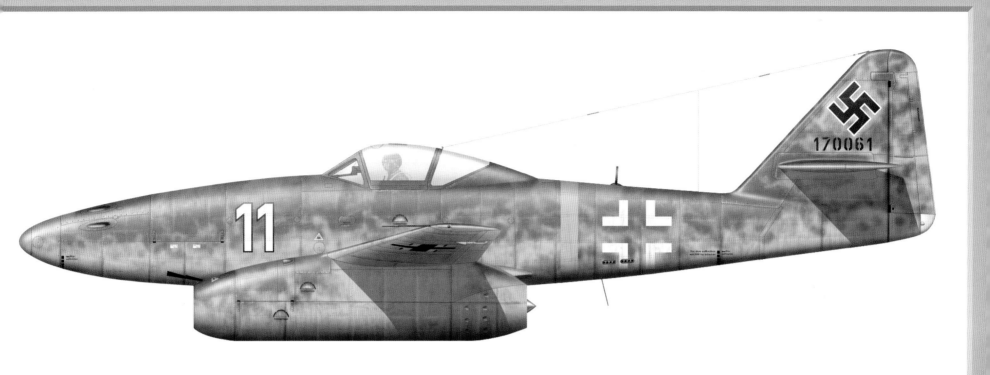

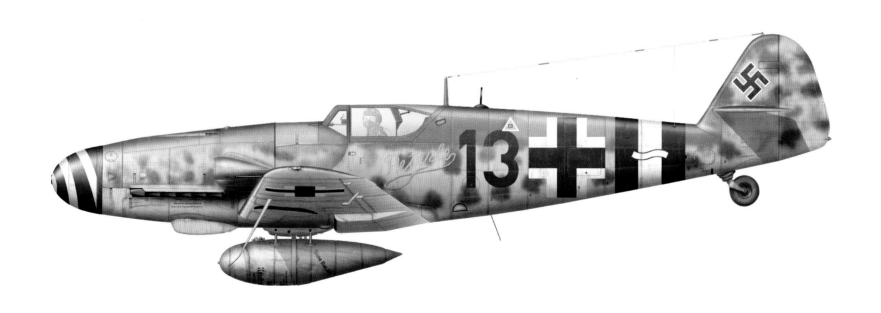

107. Me 262 A-1a

Flown by *Leutnant* Franz Schall, *Kommando Nowotny*, Achmer/Germany, October 28, 1944.

Franz Schall, born on June 1, 1918 in Austria, served as an AAA gunner until 1940. Trained as a fighter pilot, he was posted to I./JG 52 on the Eastern Front in February 1943. He had a slow start, achieving his seventh victory on July 15, 1943. On November 11, 1943, he was shot down and injured by AAA near Kerch. His rise to fame began only in 1944. On August 31, 1944, he achieved his 106th victory by claiming thirteen Soviet aircraft shot down. When he was posted to Me 262-equipped *Kommando Nowotny* in October 1944, his score stood at 117. On October 7, 1944, *Leutnants* Franz Schall and Helmut Lennartz scored the first victories of Me 262-equipped *Kommando Nowotny* when they shot down two U.S. 44 BG Liberators. On November 6, 1944, Schall achieved his next victory against a Thunderbolt. Two days later – during the mission when the unit commander *Major* Walter Nowotny was killed – Schall destroyed three Mustangs, the last piloted by 357 FG's Warren Corwin, but then both engines of his Me 262 seized. The helpless German pilot was attacked from above by U.S. 357 FG's Lieutenant James W. Kenney, and Schall was lucky to survive and bail out. In 1945, he was posted to JG 7, and when he was killed during a landing accident on April 10, 1945, he had shot down sixteen Allied aircraft while flying an Me 262.

108. Bf 109 G-14

Flown by *Leutnant* Horst Schlick, 4./JG 77, Schönwalde/Germany, November 1944.

Horst Schlick arrived as a 20-years-old *Unterofffizier* to I.(J)/LG 2 (later I./JG 77) on the Eastern Front early in 1942. Flying as the wingman of the ace *Oberleutnant* Erwin Clausen, Schlick scored his first victory against an I-16 on February 22, 1942. But his stay on the Eastern Front would be short-lived. One month later he was shot down in River Donets and barely made it over to the German lines. The majority of Schlick's successes were scored over the Mediterranean area, where I./JG 77 was deployed from May 1942. After achieving five kills over Malta, Schlick was rushed to the Battle of El Alamein, where he downed a Hurricane of No. 274 Squadron as his eighth victory on November 2, 1942. Four months later, Schlick achieved his 20th against a Spitfire over Tunisia. Schlick remained in service in the Mediterranean for more than a year. His 30th victory was scored against a 15th USAAF Mustang over northern Italy on April 16, 1944. On September 12, 1944, Schlick was one of seventy-four German fighter pilots to be shot down by fighters and heavy bombers of the U.S. 8th Air Force. But Schlick survived and ended the war flying an Me 262 with JG 7. Horst Schlick carried out a total of 480 combat missions and achieved at least 32 victories.

109. Bf 109 K-4

Flown by *Leutnant* Heinrich Hackler, 11./JG 77, Neuruppin/Germany, November 1944.

For JG 77 Herzas, Operation *Bodenplatte* – the Luftwaffe's massive strafing operation against Allied airbases in France and Belgium early on New Year's Day 1945 – resulted in a tragedy. The task was to attack Deurne Airdrome near Antwerp. The *Jagdgeschwader* took off with about sixty Bf 109s, who were guided by a Ju 88 to the target. The problem started when the formation reached Rotterdam, where the German antiaircraft batteries opened an intense fire against the fighter-bombers. The formation continued, and went down to the deck as it crossed the frontline, where it again became subject to ground fire. Because of the mist and the low flight altitude, the JG 77 pilots were unable to locate their target immediately. A total chaos broke out when some of the pilots started climbing in order to try and find the target, while others remained circling at low altitude. While they continued circling aimlessly northeast of Antwerp, Allied AAA was firing at the Messerschmitts. Scattered groups of Bf 109s managed to locate Deurne Airdrome and carried out strafing attacks that damaged fourteen and destroyed one RAF 266 Squadron Typhoon – the oldest and most worn out Typhoon in the unit's inventory. Other JG 77 pilots found and raided Woensdrecht Airdrome, which was practically deserted. Finally, the unit turned homeward, split into Bf 109s flying individually or in small groups – still subjected to anti-aircraft fire over hostile territory. The January 1, 1945 operation cost JG 77 a total of eleven Bf 109s and eleven pilots. Among the casualties was 11. *Staffel*'s *Kapitän*, *Leutnant* Heinrich Hackler. Hackler was a veteran who had served with JG 77 since 1941. Although Hackler never achieved any particularly conspicuous victory rows, the experience that he amassed turned him into one of the backbones of III./JG 77. Hackler had achieved his first aerial victory on the Eastern Front on June 26, 1941, and in May 1942 he scored his thirtieth. When he was awarded with the Knight's Cross on August 19, 1944, his score stood at sixty-seven. Heinrich Hackler's final score is unknown, at least sixty-seven confirmed victories.

110. Fw 190 A-8

Flown by *Major* Walther Dahl, *Stab*/JG 300, Jütebog/Germany, December 1944.

Walther Dahl, born on March 27, 1916, belonged to various staff positions in JG 3 since 1940. Serving with *Stab* II./JG 3, he scored his first victory against a Soviet MiG-3 on June 22, 1941. During Operation *Barbarossa*, when Dahl regularly flew as the famous *Gruppenkommandeur Hauptmann* Gordon Gollob's wingman, Dahl achieved rather modest successes. His total victory tally stood at seventeen when II./JG 3 left the Eastern Front to be shifted to Sicily in late fall of 1941. His rise to fame came when he served as adjutant of JG 3's commander, Oak Leaves holder *Hauptmann* Wolf-Dietrich Wilcke, at Stalingrad in 1942-1943. During the final stage of the Battle of Stalingrad, Dahl achieved a large number of victories in a quick succession. On October 17, 1942, Soviet 512 IAP's Starshiy Leytenant Ignatiy Biryukov force-landed his Yak-1 and was registered as *Hauptmann* Walther Dahl's thirtieth victory. On October 25, Dahl claimed three victories, next day four, and three again on November 30, 1942. On July 20, 1943, Dahl was appointed *Gruppenkommandeur* of III./JG 3, which he led in the home defense from August 1943. Under Dahl's command, III./JG 3 proved to be one of the most successful home defense fighter units during the fall of 1943. This led to Dahl being awarded with the Knight's Cross on March 11, 1944, and two months later he was assigned to lead the day fighter forces in southern Germany. In this position, Dahl became particularly enthusiastic over the *Sturmjäger* tactic, and for this reason he was on June 26, 1944 appointed *Geschwaderkommodore* JG 300, which united all *Sturmgruppen*. Finally, on January 26, 1945, his old *Gruppenkommandeur Oberst* Gordon Gollob – now Galland's successor as *General der Jagdflieger* – had Dahl promoted to Inspector of the Day Fighters. Walther Dahl survived the war with a total of 128 victories. He passed away on November 25, 1985.

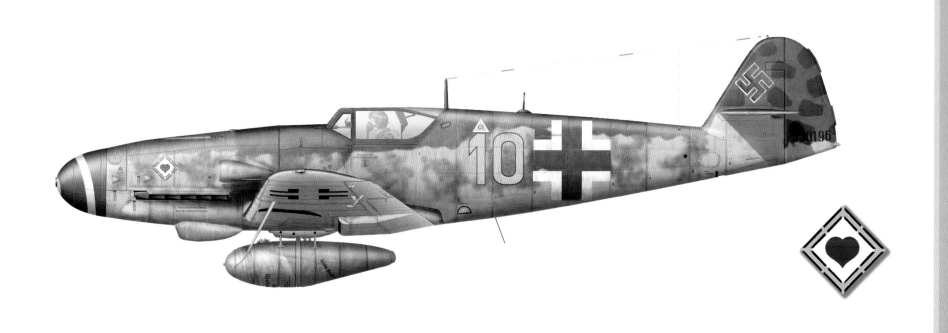

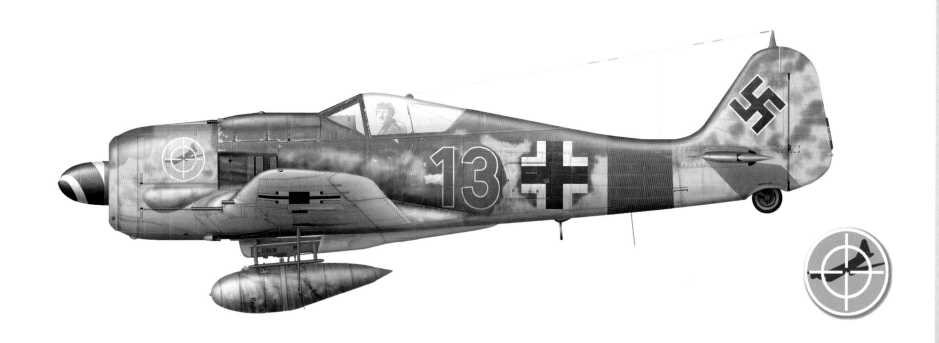

111. Bf 109 K-4

Flown *Feldwebel* Hans Rössner, 12./JG 77, Düsseldorf/Germany, December 23 1944.

The Germans were aided by adverse weather conditions that hampered Allied flight activity when they launched their Ardennes offensive on the Western Front on December 16, 1944. But on December 23, 1944, the skies cleared, and the Allied air forces dispatched approximately five thousand sorties against German troops and lines of communication. The Germans countered with an all-out effort – 800 sorties were carried out. Large-scale air battles developed. I. and II./JG 11 caught the B-26 Marauders of 9th USAAF 391 BG without escort, and blew sixteen out of the sky. In total, 9th USAAF reported thirty-five medium bombers missing, with another 188 returning with various degrees of battle damage. But in general, the Allied fighters had the upper hand. JG 11 paid a terrible price, thirty-five aircraft and seventeen pilots were lost. JG 77 also suffered heavily, registering twenty-three aircraft shot down. Among the pilots that were killed was 12./JG 77's *Feldwebel* Hans Rössner. Rössner had been posted to JG 77 in early 1944 and had been credited with twelve victories. A total of 135 German fighters were shot down on December 23, 1944. The bulk of them were shot down by U.S. fighters, who claimed a staggering 134 victories.

112. Fw 190 D-9

Flown by *Feldwebel* Werner Hohenberg, 4./JG 2, Marzhausen/Germany, January 1, 1945.

Werner Hohenberg was posted to 8./JG 52 on the Eastern Front in July 1942, after completing his fighter pilot training at *Jagdergänzungsgruppe Ost*. Later he was shifted to 7./JG 52, where he flew as Erich Hartmann's wingman. Hohenberg's most successful day in terms of aerial victories was July 5, 1943, during the Battle of the Kursk Bulge, when he achieved four victories. But the Luftwaffe's own losses also were considerable. Four days after the opening of the German offensive on July 5, 1943, only three pilots remained in 7./JG 52. On July 9, 1943, Hohenberg was shot down and severely injured. While he was treated for his wounds, he was awarded with the German Cross in Gold for his previous feats. After recovering from his wounds, Hohenberg was posted to *Stab* I./JG 2 at Usingen/Germany in November 1944. During the infamous Operation *Bodenplatte* on January 1, 1945, JG 2 was assigned to attack St Trond Airdrome in Belgium, where U.S. Thunderbolt-equipped 48th Fighter Group and 404th Fighter Group were stationed. Five JG 2 fighters were shot down by Allied ground fire as they passed the frontline. The antiaircraft artillery at St Trond destroyed another five. Among the latter was the Fw 190 D-9 piloted by *Hauptmann* Georg Schröder, the *Gruppenkommandeur* of II./JG 2. Then the return flight developed into a virtual gauntlet. With twenty-three pilots and forty-two aircraft lost, JG 2 was the hardest hit *Geschwader* on January 1, 1945. Counted among the casualties was *Feldwebel* Werner Hohenberg, who was lucky to survive being shot down, and spent the remainder of the war in an Allied POW camp. Hohenberg carried out a total of two hundred combat sorties during World War II, and achieved thirty-three victories during seventy aerial combats. He was released from British captivity on October 1, 1946.

113. Bf 109 G-6

Flown by *Hauptmann* Erich Hartmann, *Stab* I./JG 53, Veszperem/Hungary, February 4, 1945.

In 1945 the air war on the Eastern Front had definitely turned to the disadvantage of the Luftwaffe. Almost every combat sortie resulted in difficult air combats with "Stalin's Falcons" and bitter losses. Out of 753 Luftwaffe aircraft registered lost in combat during the month of February 1945, 303 were lost due to the activities of the Western Allies and 400 were destroyed by the Soviets. Only the enormous experience accumulated by a handful of old veterans of the Luftwaffe force on the Eastern Force allowed the Germans to score some successes in the air. In fact, these few Luftwaffe Eastern Front veterans were the most experienced and probably most skillful fighter pilots of the entire war. Erich Hartmann, who commanded I./JG 53 as a *Hauptmann* for a brief period in February 1945, had carried out 1,004 combat missions as the war ended. *Leutnant* Erich Sommavilla of I./JG 53 recalls how skillful fighter aces from the Western Front were handicapped against the aggressive Soviet fighter pilots late in the war. "Things only changed when we received Eastern Front experts such as Hartmann and Lipfert," said Sommavilla – although Hartmann actually carried out only one combat sortie with I./JG 53, on February 4, 1945, and shot down a Yak-9 (his 337th victory). The results of the air combats on the Eastern Front that day are indicative for the character of the air war against the VVS by that time – the Germans claimed fourteen victories against just as many losses to their own. Shortly afterward Hartmann was picked to train on an Me 262 jet fighter, but preferred to return to JG 52, where he scored his 352d and last airkill on May 8, 1945.

114. Fw 190 A-8

Flown by *Feldwebel* Rudolf Artner, 9./JG 5, Herdla/Norway, February 9, 1945.

On February 9, 1945, RAF Coastal Command's Strike Wing dispatched thirty-one Beaufighters and two Warwicks, escorted by twelve Mustangs of 65 (RCAF) Squadron – all led by Wing Commander Colin Milson – against a German coastal convoy off Norway. For two years, the Strike Wing had been carrying out almost daily strikes against Norway's western coast. But this day, the Luftwaffe would pay back dearly. February 9, 1945 went into the Strike Wing's history as "the Black Friday." III./JG 5, based at Herdla, scrambled its Fw 190s against the RAF formations, and the Beaufighters and Mustangs got entangled in a most difficult fight. Among the participating German pilots was *Feldwebel* Rudolf Artner, an experienced ace who on this day led the 9. Staffel in the air. Artner later filed the following combat report: "About 50 km north of the Sogne-Fjord, we spotted the enemy formation, which consisted of approximately 30 Beaufighters and 10 Mustang escort fighters. During a combined attack with my *Staffel*, I scored hits on a Beaufighter, which I attacked from behind, and above. The Beaufighter caught fire and descended in a flat angle. The impact was registered at 1610 hours, approximately 10 km north-west of Forde (Grid Square 06 East LM 1.5). The crew failed to bail out." 404 (RCAF) Squadron's Pilot Officers Blunderfield Jackson were both killed as Artner filed his eighteenth aerial victory. Shortly afterward, a second Beaufighter ended up as Artner's nineteenth. In total, 9./JG 5 claimed nine RAF aircraft shot down in this combat. Actual RAF losses were nine Beaufighters – six of them from 404 (RCAF) Squadron alone – and a Mustang. This was particularly hard, since the attackers failed to inflict any considerable damage to the ships. On the German side, four Fw 190s were shot down. With one of them, *Leutnant* Rudi Linz was killed – shortly after achieving his seventieth and last victory against a Beaufighter. Linz was awarded with the Knight's Cross posthumously. Rudolf Artner survived the war with a total of twenty confirmed victories.

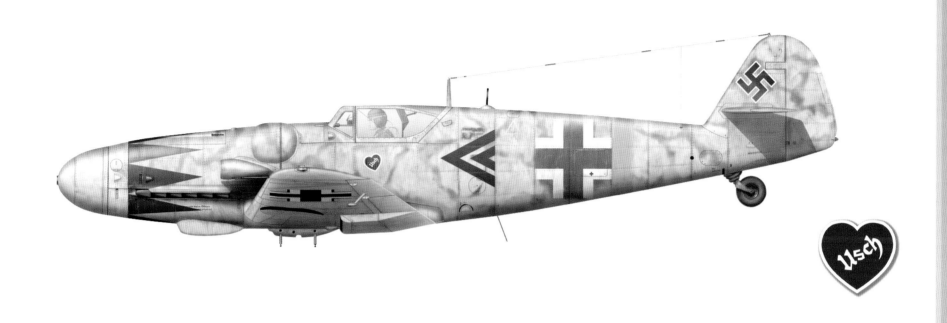

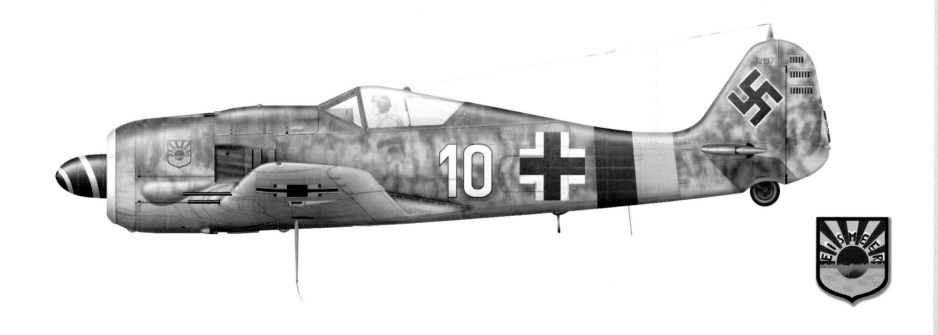

115. Me 262 A-1a

Flown by *Oberfeldwebel* Hermann Buchner, 10./JG 7, Rotenburg/Germany, April 8, 1945.

Hermann Buchner earned his fame as a *Schlachtflieger*, and he carried out 611 ground-attacks with SchG 1 between 1942 and 1944. In early November 1944, he arrived at Lechfeld to commence training on the Me 262 jet fighter with *Erprobungskommando* 262. Three weeks later Buchner had his first encounter with Mustang fighters with an Me 262, although this resulted in no loss to either side. On November 26, Buchner scored his first "jet victory" against a U.S. 7 PG F-5 (Lightning) reconnaissance aircraft, piloted by Lieutenant Irvin J. Rickey, who survived. The impact of the Me 262 cannon shells was so great that Rickey believed that he had sustained a direct AAA hit. In December 1944, Buchner was posted to *Hauptmann* Georg-Peter Eder's 9./JG 7. Due to a controverse with Eder's successor, *Oberleutnant* Günther Wegmann, Buchner was shifted to 10./JG 7 at Berlin-Oranienburg in mid-March 1945. This *Staffel* was headed by 130-victory ace *Leutnant* Franz Schall. Buchner next claimed a B-24 on March 25 and an RAF Lancaster on March 31, 1945. But the Allied overwhelming numerical superiority was too much even for the Me 262s. On April 8, Buchner's plane was shot ablaze by a strafing Mustang while landing. Next day, more than a hundred Luftwaffe aircraft, including a large number of Me 262s were destroyed in airbase raids. On April 10, twenty-seven out of fifty-five Me 262s that had been dispatched against U.S. heavy bombers were shot down. Buchner would fly no more with the Me 262. He was credited with 58 confirmed victories. Hermann Buchner is still alive.

116. Ta 152 H-0

Flown by *Feldwebel* Willi Reschke, *Stab*./JG 301, Stendal/Germany, April 14, 1945.

Willi Reschke belongs to the "generation" of the last Luftwaffe fighter aces. He was posted to his first combat unit, 1./JG 302, near Vienna in June 1944. Reschke drew his first blood during the great air battle over Hungary on July 2, 1944, when U.S. 15th Air Force dispatched 712 heavy bombers and 300 escort fighters against Budapest. During a prolonged fight, German and Hungarian Bf 109s, Bf 110s, and Me 410s claimed fifty-seven American aircraft shot down – including eight by I./ZG 76 Me 410s, twelve by the Hungarian fighter group Puma, and sixteen by I./JG 302. By destroying two Liberators, *Unteroffizier* Willi Reschke achieved his first victories. Among the U.S. losses was 4 FG's 2dLt Ralph K. Hofer, a fifteen-victory ace. Reschke soon became known as a most daring pilot, and developed into one of 1./JG 302's most successful airmen. His next kill, on July 7, 1944, in fact was achieved by conducting an air-to-air ramming of a Liberator – a feat that the reckless young pilot was able to survive by bailing out. Through August 1944, he had amassed a total of fourteen victories – all but one achieved against U.S. heavy bombers. During the combat on August 29, 1944, when he achieved his fourteenth, Reschke was mistakenly shot down by another Bf 109 of I./JG 302, but once again survived. Reschke, who then was posted to III./JG 301, continued to carry out a most determined fight while the entire Luftwaffe became conspicuously marked by defeat. On November 21, 1944, when the German fighter force lost eighty-three Bf 109s and Fw 190s in a fruitless effort to defend the synthetic oil plant at Leuna against U.S. bombers, Reschke scored the only victory achieved by III./JG 301. In the spring of 1945, Reschke was posted to the crack *Stab*/JG 301, equipped with the Ta 152 – Germany's undoubtedly best piston-engine fighter in World War II. Flying a Ta 152, Reschke shot down the Tempest piloted by 486 RAF Squadron's Warrant Officer O. J. Mitchell on April 14, 1945. On April 20, 1945, Reschke was awarded with the Knight's Cross for his twenty-five victories. Four days later, five Ta 152s became involved in a tussle with a formation of Soviet Yak-9s, ending with Reschke shooting down two Yakovlevs while one Ta 152 was lost. Willi Reschke survived the war with a total of twenty-seven aerial victories on approximately one hundred combat sorties, and he is still alive.

117. Me 262 A-1a

Flown by *Oberst* Johannes Steinhoff, JV 44, München-Reim/Germany, April 18, 1945.

When *Major* Johannes Steinhoff arrived in Tunisia to assume command of JG 77 on April 3, 1942, he had scored a total of 156 victories – all but two with II./JG 52. By that time, the balance of favor in the Mediterranean area had tipped to the Luftwaffe's disadvantage. Only two days later, Steinhoff barely survived getting shot down by a Spitfire. JG 77 filed a total of thirty-three combat losses over Tunisia during the month of April 1943 alone, and Steinhoff noted how the combat spirits among several veterans – including the famous Heinz Bär – dropped below zero. The subsequent air fighting over Italy in 1943 and 1944 further deteriorated the spirits in JG 77. Steinhoff would add another fourteen personal victories during his time with JG 77. In November 1944, he was assigned to lead the formation of the first Me 262 jet fighter *Geschwader* JG 7. Following repeated clashes with *Reichsmarschall* Göring, Steinhoff was accused of not fulfilling his JG 7 task satisfactory, and in December 1944 he was relieved from his posting as *Geschwaderkommodore* of JG 7. Shortly afterward he joined his friend *Generalleutnant* Adolf Galland in the Me 262-equipped JV 44. There he achieved his last six victories until he was seriously burned in a take-off accident on April 18, 1945. After the war, Steinhoff was appointed commander of the *Bundesluftwaffe*, and held this post until he retired on April 4, 1974. Johannes Steinhoff passed away on February 18, 1994, in Bonn/Germany. He was credited with a total of 176 victories and carried out 993 combat missions, during which he was shot down twelve times.

118. Fw 190 D-9

Flown by *Leutnant* Heinz Sachsenberg, JV 44, München-Riem/Germany, late April 1945.

Led by *Generalleutnant* Adolf Galland, the Me 262-equipped JV 44 was formed in February 1945. These jet fighters were superior to anything the Allied could launch into the air, but their weakest spot was to be attacked by hostile fighters when they took off or landed. The pioneer jet fighter unit *Kommando Nowotny* had been provided with airbase cover by the Fw 190 D-9s of III./JG 54, and Galland could use the influence that he still had to get a handful of Fw 190 D-9s and D-11s assigned to JV 44. On April 23, 1945, JV 44 reported a strength of twelve Me 262s and five Fw 190 D-9/11s. The multi-colored paint on these Fw 190 D-9s have been interpreted as an indication of the high combat spirits among its personnel. But the conspicuous red and white stripes in fact were applied only in order to avoid German AAA from opening fire against the "Doras". The most successful among JV 44's Fw 190 D-9 pilots was Knight's Cross holder *Leutnant* Heinz "Heino" Sachsenberg – the son of thirty-one-victory World War I ace and *Pour le Merité* holder Gotthard Sachsenberg. Heinz Sachsenberg had served with 6./JG 52 on the Eastern Front from late 1942, and achieved his first victory on April 21, 1943. On May 7, 1944, he was credited with seven aerial victories. One month and one day later he surpassed the 100-victory-mark. On August 23, 1944, after scoring his 104th and last victory, Sachsenberg was shot down and seriously injured in combat with U.S. Mustangs over Romania. "Sachsenberg was a good pilot," said Galland, "and we felt safer when his aircraft were in the air." However, Sachsenberg had barely recovered from his wounds when he was posted to JV 44. Maybe as an indication of this, his last combat aircraft carried the inscription "Sell my clothes, I'm going to heaven." Sachsenberger survived the war, but never recovered from his wounds, and passed away on June 17, 1951.

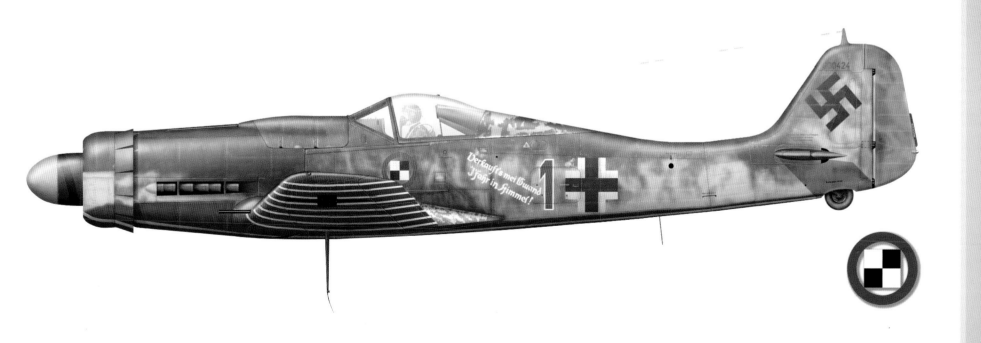

119. Fw 190 D-9

Flown by *Hauptmann* Waldemar Wübke, JV 44, München-Riem/Germany, late April 1945.

Waldemar Wübke belongs to the Luftwaffe veterans who served from almost the first day of the war until the last. He flew with 9./JG 54 as a *Leutnant* from 1940, and was among the first pilots to bring forward the fighter-bomber tactics against England. The inscription – quite ironically meant – that he painted on every single aircraft that he flew from 1940 onward stems from this time. Wübke loathed the fighter-bomber missions, and the writing "By the Order of the Reichsbahn" was to be found on the sides of boxcars that carried bombs. On October 21, 1940, he was awarded with the Iron Cross of the First Class. On July 11, 1941, Wübke achieved III./JG 54's 250th victory by downing a Soviet SB bomber. On September 2, 1942, *Oberleutnant* Wübke was appointed *Staffelführer* of 7./JG 54. On September 9, 1942, he engaged a formation of six to eight LaGG-3s and MiG-3s, managed to destroy one but got himself injured. Despite this, he was back in action two days later. On January 5, 1943, Wübke, by now 7./JG 54's *Staffelkapitän*, achieved his fifteenth victory against an Il-2 Shturmovik. But by this time the Soviet resistance in the air had grown considerably sharper, and on January 18, 1943, all that was left of Wübke's *Staffel* was three Bf 109s and five pilots. Shortly afterward, the entire III./JG 54 was shifted to France, and from the spring of 1943 it was dispatched in the home defense. On July 29, 1943, *Oberleutnant* Wübke was injured again when five Spitfires bounced his *Schwarm*. Wübke barely managed to nurse his crippled Bf 109 back to base, and then he was sent to hospital in Amsterdam. Between June 17, 1944 and April 15, 1945, Wübke served as *Gruppenkommandeur* II./JG 101. After that he was posted to JV 44's Fw 190 D-9-equipped airbase protection *Staffel*. Waldemar Wübke survived the war with a total of sixteen aerial victories, including eleven on the Eastern Front.

120. He 162 A-2

Flown by *Leutnant* Gerhard Hanf, 2./JG 1, Leck/Germany, April 1945.

Gerhard Hanf's career as a fighter pilot is illustrative to the story of the downfall of the Luftwaffe. When *Leutnant* Gerhard Hanf completed his fighter pilot training in the spring of 1943, the downfall of the Luftwaffe was already in sharp decline. In June 1943, he was posted to 9./JG 77 in Sicily, the most critical place for the Luftwaffe by that time. A total of 888 German fighters had been lost in the Mediterranean theater alone between November 1942 and May 1943. Hanf was injured in combat with Lightnings on his third combat sortie on June 24, 1943. Back in action, he barely survived a crash due to engine failure on August 21, 1943. Later, III./JG 77 was allocated to protect the Romanian oil fields against U.S. air attacks, and this led to Hanf's first aerial victory against a Mustang on April 21, 1944. On May 7, 1944 he bagged a Lightning in the same area. But the German fighter losses exceeded the successes, and combat spirits in Luftwaffe units dropped. In the summer of 1944, 9./JG 77 was incorporated with JG 1 in the home defense. On July 7, 1944, a Thunderbolt was scored as Hanf's third victory. His fifth and last airkill was achieved against a Thunderbolt on July 30, 1944. When I./JG 1 was equipped with the He 162 jet fighter in April 1945, Hanf was appointed *Staffelkapitän* of 2./JG 1. During the last weeks of the war, Hanf realized that even the He 162 was a failure, unable to fulfill its expectations. The inscription on the port side of his He 162 – *Nervenklau*, "Nerve Racker" – originates from the reckless motorcycle rides that Hanf carried out on Leck Airdrome in the spring of 1945. Gerhard Hanf was lucky to survive the war – contrary to most of the German fighter pilots who received their wings simultaneously with him.

121. Fw 190 D-9

Flown by *Oberst* Hans-Ulrich Rudel, *Stab.*/SG 2, Grossenhain/Germany, April 1945.

Hans-Ulrich Rudel, a hard-core Nazi who refused to change his political views even after the war, earned fame for his outstanding successes with a Ju 87. On his tally were to be found 519 destroyed Soviet tanks. This stubborn fighter was one of Hitler's favorites, and the *Führer* even invented a military award particularly for Rudel: The Golden Oak Leaves. In fact, of the 2,530 combat sorties carried out by Rudel – a higher number than any other airman during the war – 430 were flown with the Fw 190. Attempting to intercept a formation of Il-2s one day in December 1944, Rudel's Fw 190 suffered an engine failure and the pilot had to force-land. On one occasion in early April 1945, Rudel made a flight show in an Fw 190 D-9 for the local inhabitants near his airfield in the Sudeten area. Shortly after landing, the airfield came under attack from U.S. Mustangs and Thunderbolts, and the famous "assault ace" had no other choice than to rush to the shelter. Rudel, a highly controversial person in pre-war Germany, passed away on December 18, 1982.

122. Fw 190 D-9

Flown by *Oberleutnant* Hans Dortenmann, 3./JG 26, Klein-Kummerfeld/Germany, April 1945.

On April 5, 1945, Fw 190 D-9-equipped IV./JG 26 was assigned to carry out a strafing mission against British troop movements opposed to the German defense line at Weser on the Western Front. During the approach flight, *Oberleutnant* Willi Heilmann, 15./JG 26's *Staffelkapitän*, suddenly disappeared. This incident has been covered in several versions. According to Heilmann's post-war memoirs, his departure was preceded by a ceremony in which he had discharged his *Staffel* to return to their homes. A few years later, Heilmann wrote that he had force-landed his damaged aircraft at the German-held airfield at Bissel. Historian Axel Urbanke, who states that Heilmann remained at Bissel, where he was captured by Canadian troops on April 13, 1945, supports this. In any case, following Heilmann's disappearance, his 15./JG 26 was immediately disbanded, and its pilots were spread among the 13. and 14. *Staffeln*. Hans Dortenmann, 3./JG 26's *Staffelkapitän* who supposedly destroyed Heilmann's aircraft, was one of the most successful "Dora-9 pilots". He in fact flew the same aircraft individual (WNr 210003) from late 1944 until May 5, 1945, when he himself destroyed it on the ground at Flensburg-Weiche just as British troops were approaching the base. He achieved eighteen victories piloting this aircraft, reaching a total of thirty-eight.

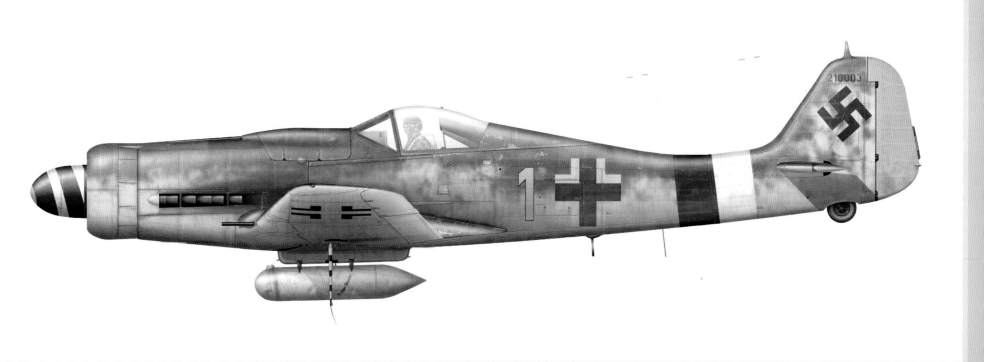

123. Fw 190 D-9

Flown by *Oberfeldwebel* Heinz Marquardt, 13./JG 51, Schmoldow/Germany, April 1945.

Born in East Prussia on December 29, 1922, Marquardt joined 10./JG 51 Mölders on the Eastern Front in August 1943. He immediately displayed some remarkable fighter pilot talents and scored his first victory on October 2, 1943. During 330 combat missions over the Soviet Narev bridgehead in Poland through October 1944, IV./JG 51 was credited with 102 victories against twelve losses of their own. *Leutnant* Peter Kalden's 10. *Staffel* took the lion's share with eighty-one of these victories. *Oberfeldwebel* Heinz Marquardt – known among his comrades as "Negus" – contributed with twenty-six to this total, thus increasing his tally from sixty-three to eighty-nine. On November 18, IV./JG 51's *Gruppenkommandeur*, *Hauptmann* Heinz Lange, and *Oberfeldwebel* Marquardt both were awarded with the Knight's Crosses. In late April 1945, IV./JG 51 operated their new Fw 190 D-9s from a base near Redlin against the Soviet air assault on Berlin, and achieved some of the Luftwaffe's last successes. During a single combat, *Fahnenjunker-Oberfeldwebel* Marquardt managed to down four Yak-3s with his Fw 190 D. IV./JG 51 claimed a total of 115 airkills during its final three weeks of combat. At 1120 hours on May 1, 1945, Marquardt took off from Redlin to lead six Fw 190 D-9s to escort twelve Fw 190 ground-attack aircraft against Soviet troop positions near Berlin. When they arrived to Flensburg Airdrome after fulfilling their mission, the Germans were bounced by six 41 Squadron Spitfire XIVs. Marquardt immediately engaged the Spitfires together with his wingman, *Feldwebel* Heinz Radlauer, and instructed the remaining four "Doras" to cover the landing ground-attack planes. Shortly after bringing down one of the Spitfires, Marquardt was himself shot down. In the confusion during the final days of the war, he was reported killed. However, he survived and was brought into Schwerin hospital, where he later was confined by arriving British troops. Thirty-five years later, Heinz Marquardt met the two British pilots – one of whom shot him down on May Day 1945: Walter Jallands and Peter Cowell. Heinz Marquardt achieved a total of 121 victories on around 280 combat sorties. Heinz Marquardt is still alive.

124. Bf 109 K-4

Flown by *Major* Adolf Borchers, *Stab* III./JG 52, Deutsch Brod/Czechoslovakia, May 1945.

Adolf Borchers was born on February 10, 1913. He married the female skier world champion Christl Cranz. Although Borchers started his fighter pilot career already in the Spanish Civil War, he had a slow beginning with his successes in World War II. However, it should be pointed out that he was able to survive despite the fact that he was in almost uninterrupted first-line service from the first day of the war until the last day. His first five victories were achieved as a *Feldwebel* with IV./JG 51 in 1940. On October 9, 1942, Borchers was appointed *Staffelkapitän* 11./JG 51. His rise to success started only in 1943, and after amassing a total of seventy-eight victories he was awarded with the Knight's Cross on November 11, 1943. By that time he had risen to the rank of a *Hauptmann*. After approximately ninety victories with JG 51, Borchers was posted to I./JG 52, as its *Gruppenkommandeur*, on June 10, 1944. By that time, JG 52 had developed into the Luftwaffe's most successful *Jagdgeschwader*. On July 24, 1944, Borchers achieved his hundredth aerial victory as the seventy-ninth German fighter pilot. On September 2, 1944, his personal 118th victory also was JG 52's ten thousandth. On February 1, 1945, he was appointed the last *Gruppenkommandeur* of III./JG 52, the *Geschwader*'s most successful *Gruppe*. At the end of the war, he was confined by the Soviets in Czechoslovakia. Adolf Borchers achieved a total of 132 victories – including 127 on the Eastern Front – on about 800 combat sorties. Adolf Borchers passed away on February 9, 1996.

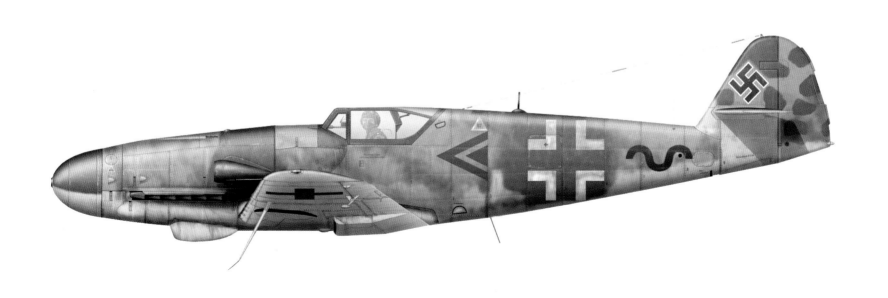

Table of equivalent ranks

A: Collar   B: Shoulder   C: Arm

Luftwaffe   **RAF**   **USAAF**

ENLISTED
1. Flieger   Aircraftsman Second Class   Private
2. Gefreiter   Aircraftsman First Class   Private First Class
3. Obergefreiter   Leading Aircraftsman   Corporal
4. Hauptgefreiter*   Sergeant
5. Stabsgefreiter**

NONCOMMISSIONED OFFICERS
6. Unteroffizier   Corporal   Staff Sergeant
7. Unterfeldwebel
8. Feldwebel   Sergeant   Technical Sergeant
9. Oberfeldwebel   Flight Sergeant   Master Sergeant

WARRANT OFFICERS
10. Stabsfeldwebel/Hauptfeldwebel Warrant Officer   Flight Officer

COMMISSIONED OFFICERS
11. Leutnant   Pilot Officer   Second Lieutenant
12. Oberleutnant   Flying Officer   First Lieutenant
13. Hauptmann   Flight Lieutenant   Captain
14. Major   Squadron Leader   Major
15. Oberstleutnant   Wing Commander   Lieutenant Colonel
16. Oberst   Group Captain   Colonel
17. Generalmajor   Air Commodore   Brigadier General
18. Generalleutnant   Air Vice Marshal   Major General
19. General der Flieger   Air Marshal   Lieutenant General
20. Generaloberst   Air Chief Marshal   General (4 star)
Generalfeldmarschall   Marshal of the RAF   General (5 star)
Reichsmarschall

* The rank of Hauptgefreiter was abolished 12 - 5 - 1944
** The rank of Stabsgefreiter was introduced 4 - 2 – 1944

Ritterkreuz

The highest decoration for the German forces was the Knight's Cross. An Approximate of 1730 *Luftwaffe* personnel were awarded with the Knight's Cross. A total of 192 were awarded with the Knight's Cross with the Oak Leaves. A total of 41 were awarded with the Knight's Cross with the Oak Leaves and Swords. Ten were awarded with the Knight's Cross with the Oak Leaves, Swords, and Diamonds.

(RK) *Das Ritterkreuz des Eisernen Kreuzes* (the Knight's Cross).
(EL) *Das Ritterkreuz des Eisernen Kreuzes mit Eichenlaub* (the Knight's Cross with the Oak Leaves).
(S) *Das Ritterkreuz des Eisernen Kreuzes mit Eichenlaub und Schwertern* (the Knight's Cross with the Oak Leaves, and Swords).
(Br) *Das Ritterkreuz des Eisernen Kreuzes mit Eichenlaub mit Schwertern und Brillanten* (the Knight's Cross with the Oak Leaves, Swords, and Diamonds).

The Structure of the Luftwaffe

The basic tactical unit of the Luftwaffe during World War II normally was the *Geschwader* ("wing").

Each *Geschwader* was identified by a number and had a prefix according to its branch of service:

Jagdgeschwader (JG) = fighter
Nachtjagdgeschwader (NJG) = night fighter
Zerstörergeschwader (ZG) = heavy fighter
Schlachtgeschwader (SchG, later SG)= ground assault
Sturzkampfgeschwader (Stukageschwader) (StG) = dive-bomber
Kampfgeschwader (KG) = bomber
Lehrgeschwader (LG) = operational training unit (formed for the purpose of training leaders).

Many *Geschwader* were also given traditional titles, commemorating a fallen "hero", such as:

JG 26 *"Schlageter"*, the name of a nationalist fighter during the French occupation of the Ruhr; JG 51 *"Mölders"*, the first Top Gun of the German Fighter Air Arm; JG 2 *"Richthofen"*, etc. It is interesting to note that this tradition has been carried on by the *Bundesluftwaffe*, which contains units such as JG 71 *"Richthofen"* and JG 74 *"Mölders"*.

Each *Geschwader* usually comprised three or four *Gruppen* ("groups"), numbered with Roman characters:

III./JG 26 = third *Gruppe* of *Jagdgeschwader* 26.

The *Gruppe* comprised three or four *Staffeln* ("squadrons"), numbered with Arabic numerals:

3./JG 26 = third *Staffel* of *Jagdgeschwader* 26.

The normal strength of a *Staffel* was twelve aircraft, in the Fighter Air Arm divided into three *Schwärme*; one *Schwarm* made up of four aircraft.

The *Schwarm* was divided into two *Rotten*, a *Rotte* consisting two pilots – the *Rottenführer* (leader) and the *Rottenflieger* (wingman).

This gives the following nominal strength of the German aviation units in World War II:

Geschwader = three or four *Gruppen* plus a *Stabsstaffel* (staff-squadron) - 120-156 a/c
Gruppe = three or four Staffeln - 36-48 a/c
Staffel = 12 a/c

The commander of a *Geschwader* was called *Geschwaderkommodore*. His rank could be *Major*, *Oberstleutnant* or *Oberst*.

The commander of a *Gruppe* was called *Gruppenkommandeur*. His rank could be *Major* or *Hauptmann*.

The commander of a *Staffel* was called *Staffelkapitän*. His rank could be *Hauptmann*, *Oberleutnant* or *Leutnant*.

Several *Geschwader* were organized into a *Fliegerkorps* ("air corps") or *Fliegerdivision* ("air division").

The largest tactical organization within the German Air Force of World War II was the *Luftflotte*, which roughly corresponded to a numbered U.S. Air Force.

The German Fighter Air Arm in World War II: Result table

Since the essence of the German Fighter Air Arm in World War II was to shoot down enemy aircraft, a publication like this would be incomplete without giving some kind of result table. A similar table was published in a previous volume on the same subject, by the same authors, and the table below has been modified according to recent research. The authors however would like to underscore that they have found evidence to correct only one of the figures in the previously published table. As far as the authors know, these are the only attempts ever made to present the whole loss and success table of the German Fighter Air Arm.

Of course the authors can not claim that the figures below are 100% exact. The true aircraft loss totals of World War II are, especially when it comes to the Luftwaffe, not known and will never be known. When it comes to the verification of aerial victory claims, things become even more difficult. Even if the loss tables of the units concerned were complete, it is very hard to decide whether a crashed aircraft really was shot down, etc. A rule of the thumb is: True losses are always higher than the loss figures given by one side and lower than the victory claims made by the other side.

The list below does not mirror the claims made by the fighter pilots. It is a well-known fact that the victory claims made by fighter pilots of all air forces generally were exaggerated. However, there is no evidence that there was any official German policy of exaggerating the fighter pilots' claims; on the contrary, each claim had to go through a thorough procedure, including research, before it was officially accepted. The following figures are a rough approximation of the actual losses in the aerial combats fought by the German day fighter pilots in World War II. These figures are based on many years of thoroughgoing studies of the aerial warfare between 1939 and 1945. Even if some details in the figures given below may be revised in the years to come, we dare to say that they are as close to the true facts as possible at this stage of historical research.

In combat	Western Front		Eastern Front	
Year	Enemy a/c shot down	Luftwaffe fighters lost	Enemy a/c shot down	Luftwaffe fighters lost
1939-40	1.500	800		
1941	1.500	300	5.000	600
1942	2.500	500	8.000	500
1943	3.000	2.000	9.000	800
1944	5.000	8.000	7.000	1.100
1945	+500	1.500	2.000	1.000
Total:	14.000	13.000	31.000	4.000

(Note: the German loss figures given are total combat loss figures, i.e. losses to ground fire, and in aerial combat.)

Comment:
According to *Gemeinschaft der Jagdflieger*, the German Fighter Pilots' Association, the German fighter pilots claimed a total of 70,000 aerial victories during World War II – 25,000 against the "Western enemies" and 45,000 on the Eastern Front. At the same time, the German Flak (AAA batteries) reported the shooting down of more than 20,000 enemy aircraft.

According to the same source, 16,400 German day fighter aircraft were lost (total loss, i.e. aircraft with more than 59 percent damage degree) as the result of hostile action during the war years. 8,500 German day fighter pilots were killed, 2,700 went missing or were taken prisoners, and 9,100 were injured.

Different total loss figures for the RAF and the USAAF are published frequently. According to Russian archives, the combat losses of the Soviet Air Force between 1941 and 1945 amounted 46,100 aircraft. Due to the fact that several Soviet records were lost during the first months of the German invasion in the summer of 1941, the actual Soviet aircraft combat losses in World War II probably were higher, totaling approximately slightly above 50,000.

Authors' note:
There has been some dispute over the use of different abbreviations of the Messerschmitt 109 and 110. While we find the use of "Bf 109" in most German official documents, the abbreviation "Me 109" is most commonly used in U.S. publications. It is not the author's intention to enter any discussion on the subject. Due to historical reasons we have chosen to use the abbreviation "Bf 109"/"Bf 110" (but "Me 210"/"Me 410"/"Me 163"/"Me 262" of the later constructions) and refer to the history of the Bayerische Flugzeugwerke (Bf), which later became Messerschmitt (Me) A.G.

Sources

Archives
Bundesarchiv-Militärarchiv, Freiburg.
Bundesarchiv, Koblenz.
Forschungsgruppe 45, Salzwedel.
Imperial War Museum, London.
Luftfahrtmuseum Hannover-Laatzen.
Monino Air Force Museum, Moscow.
Rosvoyentsentr, Moscow.
Russian Central Military Archive TsAMO, Podolsk.
WASt Deutsche Dienststelle, Berlin.

Unpublished Sources
Abschussmeldungen JG 52. Via Alfons Altmeier.
Antipov Vlad, *Patriots or Red Kamikaze?* 1999.
Barkhorn, Major Gerhard, Flight Book.
Batz, Major Willi Flight Book.
Bob, Major Hans-Ekkehard, Flight Book.
Bundesarchiv/Militärarchiv.
Bytomski, Oberleutnant Karl Flight Book.
Chronik der I./JG 54. Via Hans-Ekkehard Bob.
Düttmann, Leutnant Peter Flight Book.
Eisenach, Major Franz, Flight Book.
Flores, S. A. *The "Escuadrillas Azul" of the Spanish Air Force in World War II. Russia 1941-1944.*
— *Pilotos ex-fuerza Aerea Republicana Española en servicio de la Fuerza Aerea Rusa en la Segunda Guerra Mundial 1933-1945.*
Gemeinschaft der Jagdflieger, Germany
Gollob, Gordon. Personal diary.
Grislawski, Major Alfred, Flight Book.
Hoffmann, Oberfeldwebel Heinrich Flight Book.
JG 52 Archiv. Courtesy of Alfons Altmeier,
JG 54 "Grünherz" Archiv.. Courtesy of Günther Rosipal.
Kath, Hauptmann Otto, Flight Book.
Koller, Oberfeldwebel Heribert Flight Book.
Luftwaffe aircraft loss list. Courtesy of Matti Salonen,
Meldungen über Flugzeugunfälle und Verluste bei den sl. Verbänden (täglich), Ob.d.L. Gen.Qu. Gen. 6. Abt.
Mölders, Oberst Werner, Flight Book.
Petermann, Leutnant Viktor Flight Book.
Seelmann, Oberleutnant Georg, Flight Book.
Schilling, Oberleutnant Wilhelm, Flight Book.
Schleinhege, Leutnant Hermann Flight Book.
Späte, Major Wolfgang, Flight Book.
Staffel-Chronik der III. Jagdgeschwader 54, 7. Staffel.
Staffel-Chronik der III. Jagdgeschwader 54, 9. Staffel.
Steinhoff, Oberst Johannes, Flight Book.

Traditionsgeschichte der I./Jagdgeschwader 52. Via Alfons Altmeier.
Traditionsgeschichte III. Jagdgeschwader 52. Via Alfons Altmeier.
Waldmann, Oberleutnant Hans Flight Book.
Wolf, Leutnant Hermann, Flight Book.
Wolfrum, Oberleutnant Walter Flight Book.

Bibliography
Aders G., and W. Held. *Jagdgeschwader 51 Mölders.* Stuttgart: Motorbuch Verlag, 1993.
Anttonen, O., and H. Valtonen. *Luftwaffe Suomessa – In Finland 1941-1944.* Helsinki: 1976, 1980.
Apostolo, G. *AER. Macchi C.202.* Torino: La Bancarella Aeronautica 1995.
Avdeyev, M. V. *U samogo Chyornogo morya.* Moscow: DOSAAF, 1968.
Barbas, B. *Planes of Luftwaffe Fighter Aces, Vol 1.* Kookaburra Technical Publications Pty Ltd. 1985 Australia.
Barbas, B. *Planes of Luftwaffe Fighter Aces, Vol 2.* Kookaburra Technical Publications Pty Ltd. 1985 Australia.
Beaman, J. R. Jr. & Campbell, J. L. *Messerschmitt Bf 109 in action.* Squadron/Signal Publications, INC. USA 1980.
Beaman, J. R. Jr. & Campbell, J. L. *Messerschmitt Bf 109 in action, part 2.* Squadron/Signal Publications, INC. USA 1983.
Bergström, C. *Luftstrid över Kanalen.* Stockholm: Liber, 1983.
— *Mot avgrunden.* Stockholm: Atlantis, 1991.
Bergström, C., and A. Mikhailov. *Black Cross/Red Star: The Air War Over the Eastern Front.* Vol. I, *Operation Barbarossa, 1941.* Pacifica: Pacifica Military History, 2000.
Bergström, C., and A. Mikhailov. *Black Cross/Red Star: The Air War Over the Eastern Front.* Vol. II, *Operation Barbarossa, 1941.* Pacifica: Pacifica Military History and Classic Publications, 2001.
Bernád, D. *Rumanian Air Force: The Prime Decade, 1938-1947.* Carrollton: Squadron/Signal Publications, 1999.
Bodrikhin, N. *Stalinskiye Sokoly.* Moscow: NPP *Delta*, 1997.
— Sovyetskiye Asi. *Moscow: ZAO KFK "TAMP,"* 1998.
Bogdanov, N. G. *V nebe Gvardeyskiy Gatchinskiy.* Leningrad: Lenizdat, 1980.
Boyevoy put' Sovyetskogo Voyenno-Morskogo Flota. 4th ed. Moscow: Voyenizdat, 1988.
Boehme, M. *JG7 The world's First Jet Fighter Unit 1944/1945.* Schiffer Military History, USA 1992.
Bracke, G. *Gegen vielfache übermacht,* Motorbuch Verlag, Germany 1977.
Brown, D. E. and Wadman, D. *Camouflage, and Markings of JV 44, JG 6 and JG 1 Focke Wulf 190 Ds* Calgary; Experten Historical Aviation Research, Inc. 1995
— *"Checkmate"* Calgary; Experten Historical Aviation Research, Inc. 1998
— *Camouflage, and Markings of JV 44, JG 6 Focke Wulf 190 D-9s* Halifax: Experten Historical Aviation Research, Inc. 1993
Buchner, H. *Stormbird: Flying Through Fire as a Luftwaffe Ground Attack Pilot and Me 262 Ace.* Aldershot: Hikoki Publications, 2000.
Bucurescu, I., et al: *Aviatia Romana-Pe frontul de est si in apararea teritotiului.* Romania: Tehnoprod, 1993.
Caldwell, D. *JG 26; Top Guns of the Luftwaffe,* Orion Books, USA 1991.
— *JG 26 Photographic History of the Luftwaffe's Top Guns,* Airlife Publishing Ltd. 1994.
— *The JG 26 War Diary: Volume One 1939 - 1942.* London: Grub Street, 1996.
— *The JG 26 War Diary: Volume Two 1943 - 1945.* London: Grub Street, 1998.

Campbell, Jerry L. *Focke Wulf Fw 190 in action.* Squadron/Signal Publications, INC. USA 1975.

Chazanov (Khazanov), D. *Bitwa nad Moskwa.* Series *Nawieksze Bitwy Wieku.* Warsaw: ALTAIR, 1977.

— *Nad Stalingradem.* Warsaw: Wydawnictwo Altair, 1995.

Crandall, J. *Doras of the Galland Circus.* Hamilton: Eagle Illustrations, 1999.

Dickfeld, A. *Footsteps of the Hunter.* Winnipeg: J. J. Fedorowicz Publishing, 1993.

Ethell, J. L. *Komet; the Messerschmitt 163,* Sky Books Press, USA 1978.

Ethell, J. & Price, A. *Target Berlin,* Jane's Publishing Company, UK 1980.

Ewald, H. *Wo wir sind ist immer Oben.* Querbitzsch: Markus Ewald und Falk Klinnert, 1998.

Fast, N. *Das Jagdgeschwader 52.* Bergisch Gladbach: Bensberger Buch-Verlag, 1988-1992.

Fiest, U., N. E. Harms, and M. Dario. *The Fighting 109.* Devon: David & Charles Ltd., 1978.

Feist, Uwe & McGuirl, Thomas. *Luftwaffe Diary,* Feist Publications, USA 1994.

von Forell, Fritz. *Mölders und seine Männer,* Steirische Verlagsanstalt, Germany (Austria) 1941.

Frankland. Noble: *Bomber Offensive,* UK 1970.

Freeman, R. A. *The Mighty Eighth,* Macdonald, UK 1970.

Freeman, R. A. *The U.S. Strategic Bomber,* Macdonald and Jane's Publishing Company, UK 1975.

Freeman, R. A. *The Mighty Eighth War Diary,* Jane's Publishing Company, UK 1981.

Galland, A. *Die Ersten und die Letzten; Jagdflieger im zweiten Weltkrieg.* Munich: Franz Schneekluth Verlag, 1953.

Geroi ognennykh let. 3rd ed. Yaroslavl: Verkhnye-Volzhskoye knizhnoye izdatel'stvo, 1985.

Geroi Sovyetskogo Soyuza. Moscow: Voyenizdat, 1987.

Geust, C. –F, K. Keskinen, and K. Stenman. *Soviet Air Force in World War Two: Red Stars.* Kangsala: Ar-Kustannus Oy, 1993.

Girbig, W. *Jagdgeschwader 5 "Eismeerjäger."* Stuttgart: Motorbuch Verlag, 1975.

— *Start im Morgengrauen,* Motorbuch Verlag, Germany 1973.

— *Im Anflug auf die Reichshauptstadt,* Motorbuch Verlag, Germany 1977.

— *...mit Kurs auf Leuna,* Motorbuch Verlag, Germany 1980.

Goebel, R. L. *Mustang Ace: Memoirs of a P-51 Fighter Pilot.* Pacifica:Pacifica Press, 1991.

Golubev, V. F. *Krylia krepnyt v boyu.* 2d ed. Leningrad: Lenizdat, 1984.

Grif sekretnosti sniat. Poteri vooruzhennykh sil SSR v voynakh, boyevykh deystviyakh, i voyennykl konfliktakh. Moscow: Voyenizdat, 1993.

Green, W. *Warplanes of the Third Reich.* London: Macdonald, 1970

Griehl, M. / Dressel, J. *Focke-Wulf Fw 190/Ta 152.* Stuttgart: Motorbuch Verlag, 1997

Grinsell, R. Watanabe, R. *Focke-Wulf Fw 190.* Jane's Publishing Company, Ltd. 1980.

— *Messerschmitt Br 109.* Jane's Publishing Company, Ltd. 1980.

Gundelach, K. *Kampfgeschwader 4 General Wever,* Motorbuch Verlag, 1978.

Glantz, D. M., and J. House. *When Titans Clashed: How the Red Army Stopped Hitler.* Lawrence: University Press of Kansas, 1995.

Haase, O. *Stirb und werde: Aus zwei Jahren Russlandkrieg des Jagdgeschwaders Trautloft.* Berlin: 1943.

Hafner, and Meiller. *Flieger Fiende Kameraden.* Rastatt: Erich Pabel Verlag, 1962.

Hahn, F. *Geheimwaffen.* Heidenheim: Erich Hoffman Verlag, 1963.

Hammel, E. *Aces Against Germany: The American Aces Speak, vol. II.* Novato: Presidio, 1993.

— *Air War Europa: America's Air War Against Germany in Europe and North Africa 1942- 1945.* Pacifica: Pacifica Press, 1994.

Hayward, J. *Stopped at Stalingrad: The Luftwaffe and Hitler's Defeat in the East.* Lawrence: University Press of Kansas, 1998.

Held, W. Trautloft, H. and Bob, H. –E. *Die Grünherzjäger.* Friedberg: Podzun-Pallas Verlag, 1985.

Held, W. *Fighter!, Luftwaffe Fighter Planes and Pilots.* Arms and Armour Press. 1979.

— *Adolf Galland; a Pilot's Life,* Champlin Fighter Museum Press, 1986.

— *Der Jagdflieger Walter Nowotny,* Stuttgart: Motorbuch Verlag, 1997

— *Die Deutschen Jagdgeschwader im Russlandfeldzug.* Friedberg: Podzun-Pallas Verlag, 1986.

Hermann, D. *Focke-Wulf Ta 152, Der Weg zum Höhenjäger.* Oberhaching: Aviantic Verlag 1998.

Herrmann, H. *Bewegtes Leben: Kampf-und Jagdflieger 1935-1945.* 2nd ed. Stuttgart: Motorbuch Verlag, 1986.

Hildebrandt, C. *Broken Eagles 1, Fw 190 D.* Fighter Pictorials. 1987.

— *Broken Eagles 2, Bf 109 G/K.* Fighter Pictorials. 1988.

— *Broken Eagles 3, Bf 109 G/K,* part II. Fighter Pictorials. 1989.

— *Broken Eagles 4, Me 262 A.* Fighter Pictorials. 1993.

Hitchcock, T. *Monogram Close-Up 6, Bf 109 G, Part 1,* Monogram Aviaton Publications. 1976.

— *Monogram Close-Up 7, Bf 109 G, Part 2,* Monogram Aviaton Publications. 1977.

— *Monogram Close-Up 16, Bf 109 K,* Monogram Aviaton Publications. 1979.

— *Monogram Close-Up 9, Bf 109 F,* Monogram Aviaton Publications. 1990.

Hitchcock, T. H. & Merrik, K. A. *The official Monogram painting guide to German Aircraft 1935-1945,* Monogram Aviaton Publications. USA 1980.

Ishoven, A. *Messerschmitt Bf 109 at war,* Ian Allan Ltd, 1977.

Jagdgeschwader 54 Grünherz: Verluste 1940-1945. Edited by Günther Rosipal. Salzwedel/Hannover: Forschungsgruppe 45, 1998.

Keskinen, K., K. Stenman, K., and K. Niska: *Suomen ilmavoimien historia.* Vol.VII, *Venäläiset hävittäjät, Tietoteos.* Forssa: Forssan Kirjapaino Oy, 1977.

Kriegschronik Band XIV. Franz F. Winter, ed. *Die deutschen Jagdflieger.* Munich: Universitas Verlag, 1993.

Kriegstagebuch des Oberkommandos der Wehrmacht 1939-1945. Edited by Percy E. Schramm. Munich: Bernard & Graefe Verlag, 1982.

Kursenkow, S. G. *Jagdflieger.* Berlin (GDR): Deutscher Militärverlag, 1964.

Lipfert, H. *The War Diary of Hauptmann Helmut Lipfert,* Schiffer Publishing, 1993.

Michulec, R. *Stalinowskie sokoly.* Gdynia: AJ Press, 1995.

Mombeek, E. *Reichsverteidigung, Die Geschichre des Jagdgeschwaders 1 "Oesau"* Moombeek 1993.

Murray, W. *Luftwaffe: Strategy for Defeat 1939-45.* London: Grafton Books, 1985.

Neulen, H. W. *Am Himmel Europas: Luftstreitkräfte an deutscher Seite 1939-1945.* Munich: Universitas Verlag, 1998.

Nohara, S. *Messerschmitt Me 262,* Model Art Co.Ltd. Japan 1991.

— *Messerschmitt Bf 109 F,* Model Art Co.Ltd. Japan 1993.

Nohara, S, Shiwaku, M. & Nozaki, T. *Aero Detail 2, Focke-Wulf Fw 190 D,* Dai Nippon Kaiga Co.Ltd. 1990.

— *Aero Detail 5, Messerchmitt Bf 109 G,* Dai Nippon Kaiga Co.Ltd. Japan 1992.

— *Aero Detail 6, Focke-Wulf Fw 190 A/F,* Dai Nippon Kaiga Co.Ltd. Japan 1993.

Nohara, S. Shiwaku, M. *Aero Detail 10, Messerschmitt Me 163 & Heinkel He 162,* Dai Nippon Kaiga Co.Ltd. Japan 1994.

Nowotny, R. *Walter Nowotny: Berichte aus dem Leben meines Bruder.* Leoni: Druffel-Verlag, 1957.

Obermaier, E. *Die Ritterkreuzträger der Luftwaffe: Band 1 – Jagdflieger 1939-1945.* Mainz: Verlag Dieter Hoffmann, 1966.

— *Die Ritterkreuzträger der Luftwaffe 1939-1945: Band II – Stuka-und Schlachtflieger.* Mainz: Verlag Dieter Hoffmann, 1976.

Philpott, B. *RAF Fighter Units Europe 1942-45,* Osprey Publishing 1978.

Plocher, H. *The German Air Force Versus Russia*. USAF Historical Division, Air University. New York: Arno Press, 1966.

Pokryschkin [Pokryshkin], A. I. *Himmel des Krieges*. Berlin (GDR): Deutscher Militärverlag, 1970.

— *Na istrebitele*. Novosibirsk: Novosibgiz, 1948.

— *Krylya istrebitelya*. Moscow: Voyenizdat, 1948.

— *Nebo voyny*. Moscow: Voyenizdat, 1980.

— *Poznat sebia v boyu*. Moscow: DOSAAF, 1986.

Polak, T., and C. Shores. *Stalin's Falcons: The Aces of the Red Star: A tribute to the Notable Fighter Pilots of the Soviet Air Forces, 1918 - 1953*. London: Grub Street, 1999.

Poruba, T., Janda, A. *Messerschmitt Bf 109 K*, Hradec:JaPo 1997.

Punka, G. "Messer": The Messerschmitt 109 in the Royal Hungarian "Honvéd" Air Force. Budapest: OMIKK, 1995.

Price, A. *Battle over the Reich*, Ian Allen Ltd., 1973.

— *Focke-Wulf 190 at War*, Ian Allen Ltd., 1977.

Prien, J. *"Pik-As:" Geschichte des Jagdgeschwaders 53 Teil 2*, Eutin: Struve-Druck, 1990.

— *Geschichte des Jagdgeschwaders 53 Teil 3*, Eutin: Struve-Druck, 1991.

— *Geschichte des Jagdgeschwaders 77 Teil 1*. Eutin: Struve-Druck, 1992 - 1994.

— *Geschichte des Jagdgeschwaders 77 Teil 2*. Eutin: Struve-Druck, 1992 - 1994.

— *Geschichte des Jagdgeschwaders 77 Teil 3*. Eutin: Struve-Druck, 1992 - 1994.

— *Geschichte des Jagdgeschwaders 77 Teil 4*. Eutin: Struve-Druck, 1992 - 1994.

— *Chronik einer Jagdruppe VI./Jagdgeschwader 3*. Eutin: Struve-Druck, 1996.

Prien, J. *Jagdgeschwader 53: A History of the "Pik As" Geschwader Volume 1: March 1937 – May 1942*. Atglen: Schiffer Military History, 1998.

— *A History of the "Pik As" Geschwader Volume 2: May 1942 - January 1944*. Atglen: Schiffer Military History, 1998.

— *A History of the "Pik As" Geschwader Volume 3: January 1944 . May 1945* Atglen: Schiffer Military History, 1998.

Prien, J./ Rodeike, P. *Jagdgeschwader 1 und 11, teil 1*, Eutin: Struve-Druck, 1993, n.d.

— *Jagdgeschwader 1 und 11, teil 2*, Eutin: Struve-Druck, 1993.

— *Jagdgeschwader 1 und 11, teil 3*, Eutin: Struve-Druck, 1993.

Prien, J. / Stemmer, G.: *Messerschmitt Bf 109 im Einsatz bei der III./Jagdgeschwader 3*. Eutin: Struve-Druck, n.d.

— *Messerschmitt Bf 109 im Einsatz bei der II./Jagdgeschwader 3*. Eutin: Struve-Druck, n.d.

— *Messerschmitt Bf 109 im Einsatz bei Stab und I./Jagdgeschwader 3*. Eutin: Struve-Druck, 1997.

— *Messerschmitt Bf 109 im Einsatz bei der III. und IV./Jagdgeschwader 27*. Eutin: Struve Druck, 1995.

Priller, J. *Geschichte eines Jagdgeschwaders; das JG 26 Schlageter*, Kurt Vowinckel Verlag, 1961.

Radinger, W. & Schick, W. *Messerschmitt Me 262*. Schiffer Military History, 1993.

Rajlích, J., and J. Sehnal. *Slovensti Letci 1939-1945*. Kolín: Vydavatelství Kolinske noviny, 1991.

Rajlich, J., Z. Stojczew, and Z. Lalak. *Sojusznicy Luftwaffe, czesc 1*. Warsaw: Books International, 1997.

Rechkalov, G. A. *V nebe Moldavii: Vospominaniya voyennogo letchika*. Kishinev: Kartya moldovenyaske, 1967.

— *Dymnoye nebo voyny*. Sverdlovsk: Sredne-Uralskoye knizhnoe izdatel'stvo, 1968.

Reschke, W. *Jagdgeschwader 301/302 "Wilde Sau."* Stuttgart: Motorbuch Verlag, 1999.

Relling, A. *Oberleutnant Anton Hafner*. Rastatt: Erich Pabel Verlag, 1972.

Reis, K. *Luftwaffe Phots-Report 1919-1945*, Stuttgart: Motorbuch Verlag, 1994

Ring, H. & Girbig, W. *Jagdgeschwader 27*, Motorbuch Verlag, 1971.

Ring, H & Shores, C. *Luftkampf zwischen Sand und Sonne*, Motorbuch Verlag, 1974.

Rudel, H.-U. *Trotzdem*. Göttingen: Verlag K. W. Schütz, 1970.

Rust, K. C. *The 9th Air Force in World War II*, Aero Publishers, USA 1970.

— *Fifteenth Air Force Story*, Historical Aviation Album, USA 1976.

Scutts, J. *Bf 109 Aces of the North Africa and the Mediterranean*. Osprey Publishing 1994.

Schmidt, H. A F. *Sowjetische Flugzeuge*. Transpress Verlag, 1971.

von Seemen, G. *Die Ritterkreuzträger*, Podzun Verlag, Germany 1976.

Schreier, H. *JG 52: Das erfolgreichste Jagdgeschwader des II. Weltkrieges*. Berg am See: Kurt Vowinckel Verlag, n.d.

Seidl, H. *Stalin's Eagles: An Illustrated Study of the Soviet Aces of World War II and Korea*. Atglen: Schiffer, 1998.

Shelflin, S.W. *Airfoil, Number 3*. Airfoil Publications. USA 1985.

Shores, C. *Luftwaffe Fighter units, Mediterranean 1941-44*. Osprey Publishing Ltd. 1978.

— *Luftwaffe Fighter units, Russia 1941-45*. Osprey Publishing Ltd. 1978.

— *Luftwaffe Fighter units, Europe 1942-45*. Osprey Publishing Ltd. 1979.

Sims, E. H. *The Fighter Pilots*, Cassell, 1967.

Slizewski, G. The Lost Hopes: Polish Fighters Over France in 1940. Koszalin: Grzegorz Slizewski, 2000.

Smith, R. J. & Gallaspy J. D. *Luftwaffe Camouflage & Markings 1935-45, Vol 2*. Kookaburra Tecnical Publications Pty Ltd. 1976.

— *Luftwaffe Camouflage & Markings 1935 - 45, Vol 3*. Kookaburra Tecnical Publications Pty Ltd. 1977.

Smith, J.R., Pentland G.G. & Lutz R.P. *Luftwaffe Painting guide*. Kookaburra Tecnical Publications Pty Ltd. 1976

Smith, R. J. & Creek, E. J. *Jet planes of the Third Reich*. Monogram Aviaton Publications. 1982.

— *Monogram Close-Up 17, Me 262 A-1*, Monogram Aviaton Publications. 1983.

— *Monogram Close-Up 11, Volksjäger*, Monogram Aviaton Publications. 1986.

— *Monogram Close-Up 10, Fw 190 D*, Monogram Aviaton Publications. 1986.

Spaight, J H. *Bombing Vindicated*, Bless, 1944.

Steinhoff, J. *Kampen om Messinasundet*. Malmö: Berghs förlag, 1973.

— *Die Strasse von Messina*, Paul List Verlag, 1969.

— *In letzter Stunde: Verschwörung der Jagdflieger*, Paul LIst Verlag, 1977.

Sundin, C & Bergström, C. *Luftwaffe Fighter Aircraft in Profile*. Schiffer Publishing Ltd. 1997.

Tieke, W. *Kampf um die Krim 1941-1944*. Erbland: Selbstverlag Wilhelm Tieke, 1975.

Toliver, R. F. & Constable, T. J. *Fighter Aces of the Luftwaffe*. Aero Publishers, INC. 1977.

— *Das waren die deutschen Jagdfliegerasse 1939-1945*. Stuttgart: Motorbuch Verlag, 1973.

— *Trevor J. The Blond Knight of Germany*. TAB/AERO Books. 1985.

— *Fighter General; The Life of Adolf Galland*, AmPress Publishing, 1990.

Tullis, T. *Eagles Illustrated*. Hamilton: Eagles Editions Ltd. 2000.

Ullmann, M. *RLM-Farbtontafel*, Ullmann 1999

— *Colors of the German Luftwaffe 1935-1945*. Ullmann 1998.

— *The Last Eagle*. Ullmann 1997.

— *Oberflächenschutzverfahren und Anstrichstoffe der deutshen Luftwaffe 1935-1945*. Ullmann 1998.

Urbanke, A. Green Hearts: First In Combat With The Dora 9. Hamilton: Eagle Editions, 1998.

Valtonen, H. *Luftwaffen Pohjoinen Sivusta*. Jyväskylä: Gummerus Kirjapaino Oy, 1997.

Weal, J. *Focke-Wulf Fw 190 Aces of the Russian Front*. Osprey Publishing UK 1995.

Widfeldt, B. *The Luftwaffe in Sweden 1939 - 1945*. Monogram Aviaton Publications. USA 1983.

Windrow, M. C. *German Air Force Fighters*, Hylton Lacyu Publishers, UK 1968.

Wykeham, P. *Fighter Command*, Putnam, UK 1960.

Ziegler, M. *Messerschmitt Me 163 Komet, Das Kraftei*. Podzun-Pallas-Verlag GmbH. Germany.

Periodicals

Der Adler.

Air Combat.

Air International

Airfoil

Aviatsiya i Kosmonavtika.

Classic Wings Downunder.

The Dispatch Magazine.

Fly Past.

Jägerblatt.

Jet und Prop

Luftwaffe Verband Journal.

Militaria

Internet Sites

The Age of Information has supplied Mankind with a new and expanding forum for exchange of information, the Internet. In recent years, several Internet sites have evolved with a supply of high-quality information in the field of aviation history. The authors have received invaluable material for this book directly from and via the following Internet sites, whose owners have undertaken considerable research work. Without depreciating the value of any other Internet site mentioned below, the authors wish to acknowledge particularly the work done by Mr. Ruy Horta to establish a worldwide interface between aviation historians and aviation history enthusiasts.

Air Operations During the Battle of Kursk by Pawel Burchard. http://www.geocities.com/dedeusz/

Biplane Fighter Aces from the Second World War by Håkan Gustavsson. http://www.dalnet.se/~surfcity/

Eagles Over Norway by Andreas Brekken. http://www.stormbirds.com/eagles/

The History Net. http://www.thehistorynet.com/home.htm

Jagdgeschwader 54 Home Page by Bob Wartburg. http://www.jps.net/wartburg/index.htm

The Luftwaffe Homepage by Michael Holm. http://www.ww2.dk/

146th Guards Fighter Regiment PVO. By Vlad Antipov. http://www.geocities.com/giap_146/

SIG Luftwaffe Homepage by Olve Dybvig. http://home.online.no/~odybvig/

New Zealand Fighter Pilots Museum.

12 O'Clock High by Ruy Horta. http://www.xs4all.nl/~rhorta/

World War II Ace Stories by Dariusz Tyminski. http://www.elknet.pl/acestory/

Gemeinschaft der Jagdfliegers. www.fliegergemeinschaft.de/main/heft/heft_main.htm

Index

Also from the Publisher

The Legion Condor 1936-1939. *Karl Ries & Hans Ring.* This classic book now makes its first appearance in English. This study is one of the few books dedicated to the history of the infamous Legion Condor, the German volunteer unit that fought with pro-Franco forces during the Spanish Civil War from 1936-1939. Many of the tactics and strategies of the Luftwaffe were first formulated and used during operations in Spain. Also, various aircraft were tested and used, such as the famous Ju 87, Do 17, He 111 and Bf 109 - all stalwarts of the later Luftwaffe during World War II. Werner Molders and Adolf Galland first earned their wings as members of the Legion Condor.
Size: 8 1/2" x 11" • 288 pp.
ISBN: 0-88740-339-5 • hard cover • $37.50

The War Diary of Hauptmann Helmut Lipfert: JG 52 On the Russian Front • 1943-1945. *Helmut Lipfert & Werner Girbig.* Aerial combat over the Russian front from one who knew it first hand. Hauptmann Helmut Lipfert's vivid portrayal of his experiences in JG 52 during the last three years of the Second World War will stand as one of the truly classic chronicles of the Jagdwaffe over Russia. This book is a rare view into the air war over Russia, when Luftwaffe pilots accumulated incredible kill tallies while facing overwhelming odds against them in mass assaults.
Size: 6" x 9" • 67 b/w photographs • 224 pp.
ISBN: 0-88740-446-4 • hard cover • $29.95

Jagdeschwader 53: A History of the "Pik As" Geschwader March 1937 - May 1942. *Jochen Prien.* Jagdegeschwader 53 - or as it was better known, the "Pik As" (Ace of Spades) Geschwader - was one of the oldest German fighter units of World War II with its origins going back to the year 1937. This first volume, of a planned three volume set, covers the early years of the Geschwader from its founding in the spring of 1937 up to May of 1942. This book appears here for the first time in English, and contains over 200 additional photos not published in the original German language edition.
Size: 9" x 12" • over 700 b/w and color photographs, aircraft line drawings, maps • 400 pp.
ISBN: 0-7643-0175-6 • hard cover • $89.95

Jagdeschwader 53: A History of the "Pik As" Geschwader Volume 2: May 1942-January 1944 *Jochen Prien.* As with the first volume, this book also appears for the first time in English, and contains over 100 additional photos not published in the original German language edition. The book contains over 450 photographs, revised text and maps, and aircraft line drawings, as well as updated aerial victory and loss listings.
Size: 9" x 12" • over 450 b/w and color photographs, line drawings, maps • 352 pp.
ISBN: 0-7643-0292-2 • hard cover • $89.95

Jagdeschwader 53: A History of the "Pik As" Geschwader Volume 3: January 1944-May 1945. *Jochen Prien.* This third and final part of the narrative starts with the bitter fighting over Italy, where the Geschwaderstab together with I. and III./JG 53 had to face overwhelming odds in their struggle over both the front lines at Cassino and Anzio/Nettuno bridgehead, and over northern Italy. This final volume of the epic saga of JG 53 concludes with a list of the officers in command of the Geschwader, its Gruppen and Staffeln, a listing of all known victories claimed by JG 53, strength returns, and other appendices.
Size: 9" x 12" • over 315 b/w photographs, line drawings, profiles, appendices, name index • 464 pp.
ISBN: 0-7643-0556-5 • hardcover • $89.95

JG 54: A Photographic History of the Grunherzjäger. *Held/Trautloft/Bob.* In five turbulent years the members of this highly successful Luftwaffe fighter unit developed into such a close-knit team that even now - almost fifty years later - that bond still exists. This unique photo history was compiled with assistance from the air and ground crews of JG 54. The 400+ photographs document the story of the Grunherz-Geschwader from its formation in the spring of 1939 to the final battles in the courland pocket in the spring of 1945. Within the timespan lay the arduous years of operations in Poland, France, the Channel Front, the Balkans, Russia, Finland and the defense of the Reich.
Size: 7" x 10" • over 400 b/w photographs • 196 pp.
ISBN: 0-88740-690-4 • hard cover • $29.95

Zerstörergruppe: A History of V./(Z)LG 1 - I./NJG 3 • 1939-1941. *Ludwig von Eimannsberger.* This book is the history of V./(Z)LG 1, a Zerstörergruppe (destroyer-group) which, like most of the Luftwaffe destroyer units equipped with the Messerschmitt Bf 110 twin-engined heavy fighter, was disbanded at the end of 1940 after suffering devastating losses during the Battle of Britain. Included are photographs from the personal archives of surviving air- and groundcrewmen—nearly all are previously unpublished. Detailed appendices list casualties, air operations, documents and other data.
Size: 9" x 12" • over 500 b/w photographs • 240 pp.
ISBN: 0-7643-0479-8 • hard cover • $59.95

The Sting of the Luftwaffe: Schnellkampfgeschwader 210 and Zerstörergeschwader 1 "Wespengeschwader" in World War II. *John Vasco.* Shows for the first time in a single volume the many personalities, and the varied Messerschmitt and Junkers aircraft types flown by these units. Between the two units, they flew in more theatres of operations than any other unit. The work also contains a comprehensive loss/damage list for personnel and aircraft, drawn from the Deutsche Dienststelle records and the Quartermaster loss

returns, and appendices covering reports on several combats by the actual participants, and extracts from three Flight Log books outlining the many tasks undertaken by the flying personnel of the unit.
Size: 9"x12" • over 270 b/w photographs • 176 pp.
ISBN: 0-7643-1305-3 • hard cover • $49.95

Six Months to Oblivion: The Defeat of the Luftwaffe Fighter Force Over the Western Front 1944/1945. *Werner Girbig.* This book covers the last chapter, the decline and fall of the air defense of Germany. It is a diary of losses and a chronicle in which the fighter pilot plays the lead. It tells of the young men who joined their squadrons full of optimism and derring-do, only to give their lives to no purpose in a last desperate endeavour. In this unabridged edition, Werner Girbig gives detailed analysis of these last months of the Luftwaffe and the fall of a once mighty air force.
Size: 6" x 9" • 236 pp.
ISBN: 0-88740-348-4 • hard cover • $29.95

The Interrogator: The Story of Hanns Joachim Scharff, Master Interrogator of the Luftwaffe. *Raymond F. Toliver.* This is the story of Hanns Scharff the master interrogator of the Luftwaffe who questioned captured American fighter pilots of the USAAF Eighth and Ninth Air Forces in World War II. This Intelligence Officer gained the reputation as the man who could magically get all the answers he needed from the prisoners of war. In most cases the POWs being interrogated never realized that their words, small talk or otherwise, were important pieces of the mosaic Hanns Scharff was constructing for the benefit of Germany's war effort.
Size: 6" x 9" • over 150 b/w photographs • 352 pp.
ISBN: 0-7643-0261-2 • hard cover • $29.95

JG 7: The World's First Jet Fighter Unit 1944/1945. *Manfred Boehme.* Formed in August 1944, Jagdgeschwader 7 was equipped with the revolutionary Me 262 jet fighter, which was faster than any aircraft in existence at the time. This unit experienced all of the highs and lows associated with the introduction of such a radically new design. Thus the history of JG 7 is also the story of the Me 262, an inspired design which broke new ground in many areas of technology, and for which there was simply not enough time for thorough development. The pilots of JG 7 frequently had to make do with improvisation and faced a numerically far superior enemy in an aircraft which was technically immature. Manfred Boehme has collected many documentary sources including first hand accounts, technical records and photo archives.
Size: 6" x 9" • 168 photographs, line drawings • 288 pp.
ISBN: 0-88740-395-6 • hard cover • $29.95